AND THE PRICE IS RIGHT

SALVAGE

Books by Margaret Case Harriman

TAKE THEM UP TENDERLY

THE VICIOUS CIRCLE

BLESSED ARE THE DEBONAIR

AND THE PRICE IS RIGHT

AND THE

PRICE IS RIGHT

by *Margaret Case Harriman*

ILLUSTRATED BY Roy D

THE WORLD PUBLISHING COMPANY

CLEVELAND AND NEW YORK

PUBLISHED BY The World Publishing Company
2231 West 110th Street, Cleveland 2, Ohio

PUBLISHED SIMULTANEOUSLY IN CANADA BY
Nelson, Foster & Scott Ltd.

Library of Congress Catalog Card Number: 58-5769

FIRST EDITION

To my daughter-in-law, Sheila Morgan,

an average shopper like myself

Contents

★

CONTENTS

AND THE PRICE IS RIGHT

1

Twinkle, Twinkle, Little Star

★

EVERYONE who watched the Coronation Procession of Queen Elizabeth II of Great Britain in 1953, either on the streets of London or on television sets throughout the world, was aware that the niftiest scene stealer in the whole parade was Queen Salote of Tonga, or the Friendly Islands. A woman of noble proportions with the glossy coloring of eighteenth-century mahogany, she rode cheerily through the pouring rain, beaming and waving with a warmth as friendly as her own islands, and people were enchanted by her on sight. What few of them knew was that Queen Salote was dressed for that occasion from head to foot—a considerable distance—by R. H. Macy's of New York.

Macy's was not surprised that Queen Salote and her court knew about their Tall Girl's Shop. "We simply got a letter from the Queen asking for an outfit for the Coronation," says a Tall Girl's executive, "so we sent her six to choose from, and she kept all of them." As the biggest and best-known department store in the world, Macy's takes such assignments calmly. Through its personal shopping service the store has decorated the palace of President Tubman of Liberia and furnished and installed all of its plumbing; has supplied silk by the yard to deck the beauties of a Saudi-Arabian harem; and, in collaboration with the Red Cross, worked all of one tragic night to clothe and otherwise help restore the survivors of the "Andrea Doria."

Recently a committee from a Russian Housing Project visited Macy's and bought whole rooms and modern kitchens intact to be shipped to Russia via a forwarder in the United States and paid for by the Soviet Embassy in Washington. Questioned about the difference in Russian and American voltage for electric appliances, the committee-members said it didn't matter, and went happily on to the purchase they appeared to relish the most, which was Hide-A-Beds. Some years ago, when Macy's installed a barnyard complete with live animals as a promotion stunt, a Brazilian came in and bought a small burro he had taken a fancy to, and had it shipped home to Brazil. A few weeks later the burro was returned by freight express and was followed by a letter from the burro-fancier who claimed that it was not the burro he had ordered. "It has not the same expression around the eyes," he wrote mournfully. Sometimes the animal itself is the customer. On Valentine's Day last year Kokomo, successor to J. Fred Muggs on the Dave Garroway television show, dropped in with his trainer at the toy department on the fifth floor. He bought a Wyatt Earp suit, a cowboy suit, and an Indian suit, spending some nineteen dollars in all.

Macy's has 650,000 D.A. (Depositor's Account) customers alone, many living far away, others included in the 150,000 people who daily shop in the store on Herald Square. In the weeks before Christmas the number of daily shoppers in the store—including D.A. and C.T. (Cash-Time) accounts, as well as those who pay cash in full—increases to about 250,000, and the pre-Christmas, or peacetime, staff of around 10,000 clerks is nearly doubled. Most of the customers are satisfied customers, but there are bound to be minor incidents and no one enjoys these more than Macy's itself, once matters have been rectified and ruffled feelings smoothed. A story the late Percy Straus, whose family have run Macy's since 1888, liked to tell on himself concerns a certain Christmas Eve. As a stimulus to Christmas shoppers Percy Straus ordered placards boldly displayed throughout the store promising patrons that each and every purchase, even last-minute ones, would surely be delivered no later than Christmas Eve. Around midnight on that day he went wearily home and fell into bed. At two o'clock in the morning his bedside telephone rang, and a charming feminine voice identified itself as that of a, shall we say, Mrs. Noel of Sunnyside, Long Island.

"I just wanted to tell you, Mr. Straus," she said, "that I am perfectly satisfied with the dancing bear I bought at Macy's for my little granddaughter's Christmas."

"I am delighted to hear it, madam," replied Mr. Straus, a courtly man. "But may I inquire why you telephoned me at my home, at this hour, to tell me so?"

"Because your goddam truck just woke me up, delivering it!" roared Mrs. Noel of Sunnyside, and hung up.

Another Macy true story is the one about the D.A. customer who ordered a flagpole to be delivered in time for the Fourth of July so that he could fly Old Glory from the lawn of his new house in Connecticut. His letter specified the required dimensions and the flagpole was forthwith delivered, but when he had installed it on the lawn it turned out to be too short. After a spirited telephone message from the customer, Macy's rushed a truck to Connecticut to deliver a second flagpole and take the first one away. Alas! The second flagpole, laboriously imbedded, proved to be too long. Disgusted, the patriotic customer dug it up and threw it into a corner of the garage. Then he went into the village, bought a local flagpole to his liking, and planted it finally on the lawn with a great sweating. Exhausted, he tottered into his house, called up Macy's and gave them a piece of his mind; they could take back their lousy flagpole, he told them, and never mind sending another either. The next day was July third. In the householder's absence, possibly for a cooling swim, a Macy truck drove up, two truck drivers descended and, with a mighty effort, uprooted the flagpole from the lawn and carted it back to Macy's. "We was sent to pick up a flagpole, and that was the only flagpole we *seen!*" they both declared truthfully, later.

The patriotic customer flew the flag from his housetop that year, but he dined out on the story for some time and he is still a happy Macy customer.

Not all of the occasional grief is the patron's. Apart from what salesclerks go through from the inevitable ill-mannered shopper, even executives are often given a turn. One summer, an assistant manager of the personal shopping service went on vacation to her cottage in Vermont and was met by a wild invasion of bats. The creatures stormed the attic and the cellar, they flew down the fireplace, they whizzed and crept through the rooms, and they ruined her vacation. The first letter that met her eye on her return to Macy's was from an amateur gardener who wrote, "Dear Macy's: I

have made a bet with my neighbor that Macy's sells bat-dirt for use as a fertilizer. Please tell me that I am correct?"

The lady executive leans back and looks tired when she speaks of this today. "I had a letter all ready to send to him, but I didn't send it," she says. What her unsent letter said was simply: "Macy's has no bat-dirt in stock, but you sure came to the right girl."

The shopper who strolls, or dashes, into Macy's on Herald Square by any one of its thirteen customer entrances (there are two others, for employees only) has no more idea of what she is starting than the patron who casually visits the Waldorf-Astoria or Grand Central Station. Merely by saying "I'll take that" a single customer puts in motion over a thousand people, whether the choice is a kitchen gadget, an item on the menu, or a ticket to Seattle. Customers do not know, nor are they obliged to know, of the vast machinery behind a single purchase. Macy's customers would be staggered, but possibly bored, by statistics about the volume of merchandise that passes each year through Macy's Receiving Department; by the fact that these goods arrive from a Thirty-fifth Street entrance to receiving units extending from the sub-basement to the nineteenth floor, where they are price-marked and channeled to various departments; that there is a "marking pool" on the fourth floor from which "markers" are regularly sent throughout the store to inspect price-tags and sometimes lower them, according to advice from the buyer of each department, who has in turn been advised by the comparison shopper. All of these things are interesting, and will be dealt with later in this book, but they are not what the average shopper wants to know right off.

The average shopper, asked to consider the huge mechanism of the whole thing, says, "So Macy's is the biggest store in the world. How do you mean, the biggest store in the world?"

Well, there is a colorful answer to that question. Macy's New York alone uses, every year, 4,848 miles of cotton twine, 1,404 miles of ribbonette, 3,788 miles of gummed tape, 225 miles of Scotch tape, 2,250,000 Christmas boxes,

2,000,000 white gift boxes, 1,500,000 folding boxes, 21,000,-
000 sheets of packing tissue, 4,000,000 D.A. and C.T. statements, 5,000,000 "taken" sales checks, and 31,000,000 paper
bags for notions and hat-bar millinery.

In its executive, or nonselling, departments, Macy's uses
annually 9,000,000 envelopes, 2,000,000 sheets of letterhead
writing paper, 3,000,000 paper clips, 2,500,000 rubber
bands, 4,000 various printed forms, 18,750,000 paper towels
for washrooms, and 72,000 eraser-tips. If the pencils used
annually by Macy's were laid end to end "we could probably
get rid of some of these statistics," a tired executive recently
said. Actually, the pencils would extend sixty-three and
one-half miles.

Macy's spends about $900 a year on the white carnations
worn in the lapels of executives. These carnations are made
of cloth and cost $6 a gross. Red cloth carnations are worn
by "sponsors" (expert salespeople in charge of those less
experienced) and are relatively expensive, costing $7 a gross,
or $525 a year, since there are fewer sponsors at Macy's than
there are executives. Red carnations rose in price when it
was discovered that they required a fast-color dye, after a
sponsor got caught in the rain one day with his carnation
and Macy's had to buy him a new suit.

Throughout the store's 168 selling departments almost
half a million different items of merchandise are offered for
sale. That all of them are successfully sold is indicated by
the fact that, in 1956, the net retail sales of R. H. Macy
& Co., Inc.—the organization which is composed of Macy's
New York, the parent store, and its thirty-two branches and
affiliates—reached an all-time high of $398,261,000, a figure
which would have surprised and pleased the man who
founded Macy's.

He was a stubborn, rosy-cheeked, seafaring Quaker named Rowland Hussey Macy whose record of four failures as a merchant before he came to New York is reflected, in his own hand, on the last page of one of his early account books. Written in Boston, in 1845, this entry records:

May 13th to Mrs. Holbrook:

1 pr. hose	.25
1 pr. dimity cuffs	.08
3 yds. pink ribbon	.15

To Mrs. Hubbard:

2 papers of pins @ 8¢	.16
Total	.64
Cash to milkman	$4.10
Received	.64
Minus	$3.46

On the page following these melancholy items he wrote, in heavily flowing script:

I have worked Two Years for Nothing.
Damn.
Damn.
damn.
damn.

On a wall of the executive offices on the thirteenth floor of Macy's hangs a lithograph of an ancient dame huddled balefully in a big chair, a mobcap riding above her beaked nose, and her eye fixed in seeming contempt upon the pages of a book she is holding; a cane rests against her knee, and at her feet a large cat is distrustfully curled. This is Judith Macy, great-grandmother of Rowland Hussey Macy, who died in 1819 at the age of ninety. Her son Sylvanus, and his son John, who was Rowland's father, both followed approximately the same pattern of life. They were New England Quakers and seafaring men, merchant traders or whalers, who left the sea to run small retail stores on land, selling books, printed gazettes, shoes, and sperm candles. Rowland, born in 1822 on Nantucket Island, Massachusetts, shipped aboard the whaler "Emily Morgan" at the age of fifteen on a voyage that lasted four years. He returned with $500 as his share of the "Emily Morgan's" $90,000 cargo of whale oil and whalebone, and with a more lasting memento of the voyage; the red star tattooed on his arm which was to become perhaps the most famous trade-mark in merchandising history.

Abandoning the sea as his forbears had done, Rowland Macy went to work as a printer in Boston where he met George W. Houghton, a dry goods merchant, and before long married Houghton's sister, Louisa. It has been said that Houghton lent him the money to open a thread-and-needle store, but the first actual records of his presence as a merchant in Boston are an 1844 directory listing his dry goods store at 178½ Hanover Street and the account book dated 1844–1845 which describes the purchases of Mrs. Holbrook and Mrs. Hubbard and of, alas, very few other people.

It was not for nothing, however, that Rowland Macy was born of a long line of industrious and persevering Quakers. In 1846, he popped up again with a dry goods store at 78½ Washington Street, and cheerily ran an advertisement in the Boston *Daily Mail* featuring "DRY GOODS From Cash

Auctions Every Day." His merchandise consisted of items picked up at public auction sales, and this store also lasted only a year. In 1847 Macy was working for another brother-in-law, Samuel S. Houghton (who later founded Houghton & Dutton in Boston) in a lace-and-embroidery shop on Tremont Street. In the same year his son, Rowland Macy Junior, was born and Macy, now a family man with responsibilities, was hard pressed for the means to sustain them.

The Gold Rush of 1849 seemed to offer a rosy solution to his problems. New towns were thrusting up overnight in California, and miners, sagging with gold, must surely need supplies for themselves and a few bits of finery for their wives. Leaving his wife and son in the more civilized purlieus of Boston, Macy with his brother Charles sailed in March, 1849, aboard the brig "Dr. Hitchcock" and arrived in San Francisco a hazardous four and a half months later, having voyaged there by way of Panama. With two partners acquired in the new country they opened a dry goods and provisions store at Marysville, forty miles north of Sacramento, under the name of Macy & Co. In an advertisement in the Marysville *Herald* they announced that they were "prepared to furnish about everything necessary for the use of Miners," and that "Country Merchants, Packers, City Traders, MINERS &¢., will do well to give us a call before purchasing elsewhere."

What Macy & Co. overlooked was the fact that miners represent largely a floating population; when one mine has been worked they move on to another, thus accounting for the number of ghost towns in the West. For this reason, and doubtless for others, the Marysville Macy's went out of business almost exactly three months after it opened. On

September 23, a paid announcement in the *Herald* marked the dissolution of the partnership, immediately above another item advertising "E. W. Tracy, Successor to Macy & Co." It is not known whether E. W. Tracy was a luckless creditor who was obliged to take over the store, or whether he was just a cockeyed optimist.

By 1851 the Macys were back in Massachusetts where they undauntedly opened another place of business in Haverhill—this time under the name of a third brother, Robert B. Macy, perhaps because the credit rating of Rowland and Charles was low after the California venture. Rowland actually ran the store, however, and wrote all the advertising, announcing as the store's policy that "His Goods are all bought for Cash, and will be sold for the same, at a small advance." It was a policy from which he never deviated, nor did Macy's for the next eighty-eight years until, in 1939, the public trend toward installment-buying obliged the store to initiate its Cash-Time Accounts. "We do not profess to keep a large Stock of Goods, but we *do* keep a FAST one," the Haverhill ads further stated, and "Taking *Onward and Upward* for our motto, we challenge any competition—confident that we cannot be undersold. . . ." Haverhill competition accepted the challenge by lowering its prices until Macy's was several times forced to sell merchandise at 20 per cent below the market price in order to make good its promise not to be undersold by rival stores. Macy's usual discount to customers was 10 per cent, and at those prevailing prices dark prints cost 10 cents a yard, fast-color prints 6½ cents, sheeting from 6¼ to 8 cents a yard, and "wrought collars" from 4 to 6¼ cents each. The fractions were due, not as it is popularly supposed to their seductive effect on patrons, but to the fact that the shilling was still widely used in New England and its value in American money was 12½ cents.

R. H. Macy's name replaced his brother's in 1852 when things had begun to look a little better, and he adopted around this time a crowing cock as his trade-mark. The cock managed to crow for almost four years before the Haverhill store, Macy's fourth attempt as a merchant, also failed and closed its doors. Temporarily discouraged, Macy gave up storekeeping and was next heard of, though obscurely, in Wisconsin where he operated as a stockbroker and real-estate broker. It may be that he was a man ahead of his times. He was known, at any rate, to be a religious man and religion, with him, marched hand in hand with a devotion to business. In the back of one of his early Bibles, which has been preserved, there is a carefully penciled account of some deal involving raspberries, blackberries, and peaches to a total receipt of $6.16. Perhaps, reading his Bible, he came upon the words of Isaiah about Tyre, "the crowning city, whose merchants are princes, whose traffickers are the honorable of the earth." The nearest thing to a "crowning city" in America was New York, and there, in 1858—one hundred years ago—Rowland Macy brought his wife and son and opened up a "fancy dry goods" store in a four-story building at 204-206 Sixth Avenue, near Fourteenth Street.

The population of New York City in 1858 was 950,000. The city was growing increasingly important as a financial center and as a manufacturing and retailing market, and into its busy port streamed immigrants from the Old World to bring new blood and healthy competition. The panic of 1857 was over, and business in general was on an upswing.

New York's shopping district was mainly around City Hall; A. T. Stewart's was on Chambers Street, Lord & Taylor on Grand Street, and Arnold Constable at Canal and Mercer. Fourteenth Street was considered pretty far uptown for a store, bordering in fact on the residential district. The wealthy patrons of A. T. Stewart's and Lord & Taylor bowled along in their carriages through unpaved streets littered with rubbish and, in wet weather, awash with mud; but from the first, Macy's ads, still written by R. H. himself, shrewdly appealed to the masses of women who did not own carriages. There were plenty of omnibuses and horse-cars, the ads pointed out, going on to advise cosily, "Ladies, if walking is too bad, just take the cars."

What Rowland Macy used for money in order to open his New York store is still something of a mystery, but it is generally concluded that he was financed by long-term credit, a custom of those days, from the jobbers and wholesalers from whom he bought. Macy was a dynamic and persuasive kind of man, and besides, word of his disastrous career up to that time had not reached these gentlemen's ears in that period of slow communication. At any rate, he was able to put $20,000 into his stock. It was the same amount he had invested in Haverhill, but with a difference: in Haverhill his store had carried all sorts of dry goods, including "staples" (cloth by the yard, and so on); in New York he became a specialist, dealing only in "fancy" dry goods such as ribbons, feathers, and laces. Even so, the first few weeks were not auspicious. The store was tiny, 20 feet wide and 60 feet long, it was out of the shopping zone, and competition was lively. Rowland Macy's new account book, inscribed as always in his meticulous script, records the events of the store's opening day, October 27, 1858, and the day afterward:

October 27, 1858:
    First Day's Sales $11.06
October 28:
    Cash on hand   11.06
    Rec'd back on ins.   2.50
    Sales by ticket book   51.70

    Total $65.26

Before Christmas, though, he was able to record:

    Cash on hand $1,427.99

It was the beginning of success. His first year's sales totaled $90,000—a good omen, maybe, since it was the same sum the whaler "Emily Morgan" had made from its cargo of whale oil seventeen years earlier. At the end of the first year Macy employed fifteen salesclerks at the then standard wages of around $2 a week, paid $1,600 in annual rent, and, always a great believer in spreading the word, spent $2,800 for advertising. By 1866 he was able to repay the wholesalers and jobbers their original stake in full and to establish his credit without question by paying current bills within ten or fifteen days. Macy's ads continued to be spirited, with Macy's cock crowing over them until 1862, when the cock was replaced by Macy's red star. Many advertising experts today consider R. H. Macy to be the first man to use plain white space to attract attention. The accepted advertisements of his time were crowded little items, packing as many words as possible into the smallest possible space. These were not for Rowland Macy, with the red star to guide him into the open sea of commerce.

COME, COME, TIME, TIME,   (read one Macy ad)

COME, COME, TIME, TIME,

THE TIME HAS COME.

WHAT IS TO BE DONE? IS THE QUESTION

WHAT IS TO BE DONE? IS THE QUESTION

WHAT SHALL BE DONE?

WHAT SHALL BE DONE?

MARK EVERY ARTICLE

WAY

WAY

WAY DOWN!

Although a trifle hysterical to the modern eye, this approach was a refreshing change from the stuffy generalities that passed for advertising elsewhere at the time. Macy was also the first to quote prices in advertisements, a useful courtesy, and the customers came, came, to the store on upper Sixth Avenue whose entire four-story façade proclaimed in gilt scrollwork and other fancy lettering:

R. H. MACY

Dealer in

Carpets, Oil Cloths, Matting &¢

Importers & Retailers of

Shawls, Cloaks, Mantillas

Silks, Velvets, Merinoes, Embroideries & Hosiery

Rowland Macy and his family lived, for a time, on the top floor of the store, just between the "R. H. Macy" and the "Carpets, Oil Cloths, Matting &¢" on the sign. From their windows at home, or indeed from any window in Macy's, they could look out upon the growing popularity of Sixth Avenue and Fourteenth Street. The popularity was not due only to Macy's, of course. The city was gradually moving uptown, and the new elevated railway was being completed, with a passenger station at Fourteenth Street bringing more customers to Macy's. A pleasant print of the period, which also hangs on a wall of Macy's executive offices, shows Fourteenth Street and Sixth Avenue as a center of gaiety. Interested ladies in silks and mantillas cluster around a gypsy fortuneteller whose trained parakeet picks out their fortunes from an array of cards; glossy victorias dash to and fro, occupied by parasoled beauties and mustachioed gents; the new elevated railway looms in the background, and R. H. Macy's dominates the scene with its four-story sign and its elegant display windows extending along Sixth Avenue and around the corner onto Fourteenth Street.

At thirty-six, when he opened his New York store, Rowland Macy was a man who had been through a great deal. He was understandably hot-tempered until, by his own statement, he was cured of his rages at a Moody and Sankey revival meeting in his later years. Before that, he was subject to certain picturesque tantrums. Once, when several customers complained that the umbrellas he sold had weak handles, Mr. Macy marched to the umbrella counter, broke every umbrella over his knee, and stormed away from there. Another time, when he discovered that a floorwalker or somebody had placed a glass shade over one of the store's gas jets, Macy seized a nearby hammer and smashed the glass shade to bits. "I am paying for *all* the gaslight, and I intend to get *all* the gaslight," he explained.

There was nothing stingy about R. H. Macy, however, when it came to expanding his business. Within a com-

paratively few years he bought out all of the small stores adjacent to his own until Macy's at length occupied the space of twelve stores on Sixth Avenue and on Fourteenth Street, in addition to its livery stables on Fifteenth Street. Smart Macy delivery wagons embellished with the red star and drawn by handsome horses—regular winners in the working class at horse shows—became a familiar sight around New York and as far as Brooklyn and Queens, where Macy's had begun to make free deliveries. Joseph P. Ryan, who has sold printed forms to Macy's since the Fourteenth Street days, remembers that the New York Fire Department made quite a fuss about Macy's delivery wagons as late as the 1890's. "Them wagons is too darn fast and too darn *red*," a fire chief complained. "People think it's a hook-and-ladder roaring up the street!"

"In those days," Mr. Ryan reflects, "Macy's buyer was Charles B. Mackin, and he had to buy oats for the horses as well as merchandise for the store. He sure loved those horses. One night the oats didn't come on time, and Mr. Mackin wouldn't leave until they came. He just paced the stables till the oats got there and the horses were fed. As I recall, he didn't go home till about midnight."

Along with his store Rowland Macy enlarged and varied his merchandise to include men's wear, household goods, ready-to-wear dresses, "mechanical" corsets, and linen bosoms. Between 1860 and 1872 he installed "French and German fancy goods," drugs, toilet goods, parasols, china and glassware, silver, sporting goods, luggage, toys, musical instruments, books, costume jewelry and fancy ornaments, velocipedes, barometers, gardening sets, bathing costumes, fresh flowers and potted plants, a picnic department selling potted meats and jam and other ingredients of an outing, *and*—an eye-opening innovation at the time—a soda fountain. Macy's was no longer a "fancy dry goods" store. It was a department store, and in 1870 its sales totaled one million dollars.

Many of the newfangled notions were the inspiration of Margaret Getchell, one of the earliest of the women executives who now more or less dominate the merchandising world. Miss Getchell was a distant relative of Rowland Macy's, and had been a schoolteacher in Nantucket until the loss of one eye in an accident canceled any more mulling over theme papers in a poorly-lit schoolroom. She came to Macy's and started as a cashier, being soon promoted to bookkeeper and then to superintendent. At Macy's she also fell in love with Abiel T. La Forge, Macy's lace buyer and a buddy of Rowland Macy Junior in the Civil War. Rowland Junior, sad to say, was a disappointment to his father and disappears with scarcely a trace from the record. But Abiel La Forge married Margaret Getchell in 1869 and the couple moved into the apartment over the store formerly occupied by the Macys, who by that time had a house of their own on Twelfth Street. The complete dedication to the store which is still present in all of Macy's personnel shows itself clearly in a letter from Abiel La Forge to his bride, when he was obliged to leave her on a buying trip to Europe.

"Perhaps . . ." he wrote, "it would be well to add a shoe store and barber shop. What do you think? We bought some ladies' and gents' slippers to come out this spring . . . ; if they succeed, there is no telling what it may lead to."

To Margaret Getchell La Forge such a letter was a love letter indeed. It concerned what she cared about most, the expansion of Macy's services. Although the "shoe store and barber shop" never became crystallized in fact, the shoe department was established before long, and Mrs. La Forge flew about in a fury of creation. She was in full charge of the store for the moment, since Macy was in Europe with her husband, and the stories of her energy are prodigious. To a salesclerk dismayed at having dropped an imported toy bird to the floor and ruining its singing mechanism, she is reported to have said briskly, "Give it to me, I'll fix it." Whipping a hairpin out of her hair, they say, she fixed it. What endeared her to Rowland Macy was probably her talent for display, for publicity, and for the large gesture.

Once, it is said, she spent a week persuading two live cats to be dressed in dolls' clothing and to repose peacefully in twin cribs in the toy department as an enticement to customers. Tall though these tales may be, it is evident that Margaret Getchell had the right idea about running a store: Be Everywhere, Do Everything, and Never Forget to Astonish the Customer.

Rowland Macy agreed with all of these principles, except one. Men grew old fairly young in those days, and at fifty Macy no longer wanted to "do everything." As early as 1871 he had begun to transfer responsibilities to younger men so that, if he died, the success he had won so hard and bitterly would not be interrupted. In 1872 Abiel La Forge became a partner in R. H. Macy & Co., and in 1875 Robert Macy Valentine, a nephew, was admitted to the third partnership. Rowland Macy was still the boss, but he had the comfort of knowing that the future of his business was safe in the hands of two young men, one trained by him and the other his kin.

In 1877 R. H. Macy died unexpectedly in Paris, on a business trip, at the age of fifty-four. On receiving the news Abiel La Forge and Robert Macy Valentine, after a suitable period of mourning, bought up all shares in the store owned by any Macy heirs and announced publicly that, after the first of the year, R. H. Macy & Co., would be known as La Forge & Valentine's. The store might be known by that name today—if it had survived—but for the fact that La Forge died of tuberculosis less than a year later, before the name could be changed, and that Margaret Getchell La Forge and Robert Macy Valentine also died in rapid succession. It seemed almost like the hand of God, directed by some hardfisted sailor from his particular cloud.

R. H. Macy & Co. was now in charge of Charles B. Webster, a former floorwalker and a handsome man, whom Valentine had taken as a partner after the deaths of Macy and La Forge. Webster took as partner one Jerome B. Wheeler, a flour merchant who later married Valentine's widow. The two men controlled Macy's from 1879 until the end of 1887, and made various improvements in the merchandise and facilities, installing electric light, a Western Union office, and a Bell telephone. However, Webster and Wheeler never got along very well together. For one thing, Wheeler had alienated the Valentine family (Rowland Macy's relatives) by his marriage to Mrs. Valentine; and for another, he lacked the proper dedication to Macy's, being equally interested in some mining properties he held in Colorado. Webster, who owned the majority interest in the Macy partnership, finally dissolved it, and invited two men who were running the china and glassware department on lease from Macy's to become his new partners.

Rowland Macy never knew on earth that the future of his store depended, not on the young men whom he had trained to succeed him, but on the two sons of a quiet man with whom he had made a minor deal in 1874, when he leased him space to sell his own imported china and glass at Macy's. But Rowland Macy must have rested easier in heaven when he knew who the two new partners were—for there is no more unbeatable combination in business than the principles of an able Yankee trader and those of a discerning Jew.

The quiet man's name was Lazarus Straus; and the two new partners were his sons, Isidor and Nathan.

2

Fourteenth Street

★

L AZARUS STRAUS was a man of some distinction in his native town of Otterberg, in the Bavarian Palatinate. A farm owner and trader in grain, he was also a fiery-hearted liberal and solidly supported Carl Schurz and other crusaders in their battle for political freedom in 1848. When the movement failed Lazarus Straus sailed for America in 1852 and, with the protean adaptability of his generation, became a traveling peddler in Oglethorpe, Georgia.

Many German immigrants pinned their hopes to a pushcart in their first days in the New World, but the best of them did not remain peddlers long, nor did Lazarus Straus. Within a year he had opened a general store in Talbotton, Georgia, in partnership with a man named Kaufman, and in 1854 he was able to bring to their new home in America the wife, Sara, and four children he had left in Bavaria. The children were a daughter, Hermine (who soon had her own piano and other niceties of life in Talbotton), and three remarkable sons; Isidor and Nathan, who became the first Strauses to own and operate Macy's, and Oscar, who in 1909 was appointed America's first ambassador to Turkey.

34

The boys went to school at the Collingworth Institute in Talbotton and that was the two older boys' only formal education, for the outbreak of the Civil War soon destroyed the pleasant routine of life in the South. Isidor, the eldest, who was barely sixteen came to work in the store and two years later fell upon a stroke of good luck. Lloyd C. Bowers, one of a group of local men who had bought a fast steamer to run the Union blockade and carry cotton to England and supplies back to the South, took Isidor along to London as his secretary and assistant. When the blockade-running venture petered out, Isidor found himself alone in London with his entire private fortune of $1,200 in gold sewed into his underwear and with about $1,500 in bills of exchange belonging to his father's firm. Through various deals in cotton acceptances during the next two years, he ran his $2,700 up to about $10,000, which he brought back to America.

The war had driven Lazarus and his family out of Georgia and, after the elder Straus had invested all of his remaining capital in raw cotton, they had settled temporarily in Philadelphia. At the end of the war Lazarus made a gesture which, though perfectly commonplace to him, was never forgotten by the men with whom he had done business and which permanently secured the integrity of the Straus family. He took the money he made in cotton and went around to all the firms he had dealt with, paying every last cent on the bills which most of them had written off as a total loss because of the war. This simple feat of honesty cost him about $25,000, but it was worth millions.

Isidor, the traveled man, soon got his family out of Philadelphia and established in New York, and in May, 1866, the firm of L. Straus & Sons opened a wholesale business in glassware and china in a small store on Chambers Street. The "Sons" were Isidor and Nathan, since Oscar was only sixteen and still in school, and they gradually took over much of the operation from Lazarus who, nearing sixty, had begun to depend on his sons. Isidor was bookkeeper, merchandiser, and general manager, and Nathan was the salesman; and it was because Nathan hated being a traveling salesman that L. Straus & Sons eventually became connected with R. H. Macy & Co. In order to stay off the road, Nathan got the idea of setting up glass and china departments in various stores on a lease basis, with the Strauses supplying the merchandise and the store running the department—in somewhat the same way that a concessionaire today operates a checkroom or a restaurant. The Strauses knew Rowland Macy, having sold him china, and it was to him that they first took the new idea. In March, 1874, the glassware and china department of L. Straus & Sons opened for business in Macy's basement. It was a success from the start, with sales totaling $102,430 in the first year, and over $650,000 in 1888, the year that Isidor and Nathan Straus became partners of Charles B. Webster in R. H. Macy & Co. Eight years later Webster, whose health was not good, sold his interest to the Strauses for $1,200,000 and retired, leaving Isidor and Nathan as sole partners.

The brothers were superbly equipped for their new careers. From their father they had learned industriousness, integrity, and experience, to which each brother added his own admirable characteristics. Nathan was the showier of the two, sparkling forth with a continual stream of colorful new ideas and hunches which Isidor, like a rock in a waterfall, calmly considered and either retained or allowed to slide off him. It was Nathan who enlarged window displays, increased advertising, and thought up new departments and customer services; but it was Isidor who handled the financing and merchandising of each new project and saw to it that all ran smoothly. In their first five years of sole partnership Macy's established sixteen new departments including carpets, pictures, wallpaper, blankets, boys' clothing, and infants' wear. To obtain more space, the Strauses bought up adjacent land and built two six-story annexes on Thirteenth and Fourteenth Streets in which—a sensational departure—they installed elevators. The local press took a dim view of this novelty, one newspaper referring to the annexes as "skyscrapers" and expressing grave doubts that customers "would submit to crowding in elevators, no matter what they had tolerated in the aisles." The many European contacts of L. Straus & Sons proved useful, and in 1893 Macy's opened a Paris office, following it in 1897 with an office in Belfast mainly for the purchase of Irish linens.

Remembering how Rowland Macy had come to grief with his stocks picked up at public auction, the Strauses advertised in 1894: "We never deal in old or bankrupt stocks. We sell new and desirable goods only." This did not mean that Macy's was not as alert to close-out sales of manufacturers or to other bargains in 1894 as it was in 1956, when it was able to buy $1,500,000 worth of Capehart television and radio sets at prices which permitted their retail sale at as much as 50 per cent below the listed value. But the merchandise, however acquired, had to be good to satisfy Macy's, in the 1880's and 1890's as in the 1950's. That the quality was excellent is proven by the sturdy survival of several long-ago purchases. Mrs. Kendell, a salesclerk at the thrift tables on the main floor, has a doll that her grandmother bought at Macy's in 1883; the doll's cheeks and eyes are still bright and her dress of striped pure silk, though a little faded, is uncracked. A Mrs. Charles Meldrum, a Staten Island customer, recently came across a bolt of pink satin ribbon bought at Macy's in 1896; slightly dusty but un-faded. Miss Torretta, who works in the candy department, treasures her grandmother's wedding dress made of heavy, still-lustrous satin bought at Macy's in 1902 for a dollar fifty a yard. And only last year a Mrs. Louis La Rocco of Lindenhurst wrote a letter asking how to wash a blanket which her grandparents had bought at Macy's sixty years ago. Mr. Rutchik of the blanket department replied with full instructions.

Mrs. Charles Farrar of Teaneck, New Jersey, remembers shopping at Macy's in 1896 when she was little Ida Lamogne, aged ten. As a reward for good marks in school her mother would let her take the ferry alone from Hoboken, where the Lamognes lived, to New York and Macy's, and would give her sixty cents for the day's outing. Round trip on the ferry was six cents, and at Macy's elegant black lace rem-nants were to be had for a penny apiece, elastic for garters (a more practical purchase) at seven cents a yard, and calico (another strict necessity) at seven to eight cents a yard. There was plenty left over from the sixty cents for lunch, eked out by the licorice-strings the salesclerks at Macy's candy counter gave her. By a neat coincidence little Ida's first cousin, Charles Gildersleeve, is now a "sponsor" in Macy's Closet Shop. "Cousin Ida also remembers a mansion on Fourteenth Street which her mother told her was the Rhinelander home," he says. "It was as busy as Macy's, with horses and carriages arriving continually. I have not checked on the Rhinelander mansion to see if it really existed there at that time, or whether," Mr. Gildersleeve adds with charm, "it was just another Victorian home and a little girl's imagination."

A longtime D.A. customer, a Mrs. Bernstein, still has a bill from Macy's dated January 7, 1901. The bill, embellished with the red star, is headed:

Bought of R. H. MACY & Co.
Retailers, Importers and Manufacturers
BOTH SIDES 14th STREET—SIXTH AVENUE
TERMS: CASH IN EVERY INSTANCE

and further lists five foreign offices, in Paris, Belfast, Limoges, Rudolstadt in Thuringia, and Carlsbad and Steinschönau in Bohemia. The items, handwritten in ink on both sides of the paper, number eighty in all—including a washboiler, coffee mill, coal shovel, coal scuttle, grater, dauber, cream ladle, and flour-sieve—and come to a cash total of $16.83. For that amount, and with the number of things she bought, Mrs. Bernstein could have equipped an entire restaurant kitchen in 1901.

Prices had gone up little since 1897 when Macy's advertised in *The Sun* men's sack suits and overcoats at $9.97, calfskin shoes at $2.49, Derby and Alpine hats at $1.24, and six-year-old imported Scotch whiskey at 99 cents a bottle. In the same issue Wanamaker advertised men's overcoats "handsomely tailored" at $15 and women's suits at $12. Macy's was able to undersell competitors and maintain its 6 per cent discount because of its strictly-cash policy and because, for the most part, it bought directly from the manufacturer. The middleman was a bogeyman in those days, to be eliminated whenever possible. Operating expenses were comparatively low too, although Macy's paid its employees the standard wages of the day. In the 1870's salesclerks (mostly women at Macy's even then) had started at $3 or $4 a week, with no commissions, and "cash-girls"—the little fourteen-year-olds who ran about the floor answering the clerks' cries of "Cash! Cash!"—received $1.50 a week, plus a silver dollar and a box of candy at Christmas. Cashiers were in a higher bracket, earning as much as $8 a week. Employees worked from 7:45 A.M. until 7 P.M. and there were no bonuses, but twice a year all the help were treated to a fine outing; a picnic on Staten Island or a steamboat excursion in the summer, and a sleigh-ride in the winter.

By the turn of the century wages had risen to an average of $10 a week for salesclerks, and a system of commissions had been established. But Rose Olender of the cigar department recalls that as late as 1916, when she was first hired as a cash-girl in the flowers-and-feathers department, she was paid $5 a week for a six-day week. "Once a year I would get a fifty-cent raise" Mrs. Olender muses. "After a year I was promoted to the mail-order department at seven dollars a week. In the lunchroom I could get a good lunch, a sandwich, a big cup of milk and an apple, for nine cents. I remember what we used to call Blue Mondays during World War I. The store was closed on Mondays to save fuel, but the girls in the mail-order department had to come in to sort the mail. We had to walk up to the tenth floor because no elevators were running, and we had to keep on our coats and gloves because there was no heat. We really turned blue on Blue Mondays, and the lunchroom sent us up hot coffee every hour to keep us going." At this point Mrs. Olender sighs a long, contented sigh. "I have been very happy at Macy's," she concludes peacefully.

Fred Landeck, another employee, started at Macy's in 1902 as a wagon helper. The delivery route ran from a station depot at 148th Street to Dobbs Ferry, where the poor condition of the roads obliged the driver and Fred to pick up a fresh team of horses with which they continued deliveries as far as Hastings-on-Hudson and Irvington. Then the wagon started back to Dobbs Ferry, picked up the first team, and left the second team to rest for the next day. As everywhere in those times, horses were more pampered than men. Macy's driver and his helper started out daily at 7 A.M. and often it was after midnight when they arrived back at the station depot. For this Fred, the helper, was paid $6 a week. He retired a few years ago, and is a proud member of Macy's Fifty Year Club, which numbers twenty-four employees who worked at Macy's for fifty years or longer. Only one member still works regularly at the store.

In 1897, a fourteen-year-old boy wearing knickerbockers applied for a job at Macy's. He claimed to be sixteen, but even so the manager said he was too young and told him to go home and wait a while. The youth waited two months and then, clad in a new pair of long trousers, reapplied and was taken on as package-boy. This was William Titon who, as the final authority on all of Macy's groceries, other foods, wines, and liquors, is still active and famous as "Titon the Taster." Last year, at a luncheon given for him by Macy's top brass, he celebrated his sixtieth year with the store.

At seventy-five, Mr. Titon is a small, immaculate man who looks like a rosy apple. "I guess I got my start because I was nosy in more ways than one," he reflects nowadays. "The sense of smell, you know, is the most important part of tasting, that's why a taster can't smoke or afford to get a cold. Well, I was hauling those big baskets of merchandise to the delivery room, as a package-boy back in the old Fourteenth Street store, when they got short-handed one day in the grocery department and I was sent in to help fill orders. That's when I got nosy. Mr. Hall, the superintendent, sent me into an empty room off the grocery section to grind coffee beans from different brokers, put each lot into a separate envelope, boil water, and lay out the cups for a coffee-tasting session. Those ground coffee beans smelled so interesting I couldn't resist sniffing at each envelope after I'd filled it. Mr. Hall caught me at it. I thought he'd fire me, but he just asked me which three I liked best. I named three, and Mr. Hall sniffed them himself and said, 'Not bad.' I never left the grocery department after that.

"We roasted our own coffee in those days, in a factory on Fourteenth Street," Mr. Titon goes on to say. (He often speaks of himself and Macy's as "we.") "It was the beginning of the famous coffee known as Macy's Red Star Brand. We sold it in the bean, of course, in five-pound bags and once when we had a sale on it we sold forty thousand pounds in one day. The customers like to have trampled themselves to death. Another time," Mr. Titon continues pleasurably, leaning back in his swivel chair, "we advertised twenty-five thousand turkeys for Thanksgiving at twenty-three cents a pound. Before the sale began we kept the turkeys in barrels on the roof because there wasn't much refrigeration in those times. Well, sir, the Saturday before Thanksgiving it started to rain, and it didn't let up for five solid days. We all hustled up onto that roof and worked day and night in the pouring rain to weigh and tag those turkeys before they got waterlogged. Talk about Home for Thanksgiving! I remember I myself worked in that downpour from Sunday to Wednesday night. The turkeys turned out fine."

Asked about his own contributions to good eating and drinking, Mr. Titon waves a hand indicating correctly that

there are too many to enumerate. "I maintain the quality," he says. "I travel all over Europe every year to find things like a good Gruyère that will spread properly, or a wine, for instance, like the *Pineau des Charentes*, which was discovered accidentally when a French cellar-man poured new wine into a cask that still contained cognac. Not everybody's wine, the *Pineau des Charentes,* but interesting. Oh, and yes, I did discover the Idaho potato, in 1926 when I was buying apples in Idaho. Until then, baked potatoes were just ordinary potatoes, baked, and nobody had ever heard of a baked Idaho potato. We bought them and promoted them in advertising that told women how to cook them. Now, of course, you hardly ever hear of a baked potato that isn't an Idaho. The Governor of Idaho wrote and thanked the Strauses. Come on, we have to taste some wine now."

A small cell with a washbasin on the eighth floor is where Titon the Taster conducts his wine-tasting, along with Harold Goldberg, manager of the liquor department, and Miss Bianchi, their assistant. Titon tastes first, perched over his wineglass like a bird over a drinking cup, head tilted and eyes aware. After examining the color and inhaling the bouquet, he sips, rolls the wine over his tongue, and spits it out in the basin. "This one is vile," he will say, tasting various glasses, or "this one is young, fresh," or "this one has taken wood." The last comment means that the wine tastes of the barrel. Half a dozen wines submitted by brokers are tested in this way against Macy's Own Brand and others currently on sale, and are either added to the stock or rejected. Titon's is the last word, both on beverages and groceries, and his confidence in his judgment a beautiful thing to see. Once, when a comparison shopper reported that Macy's Portuguese sardines were too expensive as compared with competitors' prices, Titon appeared emotionally before the assembled authorities. "There are fishermen and fishermen," he explained. "Some fishermen go out early in the morning and stay out all day, and by the time they get their fish back to the docks the fish are as tired as they are.

Now, *my* sardines are the first catch of the early morning, and gentlemen, when they are brought back to the docks *the dew is still on the grass!"*

A patron who would agree with Titon on this point is Robert Montgomery, the actor, who is also a member of Macy's Board of Directors and a great one for Portuguese sardines. Quite often he can be glimpsed drifting about the grocery department, inquiring of flattered salesladies "I say, when are those Portuguese sardines coming in again?"

Like the Strauses, Mr. Titon has his own stake in posterity at Macy's; his son, Milton, has been with the store for over twenty years, and is now buyer of men's shoes. William, the elder Titon, remembers all of the Strauses, back to Lazarus. "When Mr. Lazarus died the store was closed for three days," he recalls. "Mr. Isidor and Mr. Nathan were devoted sons. Mr. Nathan was a great philanthropist, you know. He was mainly responsible for pasteurized milk in this country, and he got the city of New York to put up milk stations that sold pasteurized milk at a penny a glass, and gave it free to mothers. He was president of the Board of Health for four years, and Park Commissioner too, for a while. He had a lot of outside interests, but Mr. Isidor stuck mainly to Macy's. I remember when Mr. Isidor and Charles B. Webster used to walk around the store in high silk hats."

Isidor's firm hand on Nathan's ebullience appears in a letter he wrote to Nathan in Paris in 1893, urging him to cut down foreign buying in view of nervous business conditions at home. "As you always say 'The way to resume is to resume,' you can also say 'The way to stop is to stop,'" the letter, handwritten, succinctly advised. It was not that

Isidor's mind was narrower than Nathan's, but simply that his feet were more solidly on the ground.

All three Straus brothers were public-spirited and civic-minded and Oscar, a lawyer, had only a brief connection with Macy's before going on to be appointed U.S. Minister to Turkey, a member of the Permanent Court of Arbitration at The Hague, U.S. Secretary of Commerce and Labor under Theodore Roosevelt, and finally Ambassador to Turkey. Isidor indeed served a term in Congress in 1894, but his heart was with Macy's and he was needed there. The business was growing fast on Fourteenth Street, and Macy's had recently acquired an interest in the Brooklyn store of Wechsler & Abraham, which presently became Abraham & Straus.

Isidor and Nathan Straus both adhered to Rowland Macy's policy of not being undersold by competitors and this led to some lively turn-of-the-century battles, principally with Hearn's, a department store a few doors to the west on Fourteenth Street. Once, for example, Macy's bought a big lot of Japanese wash silks at a price enabling them to be sold at 41 cents a yard. Hearn's, also possessing Japanese wash silks, promptly put their silks on sale at 39 cents. Macy's cut its price to 37 cents, Hearn's cut *its* price to 35 cents, Macy's to 33 cents, Hearn's to 31 cents, and so on until at the end of the day Macy's silk was selling at "eleven yards for one cent" and bargain hunters were fainting in the aisles. Price wars reached such feverish heights that one Macy ad in *The Herald* dizzily proclaimed "Macy's Undersells MACY'S During This Carpet Sale!" Hearn's met this peculiar challenge with a widely-advertised weekly bargain sale, every Friday, a coup which Macy's noted with disdain in an ad which, however, carefully named no names:

Selling goods at exorbitant prices five days in the week (the ad read) and pretending to sell bargains on one particular day is not and never has been our practice. We have six bargain days every week as we always aim to give greater value than any other house.

Hearn's took this swipe personally, no doubt with reason, and launched a series of daily advertisements heaping ridicule and abuse upon the enemy. It seems almost a pity that

the Hearn's copywriter who composed these brickbats
should have died unknown and unsung; surely he achieved
a new low in poesy, if not in advertising:

> Black pots and tin pans, new kettles and drums,
> Candy and hash, fishing tackle and brooms,
> Are all very useful things in their way,
> And, with soda water, can be made to pay.
> But they are not dry goods as the jealous MAY SEE
> (Who should stick to his pots and let dry goods be),
> Will shortly find out to the loss of his profit,
> And with ninety-nine cents be a cent out of pocket.

Also:

> Some who deal in fishing tackle
> Night school should attend,
> And study up the dry goods trade
> In hopes their ways to mend.
> Elements of success they'll find
> Are, first, in keeping quiet
> (Unless they can the truth proclaim)—
> Falsehoods may cause a riot.
> And next avoid a bigger job
> Than can be managed right;
> And not to hit too big a man,
> Lest possibly he'll fight.

And, in a burst of obscure punning:

> The blind may see and better see than any one may see
> Who, while he sees, sees not.
> If he can see, how can he see? He cannot see—
> All but the name's forgot.

If this short enigma's hazy,
It's because the subject's crazy—
Just as crazy as one may see.

Macy's paid no attention to these spasms, beyond blandly continuing the advertisements and maintaining the policies which had provoked them. Finally Hearn's, maddened by this indifference, descended to what may be called prose:

Some Folks

are so wrapped up in their own conceit
that they think the world is made for
them and them only. They want the earth
and all of it. In this free country there
is room enough for all who do not want all
of this free country. We were born here and
expect to stay if some who are in the crockery
business have no objections, even if the
china man must go.

The Strauses remained outwardly unmoved by these attentions in the public prints. They were occupied with another battle anyway, this one with book publishers. Disturbed by the fact that Macy's sold their books at prices under the listed retail price, publishers had united in an effort to curtail this practice. Macy's reply to them was an announcement in *The Herald* of November 10, 1901:

We not only sell books cheaper than other stores, but everything else, except a few proprietary articles that we are not at liberty to cut. We are compelled to charge regular rates for them because we agreed to do so. But we do not care to make any more trade contracts of that sort.

A few days later another announcement stated:

> The American Publishers' Association refused to let
> us have their books because we make the prices to you
> so low . . . We consider this action an unlawful com-
> bination in restraint of trade which should be investi-
> gated . . .
>
> We mean to continue to have [the books] at from
> 10 to 25% less than any other house, no matter what we
> have to pay to secure them.

The life of a prosperous merchant was not all stress and
strain and competitive tactics, however. On pleasant days,
Isidor would put on his high silk hat and walk up to Del-
monico's on Twenty-third Street, sometimes with Nathan,
to take a leisurely two hours over lunch. Also—although
Macy's now employed over three thousand people and Isidor had his own private secretary—he spent a part of each
day meticulously answering his mail in longhand. He wrote
long letters to friends, customers, and business associates,
on all sorts of subjects: business, charities, politics, insurance, job-applications and personal favors. To the Honorable H. J. Thurber, a political acquaintance in Washington,
he wrote, "I am in receipt of your favor of the 28th inst.
informing me that the bicycle sent you is a size too large for
great comfort." Three closely written pages followed, advis-
ing Mr. Thurber that the next size would surely be too
small, and instructing him how to readjust the seat and
handle bars for greater comfort. The letter conjures up an
amiable picture of the Honorable H. J., whiskers flying,
whizzing through the nation's capital on a personally adjusted Macy bicycle. Isidor's tone could be firm. "Madam"
(he wrote to a certain lady): "Replying to your favor of the

8th inst., I would inform you that it would not be proper for me to give you a letter of introduction to President Cleveland on the mission you desire to see him." Also, he could be terse. A letter withdrawing Macy's advertising from *The Youth's Companion* because the magazine had taken four weeks to get the last ad into print occupied only a quarter of a page.

He kept a steady eye on L. Straus & Sons, which was still very much in business, and on the new Brooklyn store, Abraham & Straus, often sending a letter to Mr. A. Abraham that, although courteous, was calculated to keep that gentleman tossing in his bed for several nights.

Dear Mr. Abraham (one such document reads, in part):

I have just received a comparative statement of stock and sales covering the period from August 1st to October 31st and I find some stocks so exorbitantly out of proportion to the amount of business they have done that I deem it my duty to call your attention thereto.... First and foremost, I must take Department M, upholstery. This fastidious stock, so sensitive to the freaks of fashion, I find carrying $66,000 stock where the sales for three months foot up $35,000. . . . It is utterly impossible for you to make any money in that department under such conditions.

. . . I am sorry to observe that Department E, respecting which I have on former occasions written you, makes a most unsatisfactory showing. $111,000 stock with $50,000 sales for three months requires no comments.

I started off with my criticism respecting Department M because that cropped out before my eyes as the most conspicuously mismanaged department, but since writing and casting my eyes over the sheet again I find Department G, laces, makes a far far poorer showing. $63,000 stock on hand equivalent to 9 months sales is all but criminal. This seems to be the most incorrigible stock in your store . . .

I guess I have done enough scolding for one letter.

Sincerely yours,

Isidor Straus

Under the Straus management, benefits for Macy employees had greatly increased. Through the Macy Mutual Aid Association employees received from five to seven dollars a week in case of illness, with free medical care, and regular provision was made for funeral expenses and for retirement pensions, under an informal arrangement, for long-time employees. "Gratuity lunches" were established in the store, supplying free milk, tea, or coffee to cash-girls, stock girls, and parcel wrappers. Employees in higher echelons paid one cent apiece for these beverages. All employees could obtain soup, sandwiches, pie, and cake at prices ranging from one to four cents a serving, and Mr. Titon remembers that overtime workers were given a free supper of oyster stew. Neither the gratuity lunches nor the Mutual Aid Association was self-supporting, and Macy's made up the deficit.

Most employees worked "overtime" by present-day standards, not only at Macy's but in other stores as well. Macy official working hours were from eight to six, but clerks were obliged to arrive early in order to get the stock ready and to stay late to cover the merchandise and tidy up. They had Saturday afternoons off during July and August but such carefree periods were offset by the fact that, until

1901, Macy's stayed open evenings until ten for ten days before Christmas. What with working until almost midnight and having to be on hand at 7:45 next morning, some clerks even bedded down in the store during the holiday rush, and never got home until Christmas Day. Isidor and, to some extent, Nathan worked right along with them, and it is reported that Isidor's wife, Ida Straus, once complained that she had not seen her husband in ten days. This was a wrench for both of them, since their devotion as a couple was well-known even before it became immortalized when they went down together on the "Titanic" in 1912.

Isidor and Ida Straus had three sons, Jesse Isidor, Percy Selden, and Herbert, born respectively in 1872, 1876, and 1882. Jesse came to work at Macy's after his graduation from Harvard and an apprenticeship at Abraham & Straus in Brooklyn. It must have been a gratifying day for Isidor when he saw the arrival of the third generation in the store he loved so well, but he noted it simply in a diary he kept at the time. "September 3, 1896. Jesse came to Macy's," was all he wrote. Percy, Harvard '97, joined his father and brother the same year; but Herbert, the youngest brother, was prevented by his youth from coming to Macy's until after he was graduated from Harvard in 1903.

Nathan's sons, Nathan Junior and Hugh Grant, were even younger than Herbert, being born in 1889 and 1890. They did not enter the business until 1910, and remained with it only three years before they, along with their father, were bought out by Jesse, Percy, and Herbert, to everyone's mutual agreement. Even so, the pattern had come full circle. Lazarus Straus had had three sons, Isidor, Nathan, and Oscar; Isidor and Nathan, the two who had been faithful to Macy's, each had three sons—although Nathan's eldest boy had died suddenly as a student at Cornell. In 1866 Isidor, eldest son of Lazarus, had successfully uprooted his father from Philadelphia to New York. Now, in 1900, Jesse, eldest son of Isidor, set himself to propelling *his* father out of Fourteenth Street to a location farther uptown.

Fourteenth Street was no longer a shopping center. The city had moved uptown, and with it had gone Lord & Taylor, Altman, McCreery, Stern Brothers, and Arnold Constable. Besides, Macy's volume of business had outgrown its premises, which by now consisted of a sloppy conglomeration of different-sized buildings, and Siegel-Cooper had made it look like a dowdy cousin by building a smart, modern store a few blocks up Sixth Avenue, between Eighteenth and Nineteenth Streets. Macy's own building, or collection of buildings, had begun to go to pieces in spots; one part needed a new roof, another needed new plumbing, in another the floors had begun to slant. Isidor recognized these truths, but he shared the alarm of other conservatives over this mad northward rush. After all, they asked, how far could you *go?* New York north of Fifty-ninth Street was still considered pretty much of a howling wilderness, especially for merchants and in spite of an individualist named Bloomingdale who had settled himself at Fifty-ninth and Third Avenue.

"There's a lot of space between Fourteenth Street and Fifty-ninth," Jesse reminded his father, "and the leases on our present buildings expire in 1903. You'd better make up your mind."

Isidor consulted with Nathan who was, as usual, in favor of any innovation but left the decision to his brother. Isidor finally decided to let Jesse and Percy do some scouting around, at any rate, with an eye to a new location. Jesse and Percy prowled the town, east and west and as far north as Forty-fifth Street. They liked Herald Square. It combined Broadway and Sixth Avenue with the wide cross-town block of Thirty-fourth Street and its cross-town trolleys. The elevated railway had a station at Thirty-fourth Street, as it had at Fourteenth. To be sure, the only subway in those days was on the east side of town, and still under construction; but Jesse and Percy Straus felt that with the elevated and the trolley cars a sufficient number of customers could converge on Macy's from all directions, and they so reported to their father. Isidor approved, and plans were set in motion to secure land at Herald Square for the construction of a new Macy building.

The choice of location was a happy one, for shortly after the land was obtained the Pennsylvania Railroad announced the construction of a vast new passenger station between Thirty-first and Thirty-third Streets and Seventh and Ninth Avenues; and in 1902, the year that Macy's Herald Square opened, the Rapid Transit Commission approved plans for a subway extension from Forty-second Street down Broadway to Fourteenth Street, with a station at Macy's very door.

3

Onward and Upward

★

I N ONE WAY Herald Square was an odd place for a family
store like Macy's; at the turn of the century it was at the
core of New York's "tenderloin" district, a name which had
come to mean rich and rather fast living. According to
Mencken's *The American Language* the word "tenderloin,"
applied to the section running roughly from Forty-second
Street to Fourteenth and from Broadway to Eighth Avenue,
derived from one "Clubber" Williams, a police captain
who was transferred in 1876 from an obscure precinct to
West Thirtieth Street. "I've been having chuck steak ever
since I've been on the force," said Captain Williams, "and
now I'm going to have a bit of the tenderloin."

In 1900, Herald Square was mainly a night-blooming
neighborhood. During the day it was quiet, presided over
by *The Herald's* low gray building with its shiny printing
presses visible through the ground-floor windows and its
two bronze figures, Stuff and Guff, swinging their hammers
against the great bronze bell to tell the hours. (Stuff and
Guff, still swinging away, now preside over the center of
Herald Square itself.) Nearby was the old Herald Square

Hotel where, it was said, Hetty Green the miser multimillionairess lived in one room. A blacksmith had his forge at the corner of Thirty-fourth Street and Seventh Avenue. After dark, the Square woke to a blazing, humming life. A scarlet electric sign identified the Herald Square Theatre where Florenz Ziegfeld first presented Anna Held. A few doors away, Koster & Bial's Music Hall offered vaudeville and other attractions such as a special boxing bout between "Gentleman Jim" Corbett and James J. Jeffries who had just defeated Corbett for the championship. Koster & Bial's had its moments of grandeur, too. A plaque outside the Macy entrance at 151 West Thirty-fourth Street today reads:

> Here the motion picture began: on the night of April 23rd, 1896, on this site in Koster & Bial's Music Hall Thomas A. Edison with the "Vitascope" first projected a moving picture. In commemoration of this event, this tablet is here affixed by the Motion Picture Industry, October 4th, 1938.

The environs of Herald Square featured two high-class brothels, the Pekin and the Tivoli, and many of the brownstone houses that fronted on Thirty-fourth and Thirty-fifth Streets were equally in business in a smaller way. Ladies of the evening, wasp-waisted and ostrich-plumed, strolled purposefully around the Square, and the neighborhood was generally considered to be one where a man would not take his sister or his wife. Perhaps Jesse and Percy Straus, those right-living young men, did not fully realize the toughness of the "tenderloin" when they acquired land for the new building on Herald Square. They found it out

when every madam on the block reared back at them and refused to sell her lease for less than a million dollars or thereabouts. Nor were the madams alone in their determination to make a fast buck; legitimate businesses, too, were spurred by the hot promptings of greed. Hastily, the Strauses put the negotiations into the hands of a real-estate dealer, but it was too late to remain anonymous. Word had spread that Macy's wanted to acquire property on Herald Square and, to a man, the tenants dug their feet in and bared their fangs. One of them actually won out—or lost out, depending on how you look at it. Today there is a pie-shaped wedge of land measuring less than eleven hundred square feet, at the corner of Broadway and Thirty-fourth Street, which still does not belong in any way to Macy's. It is owned by the estate of one R. Smith.

The original owner had been Alfred Duane Pell, a clergyman, who was traveling in Spain in 1901 when the Strauses' agent approached him about buying the land. Mr. Pell sent word that he would sell for $250,000, but would not complete the deal until his return from Europe. Upon his return, R. Smith met the boat and quickly bought the property for $375,000. This Smith had been a thorn in Macy's side for many years. He operated a small dry goods store on Fourteenth Street, next to Macy's, and he had a cunning habit, when Macy customers walked into his shop by mistake, of persuading them that they were actually in one of Macy's buildings. Smith's descendants have always maintained that he wanted the Thirty-fourth Street property because the success of his store depended on its propinquity to Macy's, and he wished to move uptown along with the big store. However, most historians agree that Smith was acting for Henry Siegel, president of Siegel-Cooper. Macy's departure uptown would be a blow to Fourteenth Street and particularly to the new Siegel-Cooper store at Sixth Avenue and Eighteenth. Siegel wanted to keep the downtown shopping district alive by taking over Macy's old premises on Fourteenth Street and, as a means of negotiation, he secured the Pell property intending to use it as a weapon to persuade the Strauses to sell him their unexpired leases on Fourteenth. As his agent, R. Smith offered the Thirty-fourth Street corner to the Strauses at $375,000, the price he had paid for it, on condition that Macy's also relinquish the Fourteenth Street leases, which had still two years to run. The Strauses were not interested. The price was too high, they felt, and besides, Macy's had no intention of letting another store take over its old premises until all of the Fourteenth Street Macy customers had thoroughly learned their way uptown. Siegel finally wearied of the struggle and sold the corner at Broadway and Thirty-fourth to Smith, who could do nothing with it either. The original three-story building still stands on the corner, and its ground floor is now occupied by a Nedick's stand.

A more colorful holdout was Mrs. Laura Haskins, a widow who ran a restaurant at 117 West Thirty-fourth. Mrs. Haskins had a three-year lease on the ground floor of the building and refused to sell it to Macy's, who had already bought the leases of all the offices and apartments in the stories above her restaurant. When cajolery and cash had failed to move Mrs. Haskins by the time the George A. Fuller Construction Company was ready to clear the ground, Macy's reluctantly set about tearing the building down over her head. "Plucky widow Haskins," as the newspapers took to calling her, continued to serve lunches and dinners in a hail of plaster and falling bricks, and her clients

doggedly went on fishing chunks of mortar out of their soup just to show that their hearts were in the right place. At length Mrs. Haskins took the Strauses to court where the judge, in a kind of Solomon's ruling, decided that she was entitled to hold on to her lease, but that the Strauses were equally entitled to wreck the portions of the building in which they held the leases. The case was finally settled out of court, as were several similar lively skirmishes.

The new Macy's on Herald Square (now known as the Broadway Building) covered a block of land running westward from Broadway for about four hundred feet and extending from Thirty-fourth Street to Thirty-fifth. It was nine stories high, and contained thirty-three elevators, four escalators (a newfangled idea), its own power plant, a system of belt conveyors for packages, and eighteen miles of pneumatic tubes for cash and sales checks. It took Macy's delivery wagons, operating in a steady circuit of round trips, four days to haul the merchandise from Fourteenth Street to Thirty-fourth, even though the Strauses had pared stock to the bone in anticipation of the move. The total cost of the building, when it opened for business on November 8, 1902, was $4,800,000. The ground on which it stands is still not owned by Macy's, but is leased from various owners on long-term leases.

The new store added little in variety of merchandise (it already carried pretty nearly everything), but because of its increased space it subdivided many departments into smaller specialized sections, and it greatly enlarged its customer services, establishing gift certificates, public telephones, a post office, theater-ticket bureau, and a restaurant on the eighth floor which served one million customers in one year. The ninth floor was used mainly for exhibitions such as poultry shows and automobile shows. At one time Fred Thompson, who owned Luna Park at Coney Island, wanted to install a miniature amusement park there, but the idea fell through because with the growth of business the ninth floor came to be needed as selling space. In 1910, a tenth floor was added to the building. In its first five years in the new location, Macy's sales rose from $10,000,000 to over $16,000,000.

The store's long-established policy of refusing to be undersold by its competitors, which Macy's regarded as good ethics as well as good business, proved to be uphill work in the early years of the new century. For one thing, "name brands" bearing the trade-marks of their manufacturers were becoming popular, and the manufacturers claimed that these should be sold everywhere at the same fixed price, to be stipulated by the manufacturer. Some wholesalers, and many retailers who had suffered from Macy's low-price competition, agreed. Soon Macy's began to have difficulty in obtaining certain brands of merchandise from manufacturers or wholesalers unless the store consented to retail them at fixed prices. Through its legal counsel, Edmond E. Wise, Macy's maintained that such strictures violated both free American enterprise and the Sherman Anti-Trust Act. The first test case in the battle was a lawsuit filed by the Strauses in 1902 against the American Publishers' Association as a combination in restraint of trade. Macy's won two rounds in the lower courts, and then the American Publishers' Association had two of its members— the Bobbs-Merrill Company and Scribner's—file suits to enjoin Macy's from selling certain copyrighted novels at less than the fixed prices. The cases went through the Circuit Court, the Court of Appeals, and the United States Supreme Court before they were decided in favor of Macy's. Macy's suit against the Publishers' Association struggled through nine actions in state and federal courts, with Macy's producing evidence that the Association had threatened with coercion any nonmembers or any bookdealers who tried to sell books to the store. In 1913, the Supreme Court handed down a unanimous decision that the Publishers' Association had formed a combination in restraint of trade which was not justified by the Copyright Act, and had therefore violated the Sherman Anti-Trust Act. The Association was required to pay Macy's $140,000 as damages.

The next opponent was the Victor Talking Machine Company. Victor, in 1914, tried to regulate the retail price of its product by attaching a notice to every machine that the retailer did not own it, but had merely rented the use of it by paying royalties in a lump sum, and so must charge the fixed price or infringe the manufacturer's patent rights. Victor refused to sell talking-machines to Macy's, so Macy's bought them indirectly and sold for $89 machines that Victor had fixed at $100. In all of these battles, it has been pointed out that Macy's was actually fighting for the right to take a lower profit on sales than the manufacturer wished it to have, and at first glance this does not sound like hard-headed business tactics. However, Macy's had found its 6 per cent policy to be a good business policy, and further-more it was fighting for its belief that any firm should be free to do business in its own way as long as that way is honest. After five court trials in three years, the Supreme Court decided that the Victor license notice was in reality a subterfuge for the sole purpose of fixing and maintaining the price of Victor talking-machines to the dealers and the public. The damages paid by the Victor Company to Macy's were $154,628.

The accounts of Macy's many headaches concerning price-fixing over the years could fill a learned volume, and have in fact partially filled one (*History of Macy's of New York* by Ralph M. Hower). It may be enough to say here that with the passage of time, and certain Fair Trade Acts, the store compromised to an extent with the manufacturers. As early as 1908 it sold such items as Community Silver, Arrow Collars, Bissell Carpet Sweepers, Thermos bottles, Eastman Kodaks, Gillette razors, and a few others at fixed prices. Nevertheless it firmly declined to carry others, including Sapolio, Fownes gloves, Waterman pens, Spaulding tennis rackets and golf balls, and Edison phonographs and records. The store's determination not only to let no competitor undersell it but to oblige the customer in every possible way is as strong as ever today, and it sometimes bothers the salesclerks. In the early 1900's a customer complained that Wanamaker's was selling a certain book cheaper than the price he had paid for it at Macy's. Macy's asked him to buy a copy at Wanamaker's and to bring it to Macy's with the bill; Macy's then politely refunded to him the Wanamaker price, made him a present of the book, and also refunded the amount he had paid at Macy's. Word of this gesture naturally got around, and to this day salesclerks in various departments are occasionally confronted by lady shoppers who hand them a blouse, say, or a hat bought at another store which they have worn and which they now wish to return to Macy's for cash or D.A. credit. "But madam, the article has been worn, and besides, it did not come from Macy's!" the salesclerks courteously wail. "I know that," says Madam. "I bought it at another store (practically any other store) but when I returned it to *them* they just said, 'Take it back to Macy's. They'll take back *anything.*'" In such extreme cases, Macy's does not oblige.

The 6 per cent policy that prevails at Macy's New York is more than a device to attract customers, it is the backbone and the lifeblood of the store, important to the firm in much the same way that the Constitution and the Bill of Rights are important to the United States. Originated a hundred years ago by Rowland Macy, the policy is adhered to by the store's current management—Jack I. Straus, chairman of the board of R. H. Macy & Co., Inc., Wheelock H. Bingham, president of the corporation, Donald B. Smiley, corporation vice-president and treasurer, and Elliot V. Walter, president of Macy's New York—and nothing is allowed to interfere with it. A Macy buyer can learn this fact the hard way.

A buyer's success is rated according to the volume of business his department does, and also according to the quality of his operation. His first duty is to obey Macy's price policy, that is, to sell everything in his department (except certain price-fixed national brands) for 6 per cent less than his competitors. Also, since Macy's is not in business for its health, his department must make money for the store. This double accomplishment is achieved through a meticulously figured operation called the buyer's "mark-on," which is the difference between the selling price of an article and its cost to the store. A department can do a good volume of business and still lose money if the mark-on is not pegged at a profitable level. This is the buyer's responsibility, and it can also be his headache when he makes his monthly report to his boss, the administrator, or merchandise manager, of his department. These reports, known as "Q. Meetings," are no cut-and-dried affairs, but are conducted by the boss in much the same soul-stirring manner as King Arthur must have used to address his knights at the Round Table.

"You got to make it dynamic! You got to *live* it!" the administrator will tell his buyers in ringing tones, referring to Macy's price policy. Occasionally gloom reigns over the meeting if a buyer is obliged to admit too many "mark-downs" (articles marked down in price) during the past month. In most cases a mark-down signifies a buyer's mistake. Sometimes a buyer confesses that he has made a bad buy. "Well, buy smarter, young man," the boss tells him simply. If a buyer has been diddled outright by a vendor who, say, has lied to him about an "exclusive" which is not exclusive, it is still the buyer's fault; he should know his vendors better. Sometimes the vendor himself has been cheated or misled by the man *he* bought from. In that case the vendor and the Macy buyer weep bitter tears together, but it is still the buyer who has to take it on the chin.

Often, the buyer's dilemma is unavoidable. Price wars continue, and for a very good reason. "If I were opening a new department store in New York," a merchandising executive said recently, "the first thing I'd do would be to try to start a price war with Macy's. The publicity would be terrific, since Macy's is the biggest in the business, and it would be sure-fire because Macy's is always bound to fight back, in order to maintain its six per cent policy." In 1936, when Margaret Mitchell's *Gone with the Wind* was new, a price war with Gimbel's across the street drove its price at Macy's down to seventeen cents a copy in the space of one day. Another, later, scramble sent the price of certain Modern Library books down to eight cents, losing the store about forty-five cents a copy. These things happen. Macy's only stratagem in the book-war was to move the book department from the street floor to the fifth, leaving the valuable street-floor space free for merchandise less susceptible to sudden fluctuations. Only one customer complained about the move, according to salesclerk Rebecca Jacobson. Told that books had been transferred to the fifth floor, this lady turned pink with indignation. "Well!" she exclaimed, "I only had two chapters to go in the novel I was reading, and if Macy's thinks I'm going to waste my good time traveling all the way to the fifth floor to finish that darn book, they're crazy!" And she flounced out.

One explanation of the fact that price wars are no longer the cutthroat, cloak-and-dagger affairs they once were lies in the increased scope and skill of the comparison shopper. In the old days, a department manager who wanted to know how his prices compared with his competitors' simply sent one of his clerks across the street or around the corner to find out. Even when comparison shoppers were first employed things could get exciting, with shoppers hiding in enemy telephone booths and ladies' rooms to jot down their notes unseen, with Macy's shoppers telephoning wildly from Saks or Gimbel's and Saks or Gimbel's shoppers telephoning madly from Macy's, and merchandise everywhere being marked down five or six times in a day. There was always the danger, too, of running out of an article of merchandise—fatal, because if you did, and your competitor knew it, he would shoot his price to the top and make a killing. For twenty-three years the comparison department was managed by Hertha Hanssen, now retired, whose word on prices was final. One time Walter Hoving, currently president of Bonwit Teller but then in charge of men's wear at Macy's, objected to her ultimatum that he cut the price on some men's shirts. They had such beautiful, long shirttails, he pointed out; where else could you get such shirttails for the price they were asking? "Listen," said Miss Hanssen crisply, "unless you want to sell 'em as nightshirts, cut the price."

Today, Macy's employs a squad of comparison shoppers under the direction of Carol Carmody, a good-looking young woman. Macy shoppers need not be young or beautiful but they had better be strong and healthy, since they must walk at least six miles a day through other stores. This is worth mentioning because, just as all impoverished gentlewomen in need of a job think they can be hotel housekeepers ("I've been keeping house all my life, why shouldn't I do it for pay?"), so most inexperienced middle-aged women looking for work apply for a job as a comparison shopper ("I've been shopping all my life, why shouldn't I do it for pay?"). Nothing could be more wrongheaded. A professional shopper must not only be sturdy, she must be alert, observing, and she should have a knowledge of fabrics and materials so as to compare intelligently the quality of a competitor's merchandise with that of her home store. Shoppers should look enough like customers to mingle with them inconspicuously, but the old secrecy is no longer necessary, since most shoppers are known by this time to the selling staff in rival stores and are on friendly terms with them. In any case, everybody concerned knows that the rival store's shoppers are doing the same thing at Macy's.

Before Macy's opens at 9:45 each morning the shoppers have studied the store's newspaper ads for the day, and the ads of some twenty-seven competitors' stores as well. Then, armed with her quota of competitors' ads and with her shopping report—a neat arrangement of printed boxes to be filled in—the shopper starts out on her rounds. Although she does not actually buy anything unless it is necessary for more minute comparison, shoppers spend about eight hundred dollars a week on purchases from other stores. After thorough comparison with similar Macy merchandise such purchases are put into regular Macy stock, minus the 6 per cent discount or more, and marked "One of a Kind." Within the hour the shopper turns in her written report to the comparison department which then recommends to the buyer of each department in the store that the price of certain items be lowered, or not. Again, the word of the comparison department is final, but there are few tears since Macy's prices are generally well under the competitors' and its quality as good, or better. Sometimes a buyer will fight to maintain the price of his, or her, cherished items, pointing out that the seams in Macy's dress are better sewn, or that the wheels on a Macy bassinet are made of a more durable material. And, once in a great while, there are strange moments.

Not long ago, in preparation for a big Macy ad concerning handkerchiefs, Macy shoppers worked for two days covering other stores to see what handkerchiefs were costing elsewhere. Every shopper except one turned in her report with every box filled, representing each store she had visited. The lone exception, a new employee, had left the box concerning a certain Fifth Avenue department store blank. Asked for a reason, she explained, "That store doesn't sell handkerchiefs any more." Investigation proved that the store had, indeed, discontinued the sale of handkerchiefs a few weeks earlier. The new girl was the only one who had gone near it. But a thing like that almost never happens, Miss Carmody avers with a sigh of relief. With that single mad exception, shoppers steadily realize their responsibility to the store and its customers, and work like horses to keep both fully informed.

When there is any doubt about the comparative quality of a competitor's merchandise, the comparison department refers the article in question to Macy's Bureau of Standards on the fifteenth floor. There, mattresses and quilts are ripped apart and their stuffing examined under microscopes, a piece of carpet or a satin blouse is put to vibrating on a friction machine to test its durability, a cotton housedress is forever whirled in an automatic washer to determine whether its color will fade. The Bureau of Standards tests Macy's own merchandise to a greater extent than it tries to wear out that of its rivals. It was, in fact, established in 1927, after the store had begun selling Macy's Own Brands as one way to give the customer quality goods at Macy's own prices. Macy's Own Brands obviously had to be tested to insure quality. The Bureau also investigates new products to be put on sale in the store, and it has an honorable record of insisting on the best and throwing out the doubtful. Macy's was the first store to ban the use of lead in the paint used on toys. Some years ago the store refused to sell a certain depilatory, although it had been declared harmless by the associate dean of a well-known college of pharmacy. Dr. Ephraim Freedman, who has been in charge of Macy's Bureau of Standards from the beginning, analyzed this depilatory and reported that it contained thallium acetate, a kind of rat poison. Macy's banned it from its counters, and at least one authority which approved of this action was the American Medical Association. The depilatory has fortunately been off the market for some time now.

The Bureau of Standards also investigates all customers' complaints. If you, the customer, return a rug or a bicycle or a rocking horse you bought at Macy's with the report that it is defective somehow, you may be sure that the next day will find your rug taking the punishment of ten years' wear under the abrasion tester, your bicycle (under two-hundred-pound pressure) riding the equivalent of a thousand miles on a contraption called "The Rocky Road to Dublin," and your rocking horse, under an equal burden, rocking away on a device designed to shatter it into splinters if possible. If the articles tested are actually yours, they will not be returned to you after all the wear and tear; you will probably get new ones, or your money back—if your complaint is justified. According to Dr. Freedman, about 25 per cent of customers' complaints are justified. One customer complained that the leather jacket he bought at Macy's blew up when he lighted a cigarette. Leather is not combustible, and the jacket-wearer's insurance company asked Macy's to investigate after its client put in a claim for the jacket. The insurance people also returned the jacket, and the Bureau of Standards discovered that the front of it was spattered with lighter fluid. Another time, a doctor threatened to sue Macy's on the ground that his wife had been poisoned by arsenic contained in Macy's Own Brand of talcum powder. She had absorbed the poison through her skin, he asserted. The Bureau of Standards put the talcum through rigorous tests; no arsenic. Presently the doctor's attorney called up and said that the lady had arsenic poisoning, all right, but that she claimed her husband was trying to kill her and to put the blame on Macy's talcum. Macy's left *that* problem to the happy couple and their legal advisors.

Occasionally there is a true crisis traceable to human fallibility. Two days before Christmas, last year, somebody discovered that the Christmas trees on sale, about a thousand of them, had not been fireproofed. Dr. Freedman and his staff bundled the trees into a fleet of taxis, took them to a vacant lot somewhere and fireproofed them, and got them back to the store in time to be sold, this time safely. Another drama also took place at Christmas, three years ago. On the Saturday before Christmas the police of Toledo, Ohio, made a hurry call to Dr. Freedman. A Toledo child had bitten into a tree ornament, the kind that contains a swirling liquid, and had swallowed some of the fluid which was known to be poisonous. Her doctor, not knowing the nature of the poison or its antidote, had called the police, who didn't know either and couldn't find out because the office of the manufacturer who made the ornament was closed on Saturdays. Somebody at police headquarters in Toledo knew about Macy's Bureau of Standards, and telephoned them as a last resort. Macy's had the same kind of ornament, right there in the Bureau under examination as it happened. Dr. Freedman grabbed one, broke it open and analyzed the fluid. Then he called back the Toledo police to report it as methylene chloride and to suggest an antidote. The police called the doctor, the child's life was saved, and the whole incident, as Dr. Freedman recalls it, took less than thirty minutes.

The Bureau of Standards does a good job, but Dr. Freedman remembers that he once remarked to Percy Straus that it could do better if it had more money.

"Hell," Mr. Percy replied, "any fool can do anything if he has money."

Isidor Straus was fifty-seven years old in 1902, when Macy's moved to Herald Square. He was not only head of the firm, with his brother Nathan, he had also become an eminent and respected citizen in many fields. He had served a term in the House of Representatives, and continued to be a confidant and adviser of President Grover Cleveland; he was an active and hard-working director of many charitable and philanthropical enterprises and, in due time, he received a Degree of Doctor of Laws from Washington and Lee University. He was known for many pithy statements, such as: "If your business is active it requires all your thought; if it is not, there is all the greater reason for giving it undivided attention"; and (on a gentler note) "I should consider my life's work a failure if ever there would arise any serious differences . . . which would disturb the family union and harmony to which I happily attribute what success I may have achieved." Perhaps he was most fondly recognized for his devotion to his wife and children, and for their perfect family life.

Isidor had married Ida Blun, the daughter of a wholesale clothing merchant and manufacturer who emigrated to America from Worms, Germany. They were married in New York on July 12, 1871. "That day," Isidor later wrote in an informal biography he began for his children, but never finished, "became an epoch in the history of New York City, not by reason of its being *the* important and happy event of my life, but because the Orange riots made a battlefield of some of the streets, which also prevented some of the guests from arriving at the wedding until very late." Isidor and Ida had seven children: Jesse, Percy, and Herbert, who succeeded their father as heads of R. H. Macy; Clarence, who died in infancy; Sara, who married Alfred Hess; Minnie, who married Richard Weil and whose son, Richard Junior, was president of Macy's New York from 1949 to 1952; and Vivian, who married Herbert Sheftel and, after his death, married George Dixon Junior. The Straus family lived at 26 East Fifty-fifth Street, subsequently moving to 2745 Broadway, at 105th Street, for more sun and air, and acquiring a summer home in Elberon, New Jersey. There, on a summer day in 1904, Isidor wrote the following letter to his wife:

Sunnyside, Elberon, N.J.
July 18, 1904

My Darling Mama:

In case I should die before you, I desire to give you a few suggestions for your guidance which may prove very welcome to aid you in what otherwise might be puzzling propositions with which you may find yourself confronted.

By my will I have made ample provision for all my dear ones. Lose no time in making a will by which you dispose of your property. If my death should occur after 1907, the residue of my estate, which goes to our three sons, after paying the legacies to you and our three daughters, will be so ample, considering the value of my business interests which are entirely left to them, that the largest portion of your possessions had best be bequeathed to our daughters. If you desire to remember our grandchildren by direct bequest to them individually, you might leave to the father of each as trustee for each child a sum of about Fifty Thousand Dollars for each. Remember, this is a suggestion not a request; I loan you full power to dispose of your estate as you may deem best.

You will have no better friend or sincere advisor in all your affairs than my brother Nathan; of course you have the most devoted sons who will always strive to make your life smooth and happy, but in Nathan you and they will always have an upright and devoted counselor whose concern for your welfare is undoubted.

You have an ample income, enjoy it; deprive yourself of nothing which can contribute to your comfort and happiness. I know you are fond of doing good, indulge yourself in this enjoyment without stint and if you use up your entire interest it is the best use you can make of it.

Be a little selfish; don't always think of others. You have much left to live for, therefore don't be despairing but look forward to years of happiness with your children and grandchildren and instead of mourning disconsolately over our separation, be thankful for the happiness which was vouchsafed to us so many years. We have had more than our share of the blessings of life, therefore be cheerful and thankful and continue for many years to be the center of attraction to which all your children will flock as the fountain head of their family blessing.

Your devoted
Isidor.

To

As good a wife as ever man was blessed with.

In 1912, Isidor and Ida Straus went to Europe for a winter holiday at Cap Martin, and decided to come home in the spring on the maiden voyage of the great new White Star Liner, "Titanic." The rest of that story is well known. When the ship struck the iceberg and started to sink, Hugh Woolner, another passenger, struggled through the frightened mass of people on the slanting deck and tried to persuade the Strauses to get into a lifeboat together. "I'm sure nobody would object to an old gentleman like you getting in . . ." he told Mr. Straus. Mr. Straus shook his head. "I will not go before the other men," he said. When Mrs. Straus was urged to get into a boat she also refused. "I've always stayed with my husband, why should I leave him now?" she said simply. " Please, Mama," her husband begged, "*please* get into a lifeboat." Mrs. Straus took his hand. "We have been together so long," she said, "please let me stay now." The next time Woolner, a survivor, saw the Strauses they were sitting quietly in a pair of deck chairs. The last time he saw them, they were standing at the rail with their arms around each others' waists.

One fact which appears to have escaped historians of that terrible night is that Jesse Straus and his wife were on their way to Europe on board the "America," which passed the homeward-bound "Titanic" at sea. On the day of the disaster the "America's" captain had taken Jesse onto the bridge and pointed out far-off icebergs. Jesse hurriedly sent a wireless to his father aboard the "Titanic," begging him to tell the "Titanic's" captain to "be careful." When Jesse and his wife reached Southampton they were met by the stunning news, and took the next boat home to America. John Badenoch, head of Macy's grocery department, was also Europe-bound on the "Carpathia," the ship which finally responded to the "Titanic's" call for help. As the "Carpathia" raced toward the sinking ship Badenoch made preparations to turn his cabin over to the Strauses; but by the time the "Carpathia" arrived the "Titanic," and the Strauses, were gone.

The final cruelty was that Isidor Straus's body was recovered, but his wife's was not. It almost seems that, having chosen to stay together, they might have been permitted to do so. On April 24, ten days after the "Titanic" sank, the Educational Alliance, of which Isidor Straus had been founder and president, held a meeting at its headquarters on Jefferson Street to honor Mr. Straus's memory by a simple talk about his life and good works. This was not the memorial service more elaborately planned for the following month, and it was not widely publicized, but forty thousand people jammed into the lecture hall and so many more thronged the steps and sidewalk that railings collapsed and part of the crowd fell into an areaway. An ambulance was called, police reserves were summoned to disperse the crowds, and the meeting finally had to be canceled. The Straus Memorial held at Carnegie Hall on May 13 was more orderly, although Carnegie could not accommodate all the people who came, and about three hundred had to stand up at the back of the hall. Eulogies were spoken by Mayor Gaynor, Andrew Carnegie, and Jacob Schiff, among others, and the *Times* noted in its account that they appeared "deeply affected and spoke in a subdued voice." In 1915, on the third anniversary of the "Titanic" disaster, Straus Park, in the square at Broadway and 105th Street once overlooked by the Straus home, was formally dedicated by the unveiling of a memorial fountain. As a later tribute, the Straus sons established Camp Isida (for Isidor and Ida) in upper New York State where Macy employees could, for a nominal sum, spend their vacations and enjoy good food, swimming, archery, and tennis.

Just inside one of Macy's Thirty-fourth Street entrances there is a bronze plaque engraved with the likenesses of Isidor and Ida Straus, and with a brief account of their death. Customers hurrying by have no reason to know the correct name of this particular entrance; but every person on the Macy staff speaks of it automatically and with respect as "the Memorial Door."

4

"Mr. Jesse and Mr. Percy"

★

THERE IS A NEWSSTAND on Thirty-fourth Street, near Macy's, operated by Harold Young, who has been working at the same stand since 1906 when it was owned by one Jim Mack and Harold, a schoolboy of eight in knickerbockers and long black stockings, delivered newspapers in his free hours. Macy's has been one of his best customers from the beginning, and he knew Isidor and Nathan Straus well. "The hardest job I ever had," Mr. Young says now, "was delivering papers, every edition, to Mr. Nathan when Mr. Isidor and his wife went down with the 'Titanic.' The early editions said everybody was saved, you know, and then there was this awful doubt all day long, until the terrible truth came out in the final editions." Mr. Young shakes his head. "I felt almost as bad as Mr. Nathan."

Mr. Young remembers Jack Straus, grandson of Isidor, son of Jesse, and now chairman of the board of R. H. Macy & Co., when Jack was a boy in short pants like himself. Not long ago Mr. Young had cause to remember Mr. Jack even more vividly. He fell off a ladder in his home and broke his back. "Mr. Jack wrote me a blank check and seven peo-

ple in the store gave me blood for transfusions," he will tell
you, "and that wasn't all. When I finally came back to my
job Macy's found out that I didn't own any part of the
newsstand, just worked for it, so they arranged for me to
work out a half-ownership deal with the man who owned it.
Called me and the boss into their lawyers' offices and drew
up a partnership for us. Nicest thing ever happened to me,"
says Mr. Young contentedly. "Gave me a feeling of security.
Before that, I never really felt the job was permanent." '

The death of Isidor Straus which brought grief to Harold
Young and others like him—the "outside members" of the
Macy family—brought more than grief to Macy's; it was indirectly the cause of a considerable shake-up in the firm.
Isidor and Nathan had been equal partners. Now, Isidor's
half of the business passed to his three sons while Nathan
retained his own half. Friction was inevitable. The uncle
felt that his mature opinions and decisions should prevail,
but Jesse, Percy, and Herbert favored more modern methods of operation. Besides, Jesse and Percy were no inexperienced boys, and even Herbert, the youngest, was a man
of thirty in 1912. There was further difficulty in the fact
that Nathan's sons, Nathan Junior and Hugh Grant, were
so much younger than Isidor's sons and had come to the
store so much later that they were never really able to catch
up with their cousins. Possibly Nathan Senior's tempera-
ment had something to do with the tension that developed;
even his peaceful brother Isidor had sometimes grown impatient with his volatile ways. At any rate, although the
family relationship remained serene (as Isidor had treasured it) outside the store, matters *inside* the store reached a
breaking-point.

In 1913, a deal was made between Nathan and his three

nephews that should ring down the ages as the most courteous of all time. Jesse, Percy, and Herbert proposed that
Uncle Nathan buy their half interest in the firm, and stated
at the same time that they would be willing to buy *his* half
interest on the same terms. At first glance this looks like a
stymie, but it was no such thing. Isidor was not the only
Straus to whom family feeling was important. By their
formal offer the three brothers gave Uncle Nathan—to outward appearances anyway—the choice of accepting or de-
clining. Nathan (doubtless by a previous agreement) declined to buy their share and offered to sell them his own,
which they then bought. Thus Jesse, Percy, and Herbert obtained the full partnership they wanted, and harmony was
firmly maintained. Nathan's letter to his nephews regard-
ing the transaction reveals how deeply this kind of family
dignity concerned all of the Strauses.

> . . . Inasmuch as you have first offered the business
> to me . . . (he wrote, in part) I should feel that if you
> buy it as now proposed I should have no ground for
> complaint and would feel that you have acted in good
> faith and without taking any advantage of me. Under
> those circumstances a sale as now proposed would not
> cause any rupture in the family relationship heretofore
> prevailing between us.

The value of the business was appraised at that time at
$15,000,000, including $7,000,000 goodwill. Jesse, Percy,
and Herbert paid $7,500,000 for Nathan's half. The entente
between the two branches continued to be cordial, although
they saw little of one another. Nathan Straus died in 1931,
after an honorable career in philanthropy and public welfare. Nathan Junior was administrator of the United States

Housing Authority for some years and is now chairman of the Mayor's Advisory Council in New York and president of Radio Station WMCA. Hugh Grant Straus lives mostly in Europe. Neither is professionally connected with Macy's.

The three sons of Isidor Straus were temperamentally different, as their father and uncle had been. Jesse, the eldest, was a great merchant and famous for his crackling yes-or-no decisions; Percy was a genius at management and had a theoretical turn of mind in contrast to Jesse's, which was practical. These two complemented each other to perfection. Herbert, the youngest, was also the esthete of the family. He was a fine musician and played the cello, and he collected books, as much for their bindings as for their contents. His youth and good looks and pleasant manner made him well-liked in the store, a kind of luminous obbligato to the fanfare that emanated from the increasingly fabulous team of "Mr. Jesse and Mr. Percy"—as they were always called.

Mr. Jesse's full name was Jesse Isidor Straus and he was a stickler about using it in full, even sending his advertising manager around to newspapers now and then to see that they did not abbreviate the middle name. "It's the least mark of respect I can show my father," he said. (Jesse's son Jack is formally named Jack Isidor Straus, and he too has always greatly respected his father, although the pressure of modern times causes him to sign himself simply "Jack I. Straus.") Mr. Jesse, according to those who knew him, was a lean, whipcord kind of man "with a glint in his eye." To quote one of his executives, "he had courage, a sense of humanity, a respect for the individual, and a constant vision of Macy's as the biggest store in the world." He was also something of a disciplinarian. If he found that an executive had left the office before six, he would call him up at home and amiably chat with him about nothing in particular— thereby letting the uneasy shirker know that *he* knew the man had left early. Arriving punctually at 8:40 in the morning, Mr. Jesse would stand casually at the executives' elevator, smilingly greeting the members of his staff as they came in the door. 8:45 was check-in time for executives, and at fourteen minutes to nine Mr. Jesse's smile disappeared and he began looking at his watch and noting who was late. He looked forward with zest to each day in the store, and saw no reason why everyone else should not feel the same eagerness. Once, arriving extra early, he found the elevator occupied only by himself and a lesser toiler who had asked the operator to let her off at the eighth floor. The operator shot past the eighth and delivered Mr. Jesse first to the thirteenth, where the top brass dwells. As the door slid to behind Mr. Jesse, the lesser toiler sighed and said, "Now that you've taken God to heaven, would you mind letting me off at the eighth?"

Mr. Jesse's discipline sometimes had the effect of making even the top executives who liked and admired him most feel that they were back in school. In 1926 Kenneth Collins, a young Harvard teacher, called on him with a view to getting some money for Harvard's Peabody Museum. Mr. Jesse wrote him a check and then asked, "What are you doing this summer?" Collins replied that he had thought of going West to work in a silver mine. "We need somebody to write good English around here," said Mr. Jesse and persuaded Collins to go to work as copy chief in the advertising department. In a little over two years Collins became advertising and promotion manager, and remained with Macy's seven years in all. During that time another store offered him a job with more money and Collins told Mr. Jesse about it, explaining candidly, "I want a million dollars in the next four years." Mr. Jesse said "You'll get it," and raised him to $50,000 a year plus stock in the company. In the twenties Mr. Jesse, then in his fifties, had come to have a fatherly affection for his young executives, including Collins. "Now, I want to talk to you *in loco parentis*" he would say, when he wished to give Collins hell about something. But more often his reprimands were of a devious kind, calculated to make a budding big shot look like a small boy. In 1928, a customer wrote Macy's that a clock she had bought there in the year of the Spanish-American War had just stopped running, and asked where she could have it repaired. The letter came to Collins's attention and, seeing a great angle for advertising and promotion, he wrote to the lady assuring her that Macy's would be happy to repair her clock, and then ran a huge newspaper ad featuring the correspondence and implying that Macy's could and would do *anything*. The next day five hundred people turned up at Macy's with ancient, long-stopped clocks to be repaired. Collins, abashed, worked overtime for a week to compose five hundred letters explaining why Macy's was not able to repair this avalanche of clocks. About six thirty on the last day Mr. Jesse strolled into his office.

"Have you written all those letters?" he inquired.

"Yep," moaned Collins, exhausted. "Just signed the last one."

"Well," said Mr. Jesse, "I only wanted to teach you a lesson. All your letters have been intercepted, and the clocks are being repaired. Now you won't go off the deep end like that again, will you?"

Mr. Jesse had instructed Collins's secretary to take dicta-

tion on all the five hundred letters and to have Collins sign each one, but not to mail them. "I felt just like a kid kept in after school to write *I will be good* five hundred times," Collins says now, "but I never stuck Macy's neck out again."

Although Mr. Jesse won this moral victory over Collins, Collins won at least one popular victory over Mr. Jesse. As punctilious about his store's name as about his own, Mr. Jesse wanted it called "R. H. Macy & Co." in all advertisements, and so referred to on all occasions. "But the people call it 'Macy's'!" Collins objected, and "Macy's" it remained.

Percy Straus, a scholarly-looking man wearing pince-nez, liked to walk through the store during business hours, and prided himself on knowing every employee by name—at least, until the number of employees became so vast that no one man could have remembered them all. "Julia, you look so *young!* What do you use to keep the gray hairs away?" he would inquire of some faithful salesclerk. Although he did not wear the frock coat and the carnation that marked the floorwalker in those days, customers sometimes mistook him for one, and Mr. Percy would happily direct them, give them information, or help them straighten out their purchases. One Christmas season he came upon a clerk trying to explain to a customer that the ornament she wished to buy was part of the store's decorations and was not for sale. Mr. Percy tapped the clerk on the shoulder. "You can sell it," he murmured. When the pleased customer had departed, Mr. Percy further instructed the salesclerk. "If a customer comes in here and wants to buy one of the *escalators,*" he told her, "sell it."

Another time, he noticed a wrapping-clerk, new to the store, chewing gum violently as she worked. Mr. Percy stepped up to her politely. "Young lady, I would appreciate it if you would remove that chewing gum," he requested.

The new clerk looked him up and down. "Listen, buster," she said, "you get yourself a tailcoat and one of them carnations, and *then* you can come around here and tell *me* what to do!"

Selling escalators and banning chewing gum were a small part of Mr. Percy's worries. One of the earliest problems that faced the three sons of Isidor Straus when they took over the store was one of administration. Like some great, sprawling behemoth with a peanut-sized brain, Macy's had physically outgrown its administrative system. The business itself was terrific, but its direction from the top was inadequately organized. Things soon got so bad that the store more than once had to run newspaper ads apologizing for poor service. At the regular meetings of Mr. Jesse, Mr. Percy, Mr. Herbert, and their advisors a strange truth came to light; with the store's growth in size the personal relationship between Strauses and employees had necessarily thinned, and nothing had been arranged to take its place. Old-time salesclerks, missing the fatherly presence of Mr. Isidor and Mr. Nathan, had to content themselves with a daily glimpse of Mr. Percy or Mr. Herbert—Mr. Jesse was busy mainly in his office. New clerks, who had probably never met any Strauses whatever, were unaware of the store's former "family" atmosphere and team spirit, and they grew careless. Macy's was not alone in this dilemma; times were changing, and the day of the small businessman, even of the large individualist, with his direct contacts was giving way to big business and its organized channels of communication. Macy's had to do something about it, and the crisis became so acute that Mr. Percy, who had just mar-

ried Edith Abraham, was summoned back from his honeymoon to share in the discussions.

It took the brothers many years to organize a system of
administration that is, in fact, still being perfected almost
from day to day. Among their earliest moves was the establishment of a Board of Operations and an Advisory Council
whose members included Edmond Wise, the attorney, and
such pioneers of the present-day Macy's as Ernest Katz, Sylvester Byrnes, Adam Treu, Louis Chamansky, William J.
Wells, John Badenoch and Joseph Mayer. Many of the business reforms achieved by the Strauses with the aid of these
men are too technical to investigate here, but a few will
illustrate the trend of improvement. Under the Strauses'
direction members of the Council regularly visited other
stores—Altman's, Lord & Taylor, Wanamaker's, and even
Strawbridge & Clothier's in Philadelphia—to observe their
methods of operation and to carry away any ideas which
seemed adaptable to Macy's. Salesclerks were given two
hours off every month to visit Fifth Avenue stores for the
same purpose, and prizes were given to those who offered
the best suggestions. William Pitt, who had been store manager since 1887, was retired and succeeded by Sylvester
Byrnes, whose title was changed to "general manager." The
old-time frock-coated floorwalker rather pompously patrol-
ling the aisles disappeared, and was replaced by a bright
young man in a business suit who was called a "service manager" and whose function, in addition to pampering the
customers, was to give the clerks in his department the as-
surance of a friendly authority close at hand which they had
so sorely missed. The quality of the personnel itself improved when Macy's passed the word to all colleges and
universities that the store was interested in employing col-

lege graduates—a liaison which was later to develop into the present Training Squad. *Sparks,* a monthly house magazine full of news and pictures of the staff, was first printed in 1918; *Sparks* has now become a weekly newspaper called *The Macy Star.* And, a year earlier, at least one totally new job was created when a woman was employed full-time to interview customers concerning their likes and dislikes, and to report her findings to the Strauses and their Advisory Council.

Macy's had employed women executives since the days of Rowland Macy and Margaret Getchell, but it was not until World War I that they became notable in numbers and authority. Wartime wages had put money into the pockets of the average consumer, and Macy customers formed the habit of buying silk stockings for themselves and silk shirts for their husbands, and even of reading *Vogue* and becoming style-conscious. Before that time, Macy's had not been any more style-conscious than its patrons. A Macy buyer (usually a man) would roam the market and buy so many bolts of dress goods or, indicating fifty or a hundred feet of a rack of wholesale ready-mades, would say, "I'll take from here to there." Money in the customer's purse, and *Vogue,* changed all that and started Macy's on the stimulating path of "trading up," as it is called in the business. "Trading up" simply means emphasizing style as well as quality, and letting the clientele know that expensive items are available as well as cheap ones. Since fashion is traditionally woman's domain, this trend opened up a whole new field for women executives, and perhaps especially for women buyers.

The layman is apt to think of a "buyer" as someone who spends all his (or her) time dashing around the wholesale market and taking off on jaunts to Europe to inspect the foreign marts. Both these duties are in fact included in his job, but the truth is that a buyer spends about as much time in the store as he spends outside it. A buyer must regularly interview vendors (people who want to sell him something or from whom he wishes to buy something), he must regularly confer with the big bosses (the president of the store, the president of the company, and the chairman of the board), and since he is ultimately responsible for all the merchandise in his department he must be thoroughly familiar with every item in it, and with every nuance of change. He must be an expert on textiles, fashions, and trends, and he is also involved in problems of operating, display, customer-service, and personnel. Except for certain suggestions from on high, and an occasional brush with the comparison shopping department, a buyer's authority is supreme. He has a staff of senior assistants and junior assistants who work under him, and a good, experienced buyer can make as much as $30,000 a year.

"Buyers usually have crummy offices," explains Mildred Jay, Macy's furniture buyer, approached in her cubbyhole on the ninth floor, "because they like to be near their merchandise." Miss Jay came to Macy's thirty years ago when the furniture floor was in charge of a Mr. Cowlishaw, a man who had had a colorful career. He had started out as a professional bicycle racer, and had then become secretary to one of the Strauses before being promoted to furniture buyer. In the early twenties, Mr. Jesse, Mr. Percy, and Mr. Herbert attended a course of lectures on merchandising and good taste given at Columbia University by one Ruth Wilmot, and invited Miss Wilmot to visit Macy's and bestow a few words of advice. Miss Wilmot's first remark on being conducted to the ready-to-wear dress department was,

"For heaven's sake, get that figured carpet with all the roses *out* of here! It distracts from the dresses." The Strauses, impressed, offered her a job and established her in the Corner Shop on the furniture floor, where she sold antiques and also popularized French Modern. With propinquity and the passage of time, Miss Wilmot and Mr. Cowlishaw fell in love and were married. In September, 1929, a month before the stock-market crash, they sold out everything they owned in the stock market for a pleasant amount of cash and retired to Arizona to raise cattle. The Cowlishaws' romance is only one of about a hundred which have flowered in Macy's over the years.

"A buyer must have plenty of initiative," Miss Jay continues, returning to the theme, "and a slight streak of Machiavellian cunning doesn't do any harm. Once, when some of my assistants and I were hunting antiques outside of Philadelphia, we came upon an inn that had several really beautiful old pieces in the entrance hall. The owners wouldn't sell them or even let us look at them properly, so we had dinner there, and every so often one of us would stroll out to the hall and sort of *lean* against one of the pieces to get the height and general dimensions. Macy's managed to put out some good reproductions of that furniture—sold, of course, *as* reproductions." During Miss Jay's early days at the store the Fifth Avenue Theatre, a movie house, asked Macy's for an estimate on a decorating job, but declined the estimate as being too high. Miss Jay and Elliot V. Walter, then business manager of the decorating department, piled enough slipcovers into a taxi to cover all the orchestra seats in the theater, hustled them over, and slipcovered every seat. *"Now,* look!" they besought the owner. "Isn't it worth it?" Macy's got the job, and such initiative eventually benefited Miss Jay and Mr. Walter, too. Miss Jay's position as furniture buyer is one of the top jobs in any department store, and Mr. Walter is now president of Macy's New York.

"This thing called *trend* is important," says Nicholas Saulnier, Macy's buyer of men's shirts and pajamas. "One year, everybody wants long points on their shirt collars, for instance. Last year, everybody wanted shorter points. Macy's keeps abreast of the times and the trends, but we don't go overboard on offbeat items. When television was fairly new and the tidings got around that white photographed badly, we ran a big ad featuring blue evening shirts for television actors. We didn't get any flood of television actors, so we discontinued the blue evening shirts. We stick pretty much to the conservative items we have found to be in demand with the wives, who do about seventy-five per cent of the shopping of men's wear—at Macy's, anyway. Most of our merchandise is Macy's Own Brand, made for us by tailors and manufacturers under contract to us, and we also have a custom-made department for men who want their shirt fronts one color, for example, and the rest of the shirt another. That's not as offbeat as you might think," Mr. Saulnier adds, in response to a startled look from his listener, "it's just popular. We carry some pretty expensive merchandise, too. A soft-collar shirt in Sea Island cotton can cost fourteen ninety-nine at Macy's, and some sports shirts go as high as twenty-eight dollars. Of course, we sell shirts for a dollar ninety-nine as well."

"Wearing apparel is not the only thing that has become style-conscious," says William H. Winner, buyer of Domestics, a category which includes blankets, sheets, towels, and table linen. "When I first came to Macy's in 1927 the only kind of bath towel anywhere was plain white, with maybe a daring colored stripe at the bottom. Well, look at 'em now! Towels any color you want to match your bathroom tiles, table linen to harmonize with your flower centerpiece, blankets and sheets practically any color in the rainbow." Mr. Winner, a Sunday painter, used to go to art school nights, and the acres of blank white in the domestics department depressed him during the day. "I wanted to liven up the merchandise," is the way he puts it. His real chance did not come until 1932, when Macy's put on a furniture show called Forward House and directed by Helen Needham, a decorator from outside. "Can't we do something *different* in *towels* for the Show?" wailed Miss Needham, and Winner required no more encouragement. With the blessing of the Strauses and the help of Phyllis Brackett, a Macy stylist, he commissioned a small mill to make bath towels and face towels in bright and pastel colors. Macy's was the first to do this, says Mr. Winner. Representatives of the big mills, such as Cannon and Martex, came to the show, liked what they saw, and followed suit, and presently so did the manufacturers of blankets and sheets and table linen. Mr. Winner, a buyer for twenty-eight years, is still impressed by Macy's power as a pioneer, and also by the respect the store commands from manufacturers and wholesalers everywhere.

"In the market," he says, "Macy's is not an account—it's a territory."

The artist in Mr. Winner rejects the popular notion that a buyer is a tough guy, hard to handle, and he is slightly irritated by the gag that once went round concerning the strong man at a sideshow who squeezed a cocoanut dry and was challenged by a spectator, who promptly squeezed three more drops of milk out of it. "Who are you?" demanded the

strong man. "I," replied the spectator, "am a Macy buyer." This, says Winner, is purely apocryphal, but he does admit that buyers were tougher in the old days, and he cites his own first boss at Macy's, a man named Milton Spier who was domestics buyer from 1919 and is now retired. Mr. Spier was a brooding, cigar-chewing type whose devotion to Macy's was so keen that he kept his account books in code lest they fall into the hands of competitors. For six months he wouldn't let even Winner, his assistant, have the key to the code, until Winner finally argued, "Suppose, God forbid, a taxi hits you. Nobody will know the code!" Spier was a great friend of Jesse Straus and of Jesse's wife, the former Irma Nathan, and he had, of course, seen their son Jack grow from youth to manhood. One day in 1924, an attractive young woman came up to him in the domestics department and said, "Could you tell me, is Mr. Spier here?" Mr. Spier was cogitating on his favorite subject, Macy's, and had no wish to be interrupted by this stranger, no matter how attractive.

"Naw," he growled. "Spier's up on the roof flying his kite. He does it every morning at eleven thirty."

"Oh, I'm sorry," said the young stranger, preparing to back away. "I just wanted to introduce myself to him. I'm Mrs. Jack Straus."

The reorganization achieved by the Straus brothers after they assumed full ownership of Macy's had a beneficent effect on working conditions in the store. By 1915, opening hour had been mercifully delayed until nine o'clock, and in 1918 closing hour was fixed at five thirty during the summer. For a while the store was closed on Saturday afternoons during July and August, but Saturday closing has been an on-and-off experiment across the years and it spasmodically ceases when somebody in the top echelon happens to look out of a window on Saturday and beholds the crowds streaming to Saks-34th or Gimbel's across the way. Between 1914 and 1915 the minimum wage for salesclerks rose from $10 a week to $15, and by 1919 it had increased to $20, plus bonuses and commissions on sales. Salesclerks worked in clean, well-ventilated, and well-lighted quarters, individual lockers were installed for their use, and the cafeteria and rest rooms were greatly improved. As a final boon, clerks were allowed to sit down occasionally during working hours —a privilege which had not been granted to them up to that time. Collapsible seats were fixed in the wall behind counters, where a girl might collapse during a lull, and she was also allowed a twenty-minute rest period every so often in the employees' sitting room. By 1918 the Macy Mutual Aid had acquired a store staff of two doctors, one dentist, one chiropodist, three nurses, and two assistants, administering thirty thousand treatments in one year at a cost of $24,300, of which membership dues paid about $18,000, the Strauses contributing the rest. All of these benefits were accomplished long before Macy's was unionized, and years before they became compulsory.

Another innovation, established in 1915 and still in force, was the Earn and Learn Co-operative Program, a project of New York's Board of Education. By this system high-school juniors and seniors can work alternate weeks at standard wages, and their records in the store—as stock boys, stock girls, messengers, or sometimes even salesclerks—are counted along with their school grades as credits toward a diploma. In this way high-school students can gain experience and make a little money without their school grades suffering, and their employers benefit equally from the opportunity to grasp the twig while it may still be bent. The Earn and Learn Co-operative Program is by no means unique with Macy's, nor is it limited to department stores. The Board of Education has part-time jobs open in practical nursing, accounting, photography, and a dozen other trades and professions. But Macy's was one of the first stores to co-operate in the plan, and it is pleased with its record. The store has had as many as two hundred Earn-and-Learners in its employ at one time, and several of them have risen to executive positions. One is Helen Dooner, a vibrant blonde who looks like a young Vivienne Segal, and who is assistant superintendent of the street floor. Another is Fred Acito, a good-looking young man who came to Macy's in 1930 as an Earn and Learn messenger, and roller-skated his messages all over the packing department on the nineteenth floor. Mr. Acito, his roller-skating days behind him, is now supervisor of the packing department.

Through all the reorganizing and administrative headaches Macy's customers kept coming, in a wave of style-consciousness that now and then approached hysteria. One treasured customer arrived daily carrying a small live monkey in her monkey-fur muff. "That little animal was *always* getting away and jumping up on the pneumatic tubes along the ceiling," recalls Nellie Nikolassy, a marker. "My! He was a dear little thing!" Another piquant patron, definitely Occidental otherwise, slithered along the aisles wearing a sari and sandals and a caste-mark on her forehead. It was clear that the mad twenties were just around the corner.

In 1914, the ownership of the Macy building was transferred from L. Straus & Sons (who had figured in the leases) to Jesse, Percy, and Herbert Straus, who thereupon absorbed the old firm. Five years later the business was incorporated, with the Strauses holding all the outstanding stock. In 1922, Macy stock was first put on the market and made available to the public. The Strauses now own less than 50 per cent of the stock. Although the stores are directed by Jack I. Straus, Wheelock H. Bingham (president of the corporation), Donald B. Smiley (vice-president and treasurer), and their executive colleagues, Macy's is now substantially owned by the public. This is inevitably a sign of the times, but what that lifelong individualist, Rowland Macy, would have said to it is anybody's guess.

5

Come Kiss Me,
Sweet and Twenties

★

JUST BEFORE the first World War Irene Castle encouraged American girls to stop wearing corsets, simply by wearing none herself and displaying her own natural, lithe slimness. The corset of that day was a boxlike trap with many bones and steel ribs, and old-fashioned mothers declared it an absolute necessity—"to support your vital organs, dear." Nobody then had ever heard of the simple device of holding in the stomach and supporting the vital organs by posture alone, and it may have been the intermediate process of learning that developed the caved-in contortion later known as "the debutante slouch."

Department store ads in 1919 still featured corsets, and the ungainly bunch of batiste or nainsook worn over the corset and called a "corset-cover." Girls dashing off to a party were discreetly pinched by their mothers before departure to make sure they were properly whaleboned, and stories began to fly around about this or that daring "flapper" or "deb" who had firmly removed her corset in the girls' room on arriving at a party and had checked it with the maid in the cloakroom. By the early 1920's "parking your corset" was an accepted routine, and there were as many of these contraptions as there were coats in the average checkroom. Some girls brought along a wisp of pink elastic to hold up their stockings in the absence of the many garters dangling from the abandoned corset, but most merely twisted the stocking below the knee and tucked it in, creating the horror known as "the rolled stocking" which persisted even after skirts went up above the knee, and above the stocking itself. By 1926 department stores, trying to please both mother and daughter, had begun to feature "brassiere and corset combinations" which were made of batiste and rayon, replaced bone and steel ribs with elastic, and were a long step toward the present-day "bra" and girdle. They also produced "the flat look" then so earnestly desired by women of all ages.

A slight vignette of the New York that surrounded and invaded Macy's in the 1920's might be rewarding at this point.

Sherry's was a favorite place for coming-out parties, and the popular night clubs were the Lido, Montmartre, Silver Slipper (with Rudy Vallée), and the Palais Royale (with Paul Whiteman). Nobody ever knew why the "Royale" in "Palais Royale" was spelled with an "e," since the French word "palais" is masculine, and nobody much cared, but it was generally felt that the management spelled "royale" that way in the hope that the customers would pronounce it in the French manner. Dancers at these pleasure domes danced the foxtrot, the Charleston, the shag, and the toddle to "Chicago," "Pretty Baby," "I'll Build a Stairway to Paradise," "Avalon," "Whispering," and (in 1925) "Mountain

Greenery," and the romantic songs for playing on the banjo-mandolin and uke, and humming on the campus at proms, included "The Man I Love," "My Blue Heaven," and "The Birth of the Blues." The flaming youth of the 1920's were often simpler than they have since been pictured, and another favorite group song was that rousing ditty, "Abdullah Bulbul Amir."

KDKA, the first radio station, broadcast the results of the Harding-Cox election in 1921, and the Westinghouse people hit on the idea of building their own radio station and using a tent on the roof of the Westinghouse building as a regular broadcasting studio. This project was not a success; the studio kept blowing away. Earphones were still being worn by the listening public, and in 1923 a good headset cost about three dollars. Radios themselves were naturally more expensive. In 1925, a one-tube Crosley radio cost $14.50.

The theater was rich and varied in the postwar decade. Of the hundreds of stars and plays during that period some of the most memorable were: John Barrymore as *Richard III* and *Hamlet,* John Drew and Mrs. Leslie Carter in *The Circle,* Lenore Ulric as *Kiki,* George Arliss in *The Green Goddess,* Katharine Cornell in *A Bill of Divorcement,* Joseph Schildkraut in *Liliom,* George M. Cohan in *The Tavern,* Pauline Lord as *Anna Christie,* Jeanne Eagels in *Rain,* Helen Hayes in *What Every Woman Knows,* Lunt and Fontanne in *The Guardsman,* Ina Claire in *The Last of Mrs. Cheney,* Noel Coward in his own play, *The Vortex,* Osgood Perkins in *The Front Page,* and Leslie Howard in *Berkeley Square.*

The musicals were wonderful. Fred and Adele Astaire in *Lady, Be Good!,* Marilyn Miller in *Sunny,* Helen Morgan in *Showboat,* W. C. Fields, Fannie Brice, and Will Rogers in *The Ziegfeld Follies,* Beatrice Lillie, Gertrude Lawrence, and Jack Buchanan in *Charlot's Revue,* Fred Allen, Clifton Webb, and Libby Holman in *The Little Show,* and practically everybody in successive editions of *The Music Box Revue.*

This was the decade in which the movies were translated from silence to sound, progressing from the early Chaplin, Pickford, Fairbanks, and Valentino films to (in 1927) the first talking picture, *The Jazz Singer,* with Al Jolson. The consequent turmoil in Hollywood resulted in few good pictures until the thirties, and the rest of the decade was interesting mainly because of the headlong rush from Broadway to screaming Hollywood of many established stage stars and dozens of young actors and actresses who were just getting started on the New York stage. The famous names included John and Lionel Barrymore, Ruth Chatterton, George Arliss, Maurice Chevalier, and Jeanne Eagels. Among the more obscure players, then just starting in the theater, were Robert Montgomery, Ann Harding, Basil Rathbone, Claudette Colbert, Herbert Marshall, and Humphrey Bogart. Mary Pickford and Douglas Fairbanks chose for their first "talkie," and first co-starring picture, *The Taming of the Shrew,* which became chiefly notable for a certain screen credit that flashed before the eyes of startled audiences everywhere. It read:

The Taming of the Shrew
by
William Shakespeare
With Additional Dialogue by
Sam Taylor

Best-selling books in the twenties were Booth Tarkington's *Alice Adams,* Sinclair Lewis's *Main Street,* A. S. M. Hutchinson's *If Winter Comes,* Joseph Hergesheimer's *The Bright Shawl,* Erich Remarque's *All Quiet on the Western Front,* Michael Arlen's *The Green Hat,* Carl Van Vechten's *Peter Whiffle,* Edna Ferber's *So Big,* Edith Wharton's *The Age of Innocence, The Outline of History* by H. G. Wells, and a little atrocity called *The Sheik,* by E. M. Hull.

In some ways, it was truly an age of innocence. Nice women did not smoke, and even the most daring cigarette advertisements pictured a girl gazing at a man lighting his own cigarette and coyly murmuring, "Not at all—the aroma is delightful!" or, in a moment of extreme recklessness, "Blow Some MY Way!" Sometimes the innocence verged on wackiness. Crowds gathered to watch "Shipwreck" Kelly do nothing whatever except sit atop a flagpole for forty days and forty nights, or whatever it was; or to regard, stony-eyed, the antics of "marathon" dancers—crazed couples who, for a prize, danced together (or rather, shuffled around a floor together) for three or four thousand hours until one or the other fell to the ground in a faint. Millions worshipped at the feet of Aimée Semple MacPherson, or Billy Sunday, or Dr. Emil Coué, who commanded his followers to repeat constantly to themselves, "Day by day, in every way, I am getting better and better"—a kind of ominous hint of the Power of Positive Thinking that was to follow.

Often, both innocence and wackiness disintegrated under the impact of shocking crime, as in the Leopold and Loeb murder, the Hall-Mills murders, the Valentine's Day gangster massacre, and the brutal "sashweight murder" of Albert Snyder by his wife, Ruth, and her corset-salesman lover, Judd Gray. It was Ruth Snyder's last words as they strapped her into the electric chair that Alexander Woollcott hailed as probably the most inept remark of all time. "Father, forgive them, for they know not what they do," the confessed husband-killer piously declaimed.

In the early 1920's the fashionable party dress for women was the beaded dress, particularly the tubular dance frock with a deep beaded fringe at the knee-length hemline that stood straight out in the air when a girl's partner whirled her. On a trip to Paris Edwin I. Marks, a young man who had come to Macy's as assistant to Louis Chamansky, bought two thousand of these beaded dresses.

"Two *thousand!*" exclaimed his boss, when he reported the purchase. "What are you planning to do, hang beads all over all the women in New York?"

"Why not?" replied Mr. Marks smoothly. And, in fact, the beaded dresses were such a success that customers were soon waiting in line to get into Macy's fitting-rooms. Marks informed Mr. Jesse that more fitting-rooms were needed. "The lines of customers are so long they reach halfway across the department," he complained. Mr. Jesse regarded him with the tolerance due a relative-by-marriage; Mr. Percy had married Marks's cousin, Marks's uncle was Mr. Abraham of Abraham & Straus, and Mr. Jesse and Mr. Marks had known each other as boys when they spent summers at Isidor's camp on Grindstone Island in the St. Lawrence.

"There is no rush about new fitting-rooms," Mr. Jesse finally pronounced. "When the customers are *not* standing in line, we will begin to worry."

Marks succeeded Chamansky as division merchandise manager upon the latter's retirement, and he remembers

the decade from 1920 to 1930 as the era when he and Joseph
Mayer, who then ran the Paris office, first emphasized style
and chose specialists (later called "stylists") to accent and
maintain it. Macy customers soon got the message. In no
time at all even wealthy women from uptown began to investigate. "Macy's literally could do no wrong in those
days," says Mr. Marks now, and cites as an example the
kind of dialogue that habitually recurred in the dress department:

> WEALTHY CUSTOMER (*pulling $39.95 dress off rack*):
> I saw this *same dress* yesterday at Bergdorf's for *a hun-
> dred and fifty dollars!*
> MARKS (*exhibiting the old-school rugged honesty*):
> That's impossible, madam. Bergdorf's dress is of *much*
> better quality, the seams are hand-sewn, the lining is
> pure silk, the workmanship is superb . . .
> WEALTHY CUSTOMER (*disappearing to fitting-room
> with a buying gleam in her eye*): Don't tell *me!* I
> SAW it!

When Macy's realized that a shopper with a full purse was
never so happy as when emptying it, the store sensibly began the policy of "trading up" (selling expensive items as
well as cheap ones) which eventually flowered into its Little
Shop where, today, Mrs. Plump-Purse can spend $56.25 on a
French cotton print or $185 for a cashmere coat as han-
dily as she could do on Fifth Avenue.

In ten years Macy's sales increased from $35,800,000 in
1919 to $98,500,000 in 1929. On one certain day sales ex-
ceeded $900,000 in nine working hours—almost as much
as Rowland Macy had sold in the entire year of 1870.

Through all the prosperous excitement Mr. Jesse continued to move crisply, Mr. Percy more softly. Throughout the store Mr. Jesse had the reputation of being telepathic and having second sight, since nothing happened in its farthest corner that he was not immediately aware of. In a way this was fortunate, since he also had a talent for solving merchandising problems with apparent ease. One time the glove buyer, Lena Rabenau, was having trouble selling some imported French gloves at $5.94. Mr. Jesse called her to his office.

"We will run an ad featuring *only* the French gloves at $5.94," he told her. "That will bring the people in. When they come, instruct your clerks to show them *only* domestic gloves at $2.94 and $3.94."

"But how will that help my $5.94 French gloves?" asked Miss Rabenau, bewildered.

"The customers will ask to see the $5.94 gloves because of the ad," Mr. Jesse explained, "and after they have thoroughly seen the $2.94 and the $3.94 gloves *first,* the comparison will be so striking and the French gloves so much better that they can't *help* buying them."

The $5.94 French gloves sold out on the day the clerks began teasing the customers about them.

No detail was too small for Mr. Jesse's attention, and the extravagance of the twenties did not affect his thrift in business. When a ten dollar shortage appeared in the accounts at the close of business one day, he ordered that it be traced to its source forthwith. It took the firm one month, and cost two thousand dollars, to trace it. When a poor but popular employee died, her co-workers took up a collection for the funeral, and approached Mr. Jesse. "We have less than a hundred dollars so far, and we need a hundred and eighty-five. The Mass alone costs thirty-five dollars," they told him.

Mr. Jesse gave them enough to make up the hundred, and not a penny more. "One hundred dollars is the decent limit for a funeral," he declared. "Anybody who can't be buried for a hundred dollars is simply frivolous."

That remark echoed through the store, as did another of Mr. Jesse's pronouncements, arising from the unfortunate incident of an employee whom he had charged to deliver a message to a staff member relaying it to another employee for delivery.

"I'll do my own deputizing!" roared Mr. Jesse, when he learned that the staff member had received his message second hand. The unlucky employee was fired, and so were two or three others who ignorantly offended in the same way, and each time Mr. Jesse firmly repeated the law: "I'll do my own deputizing!" His statement became so famous that, several years after the first offense, a raw underling summoned to Mr. Jesse's office to deliver a message from Mr. Jesse to a Mr. Klein in the store, appeared in fear and trembling, took the message, vanished from the store, and did not come back to work until the next day. Mr. Jesse summoned him again.

"And where have *you* been?" he demanded coldly. "I told you to deliver my message to Mr. Klein, not to take the day off."

"I did deliver your message, sir," quavered the underling, "but Mr. Klein was a little hard to find. You see, he was in Philadelphia."

Only slightly shaken, Mr. Jesse left his office on some errand of his own. In the hall, he met Miss Margaret Sharkey returning from lunch. Miss Sharkey is a forthright kind of woman, jolly and slightly crew-cut, who came to work at Macy's in 1920 and is now the firm's assistant treasurer.

"I've been trying to get you on the phone since twelve o'clock," Mr. Jesse accused her. "You must have left for lunch early."

"No, I left at twelve," said Miss Sharkey.

Mr. Jesse glanced at his watch. "And it is now ten past one. What have you been doing all that time?"

"I grabbed a bite of lunch and got a haircut," Miss Sharkey told him.

"You got a haircut—on Macy's time?" Mr. Jesse acidly inquired.

"Well," said Miss Sharkey, "it *grew* on Macy's time."

Miss Sharkey is the first to point out that Mr. Jesse had a kindly side to him. Charles B. Webster, the former Macy partner, had left $1,325,637 in his will, "to improve conditions of unmarried working women" through the establishment of a hotel where girls earning less than $35 a week could receive room and board at a nominal fee in wholesome and pleasant surroundings. The will also stipulated that the establishment was to be set up under the direction of the executors of Webster's estate; Josiah Webster, his brother, and Jesse Straus. Webster House, named for its founder, was duly established, around 1917, on West Thirty-fourth Street, and Mr. Jesse devoted a good deal of his time to its problems. Even in dealing with poorly-paid working girls, he was obliged to use his native caution. Some girls, applying for residence, lied about their incomes, so Mr. Jesse promptly assigned a plain-clothes detective to keep watch from the parlor, to see which girls came home from work in a cab, and which girls owned fur coats or other evidences of luxury. This was only fair, of course, to the truly deserving poor. Webster House prospered to a point where Mr. Jesse felt that it might be completely self-supporting if the cost of food were cut by a dollar a day. He consulted Miss Sharkey, who had helped to organize the residence.

"Don't cut the food allotment," Miss Sharkey advised him. "Use that dollar a day to vary the food a little. Put in a grill so that the girls can have a steak or chops occasionally, instead of that everlasting pot roast and stew. Give 'em a little fresh fruit for breakfast. Goodness! Do you realize that those girls have a standard breakfast, day in and day out, of prunes, toast and coffee?"

"What's the matter with prunes?" Mr. Jesse wanted to know. "*I* eat prunes for breakfast every day of my life."

"Ah," sighed Miss Sharkey, "but would you, if you had to?"

Presently the Webster House girls got—not fresh fruit juice, as Mr. Jesse had sarcastically suggested—but an apple, an orange, or a banana for breakfast; "something solid that they can put into their lunch-boxes," Miss Sharkey had ordained.

Mr. Jesse's philanthropy also made itself felt closer to home. He bought and presented a cardiograph machine to the hospital in Mount Kisco where he had a summer place— ("You forgot to take two per cent off for cash" he growled to his secretary when signing the check). And when the Straus nursemaid, a widow with two children, became ill and died, he sent her daughter through Mt. Holyoke and later saw to it that she had a good job at Bamberger's. When the girl contracted tuberculosis Mr. Jesse not only sent her to Trudeau Sanatorium, where she happily recovered; when his secretary, following instructions, brought the girl to the station to put her on the train for Saranac, both Mr. and Mrs. Jesse were there to see her off.

Jesse Straus and his wife had three children of their own: a daughter, Beatrice, a son, Jack, born in 1900, and a younger son, Robert. Beatrice is now married to Dr. Robert L. Levy, the heart specialist. Robert Straus, a former New York City councilman, was in the publishing business for a while and is now an investment manager, and has no connection with Macy's. For a time it looked as though Jack Straus might have no connection with Macy's, either. During his schooldays and his years at Harvard he had become a skilled jazz pianist, and he wanted to make music his life's work. Jesse firmly sent him to Paris to work in a bank, and as Jack says now, "I found that I had no important talent for music beyond being able to play at parties, and that I really *liked* business."

In 1921, Jack Straus—like his father and grandfather, the eldest son of the eldest son—came to Macy's. His early training there included such unsensational chores as selling stockings at the thrift tables on the main floor. Anxious to prove his worth, he would from time to time attempt to make a suggestion about the store to Mr. Jesse, but each time (as Mr. Jack recalls it), before he got his mouth well open to utter the words, Mr. Jesse would cut him off with a prompt "No." Being the eldest son of an eldest son like Jesse was quite an education in itself, Jack found, as he dizzily adapted himself to his father's rapid changes of pace. In 1933, Jesse Straus was appointed U.S. Ambassador to France. Preparing to leave Macy's, he summoned Jack and spoke almost the first affirmative words he had ever addressed to his son. "I am leaving all my affairs in your hands," he said. From that time, whenever Jack on a trip abroad called on his father at the Paris Embassy and mentioned any problem connected with Macy's, Jesse would cut him short, as in the old days, but with a difference. "I don't even want to hear about it. You're in charge," he would say.

History repeated itself in more ways than one in the Straus family. Just as Nathan's sons had drifted away from any active association with Macy's, so did Percy Straus's sons—although one of them, Ralph Straus, is a director of the firm. Of the other two, Donald Straus is a vice-president of the Health Insurance Plan of Greater New York, and Percy Straus Junior, a retired attorney, is an art collector, a big game hunter, and a connoisseur of arms and armor. However, Herbert's two sons, Edward and John, are respectively head of Macy's Garden State Plaza and merchandise administrator of the New York store. Oliver Herbert Straus, a third son of Mr. Herbert, is a distinguished researcher in electronics and is not connected with Macy's. Jack's son, Kenneth, now thirty-three, is in charge of Macy's Flatbush store. And Gerald Levy, Jack's nephew, is television buyer for Macy's New York.

Mr. Percy, a gentler edition of his brother Jesse, nevertheless combined his kindliness with a fierce attention to details. "Aren't you a very *little* girl to be handling that heavy thing?" Birdie Schwartz of the fabrics department remembers him saying to her one day in the twenties as she struggled to reroll and replace a heavy bolt of brocade; and he took the bolt from her, deftly rolled it, and returned it to the shelves. Such thoughtful gestures, though, were usually followed by a quick brushing of his palm along the counter to make sure it was free from dust, and he daily scrutinized the length of the white marble staircase which then led from the ground floor to the balcony. If its dazzling surface revealed one blemish, scrubwomen with mops and pails were put to work forthwith, no matter how thick the crowds. Mr. Percy could be as strict as his brother toward employees, too. Once a messenger delivering some Macy groceries to the Straus apartment dropped a bottle of olives and broke it. Mr. Percy, who was at home, called up the store.

"If this messenger reports this breakage, it should be taken out of his wages," he directed. "If he does *not* report it, he is dishonest and should be fired."

The messenger reported nothing, but surprised everybody by buying, and paying for, an even larger bottle of olives and delivering it intact to a gratified Mr. Percy.

"Where did you get the money?" the department manager asked him, knowing a messenger's salary.

"Out of petty cash," replied the messenger airily.

Westward the course of empire takes its way, and in the case of Macy's in the 1920's, also southward. In 1923, the Strauses bought a controlling interest in the La Salle & Koch Company, a leading department store of Toledo, Ohio, and two years later bought control of the Davison-Paxon Company in Atlanta, Georgia. In 1929, for $26,000,000 they acquired L. Bamberger & Company of Newark, New Jersey, and thereby found themselves also in the radio broadcasting business, since radio station WOR belonged to Bamberger's. The Strauses appointed their own local siren, "Martha Manning," who every morning wooed housewives over the airwaves with tales of the bargains to be found that day at Bamberger's and Macy's. "Martha Manning" became a celebrated household god, or goddess. "My!" an old Macy customer recently exclaimed, "Martha Manning was as much an early-morning fixture in my house as morning prayers were in my great-grandfather's." WOR won distinction, too, on the day that the dirigible "Shenandoah" broke loose from its Jersey moorings and was lost for several hours. WOR was the only radio station that stayed on the air, and it finally traced the dirigible in its mad careenings, and located it safe and sound.

Macy's sold WOR in 1952, but the firm is still indirectly in the broadcasting business. A trust called The Retirement System for Employees of R. H. Macy & Co., Inc., owns the television studio at 101 West Sixty-seventh Street, now leased to the National Broadcasting Company.

By 1924, the Herald Square store was bursting at its seams with business, and a new twenty-story building was erected, west of the store and adjoining it. This is now known as the West Building. In 1929, the construction of the Seventh Avenue building completed Macy's domination of the entire block from Broadway to Seventh Avenue and from Thirty-fourth to Thirty-fifth Street. Lease trouble plagued the Strauses on Seventh Avenue as it had done on Herald Square. A Fanny Farmer candy store and several other shops with leases on the ground floor of the existing building declined to vacate when Macy's wished to erect its new towers; so the Straus architects serenely (and with the tenants' consent) tore the building down to its first two stories, and constructed the new Seventh Avenue building on top of them —with business proceeding as usual on the ground floor. Just as there had been one small holdout in 1901, on the corner of Broadway and Thirty-fourth Street, so there was one small standpatter in 1929, on the corner of Seventh Avenue and Thirty-fifth Street. The Strauses refused to pay the exorbitant price demanded by the owner of this plot, as they had refused to pay that of R. Smith twenty-eight years earlier. The slice of land, still not controlled by Macy's, is now occupied by a cigar store and an orange-drink stand.

Pictorially, Macy's improved steadily during the 1920's, from its display windows to its merchandise display inside the store. In the old days the man in charge of the windows was called a "window dresser," and window dressing was all he did, the interior display being left to the casual touch of some clerk or other whom the floorwalker would suddenly remind to "flip a bit of that ribbon over the rack" or "line up those gloves more nicely." Macy's had been a pioneer in striking window displays as far back as the 1880's, when the Fourteenth Street store was famous for its annual Christmas pageant of an endlessly moving belt of toys. But even at Macy's Thirty-fourth Street, in the first half of the 1920's, windows were a sad example of overcrowding and under-designing, and those which featured fashions were, on the whole, a sorry tableau. Mannequins were ghastly wax creatures with real hair and glass eyes, and on a hot day with the sun beating on the glass they often became more interesting, pictorially speaking, than decorative. "I would come back from lunch, and their chins would be on their chests," says Irving C. Eldredge, Macy's display manager from 1923 until he retired in 1949. Moreover, most of the mannequins were made in Germany, Austria, or Switzerland, and their stolid frames and features in no way suggested the "race-horse" look that American women were learning to desire and acquire.

Irving Eldredge, long the dean of display managers in New York, was a Brooklyn boy whose grandmother lived in New York, just around the corner from the old Macy's on Fourteenth Street. As a child, he remembered pressing his small nose against Macy's magical Christmas window

with its endless belt of toys. In 1923, he had a good job as showroom manager at Orsenigo & Company, furniture manufacturers, from whence he was persuaded by that demon persuader, Jesse Straus, to turn his attention to Macy's. At the end of their first interview, Mr. Jesse picked up his desk telephone, called Orsenigo's, and held a brief conversation. "I just wanted to make sure that, if you don't work out at Macy's, Orsenigo's would take you back," he explained to Eldredge, afterward. Eldredge was then given a sort of preliminary test. Joseph Mayer, at that time a merchandise manager before he became head of the Paris office, took him for a walk along Fifth Avenue, asking his opinion of the window displays they passed, and also of various costumes worn by other promenaders, and of the current books, plays, and art exhibits. Mr. Eldredge does not now recall any scintillating remarks he may have made during that stroll, but Mr. Mayer seemed satisfied, for they had gone no farther than Lord & Taylor's at Thirty-eighth Street when he abruptly turned homeward, to Macy's, saying, "Okay, you're hired."

In 1925, Eldredge went to France for the Paris Exposition, and there beheld a sight that filled him with joy. It was the new breed of mannequin, created by Seigel of Paris. This doll, in every sense of the word, was made of papier-mâché (non-melting), her coiffure was a lovely, sculptured affair of milliner's horsehair, and she wore a fashionable expression, as of one lightly sniffing the wind. Eldredge brought twenty-five of them back to Macy's. Sensational though they were in 1925, Seigel's mannequins have been greatly improved in succeeding years by such American mannequin-makers as Lillian Greneker, Cora Scovil, Lester Gaba, and D. G. Williams, the firm which mainly supplies Macy's. For one thing, today's mannequins are taller, so that clothes look better on them; and too, they have flexible waists and natural-looking arms and hands.

Mannequins, though important, are but one detail of the display manager's job. At Macy's, he is responsible for forty-five windows, which are changed weekly, as well as for all displays inside the store, including the lighting and decorating of every specialty shop. He has a staff of fifty-eight people, numbering window decorators, interior display artists, an art staff, an architect, and a theatrical lighting specialist. The theatrical lighting used in many window displays presented quite a problem when it was first installed. Each window is equipped with a sprinkler system in case of fire, as required by the New York Fire Department, and the heat from the spotlights was so intense that it regularly set off the sprinklers—providing a free show for spectators which was not precisely the one Macy's had intended. In order to continue the use of theatrical lighting, which had proved to be very effective, all forty-five windows had to be air-conditioned.

Macy's was the first store, possibly the only one, to have a telephone connection from the sidewalk to the interior of its windows, so that the display manager might direct his decorators from outside, at the proper artistic distance. Each Macy department pays, out of its budget, for every window display featuring that department's specialties, and this ensures a calm system of rotation free from favoritism or petty squabbles. The display manager also sees to it that a window display is co-ordinated with the store's newspaper advertising, so that a featured item hits the customer twice before the actual purchase; once in the ad, and once in the window.

In 1956, Macy's spent over $500,000 on display in Macy's New York alone. This sum includes salaries of display artists and such extra treats as the Fashion Show in the Sky, at which twelve miniature mannequins were used to display Macy ensembles to a group of fashion writers while flying six thousand feet above New York in an Eastern Air Lines plane. The aerial fashion show fell somewhat into disfavor after its first and only take off coincided exactly with the Great Hurricane of September, 1938. Mannequins, display men, and fashion writers were tumbled about for what seemed hours in a craft blown about the heavens like an autumn leaf before the pilot finally managed to land.

In 1900, a book was published entitled *The Art of Decorating Dry Goods Windows and Interiors* by an expert on the subject, one L. Frank Baum. Later that same year, L. Frank Baum also wrote *The Wonderful Wizard of Oz*, proving that he knew that display men can be wizards as well as artists. A Macy window, for instance, can be assembled overnight in an emergency. Generally, however, the windows are planned about a year in advance and involve much discussion between display staff and store stylists as to what future "trends" will be. The display manager and his colleagues begin planning next year's Christmas windows about five minutes after this year's Christmas windows are opened to the public. They wait five minutes, so as not to miss what is probably the most magical moment of the year at Macy's.

The moment occurs when Macy's famous Thanksgiving Day Parade comes to a halt in front of the store and, amid a sudden stillness in the crowd, Santa Claus rises from his great throned sled and gives a signal.

Then . . . slowly and breath-takingly, the curtains go up on . . . the Christmas windows!

Jimmy Morgan is a stock boy in Macy's pet shop on the fourth floor. Actually Jimmy is no boy, he is a man of rather dignified presence; but stock boys, like bellboys and messenger boys, are never permitted to grow up. Jimmy had a colorful career before he came to Macy's. Like R. H. Macy before him he ran away to sea at fifteen from his home in New England. Joining the American Merchant Marine, he worked in engine rooms and as steward and, during World War II, was torpedoed four times and gravely wounded. When Jimmy drifted to Macy's as a stock boy, some time after the war, he was still involved in a technical discussion with the government concerning the payment to him of certain compensatory sums. These things take time. At length Jimmy won his claim and, with it, a fairly handsome amount of money. His department manager counseled wise investment but Jimmy, a bachelor, hankered for the leisurely life. He quit his job, bought a fancy wardrobe, and thereafter Macy's saw him only at closing time when he would arrive to collect certain cronies in the store and treat them all royally to roast beef and grog at a neighboring tavern. When cold weather came on Jimmy went to Florida, dispensed large hospitality at various places of amusement, and eventually turned up again at Macy's, broke but cheerful, and quite ready to resume his career as a stock boy. He has been there ever since.

The high point of Jimmy's year comes in November, with Macy's Thanksgiving Day Parade. He is the clown in the Pierrot hat and the slap shoes, with the little dog on an eight-foot leash, who marches, runs, and gambols in the Parade. Jimmy has written his own account of this annual big moment:

> It's Thanksgiving Eve (he writes)—I am on my way home. Although a small cog in the wheel, I have attended meetings and helped to plan and prepare for the coming Parade. Tonight it means early to bed; for in the morning I have to be up at dawn to make up at home for my clown act, which also includes my dog—Santa's Little Princess.

On arriving at the store, I chip in to help with the make-up of other clowns who are also in the Parade. Then comes bus time, and we all take off for the starting point of the Parade.

While standing around, waiting for the Parade to start, one wonders if one's efforts and labors are worth it.

The Parade starts—Santa's Little Princess and I are there, marching along and handing out candy to the children who are lined up all along the sides of the street.

While marching down the avenue I see a little child in a wheel chair, crying as if her heart will break. In my mind I say, "This should never be!" So back we step, Little Princess and I, and slowly approach the child. Within a few seconds the dog and I, who both love children, leave her smiling and happy.

This episode was one of my happiest moments at Macy's—just knowing that my dog and I had helped to brighten up this little child's life made my own Thanksgiving a happy one, long to be remembered.

The Thanksgiving Day Parade has been an annual event at Macy's since 1927, with the exception of three years during the war. For weeks beforehand the excitement that runs through the store is more like the thrill that pervades a circus ground than the backstage confusion of an amateur performance—for this is strictly a professional show, even though it is put on by amateurs in show business. The production team under Producer-Director Ed Hill (who is, in off-Parade moments, senior department manager of Macy's controller's office) is divided into Marshals, Section Leaders, and Supervisors in charge of costumes, floats, balloons, grandstand arrangements, comedy acts, and a hundred other details. All of the Supervisors and other impresarios are, naturally, recruited from Macy's staff.

Along about the middle of October *The Macy Star* comes out with a casting-call aimed at every employee in the store and containing many spirited challenges: "Can you walk on stilts? Balance a broom on your nose? Skate like a son of a gun? Be a beautiful baby (and ride in a carriage yet)? Or how about clowning as a weight-lifter (with muscles supplied by Macy's)?" Every year there are plenty of standard acts, like Jimmy Morgan's, but Macy's, like any casting director, is always on the lookout for new talent. Volunteers apply to designated Section Leaders, and auditions and rehearsals begin—in the basement, on the roof, or in any clear space between—during off-hours, before the store opens mornings and after it closes at night. Last year, the Bicycle-Built-for-Five act practiced in the sub-basement while trick roller-skaters spun madly all over the controller's office and on the terrace outside.

Elsie Angiono and Mary Lyons, two bright girls in the training department, are in charge of the comedy acts and, as showmen everywhere must do, they sometimes encounter moments of pathos. A new employee came to them last year and said mournfully, "I have no talent for anything, but I *do* so want to be in the Parade!" Elsie and Mary solved that one, all right; they made her a bearded lady on a sideshow float. Another dilemma arose from the fact that all the girls' costumes are sizes 10 and 12 because they are rented from circus supply houses and circus girls are usually tiny. A long-time employee approached Elsie and Mary in tears. "I've

OFFICES

been in the Parade every year for twenty years," she wept, "and my niece and nephew will be heartbroken if I'm not in it this year, and so will I! But I just can't get into a size ten or twelve any more!" The girls fixed that, too. They rented a special costume for her, and sent her happily into the marching line as Bo-Peep.

At about eleven o'clock on the night before Parade Day, mysterious elves start work at Seventy-seventh Street and

Central Park West where the Parade will start early next morning. These are goblin workers sent by the Goodyear Company of Akron, Ohio, to inflate the vast helium balloons such as Mighty Mouse and Gorgeous Gobbler, which are manufactured by Goodyear. First the workers spread canvas on the street so that no surface roughness may puncture the rubber; then they spread netting over each balloon and attach guy ropes under the netting; and finally they inflate the balloon which, in the case of the biggest ones, can take three hours. The Goodyear people are anxious to have everyone use the proper technical term "inflate" ever since one Thanksgiving when a Goodyear executive, peacefully at home in Akron, turned on his radio to listen to the Parade, and was just in time to hear the announcer exclaim in excited tones, "And now the balloons are all blown up!" Not until he had put in a frantic long-distance call to Macy's was he sure that they hadn't all exploded.

The balloons do not explode because the helium is carefully balanced in separate compartments, and even if a balloon is snagged or punctured by a lamppost or other projection, the helium in its other compartments holds it aloft. Last year Mighty Mouse struck a horizontal flagpole on the Hotel Astor at Forty-fourth Street and lost a compartment, but he managed to reach home grounds at Macy's before he lay down and died. All of the balloons are manned, with guy ropes, by volunteers among Macy employees, who take over from the Goodyear men as soon as the balloons are inflated and the netting slipped off. It requires fifty-five men on the guy ropes to handle Mighty Mouse alone.

Other hitches can occur, besides high winds tossing the big balloons into buildings, lampposts, or trees. It can rain on Thanksgiving morning—but, somehow, it seldom does. Or, even, one of the comedy acts can be *too* good. The first year the Macy Parade was televised, a TV cameraman was so fascinated by a certain comedy quartet that he asked them to repeat the act for the camera. When the advance guard of the Parade arrived at Macy's at noon, the appointed hour, Santa Claus and the rest of the show were still at Forty-second Street.

Like the circus, the Macy Parade became for a time a little over-sophisticated, until Mrs. John Straus stood up at a meeting a couple of years ago and said firmly, "This Parade no longer seems to be for the children! It's getting to be too grand, too glossy, too much of a Broadway production. Why, this year, we had a whole float featuring the stars of *The Pajama Game!* I think we ought to simplify it, go back to what it used to be—a big show, and a big treat, mainly for the *kids*."

The men around Macy's seldom disagree when a woman speaks, having learned from experience that about some things, women know better than anybody. Macy's Thanksgiving Day Parade is, once more, strictly for the children. Last year, its professional attractions were headed by Roy Rogers and his family.

6

The Girls

AT THE BEGINNING of the 1920's department store advertising had come a long way from the packed newspaper paragraphs of the 1870's, and from Rowland Macy's own exclamatory style with its

COME, COME, TIME, TIME,

COME, COME, TIME, TIME,

THE TIME HAS COME!

Advertisements were fairly sleek and attractive, and line drawings of pretty girls had almost completely replaced the stodgy photographs of Mother or Little Sister wearing the latest fashions or adorning the newest car. Advertising still retained a kind of stuffy grandeur, however, and even as late as 1916 some Fifth Avenue stores refused to allow their fashion ads to be illustrated in any way, on the ground that no well-bred woman would be found dead wearing a dress that had been displayed in the public prints.

The advertising department of a store in those days was far from being the bright, humming beehive it now is. Generally it was a small room staffed by the advertising manager, usually a retired newspaper man, and one or two helpers. Under this relaxed regime so many typographical errors and even misquotations of prices crept into the store's newspaper ads that Macy's, for one, finally hung a sign next to the employees' lockers in the sub-basement. This sign announced that One Dollar would be paid to any employee who found an error in any of Macy's ads, and it particularly interested Estelle Hamburger, a girl in her teens who was pinch-hitting as secretary to a Mr. Byrnes, the store manager, for two weeks while his regular secretary was on vacation. Miss Hamburger was getting $12 a week in her secretarial job. After she saw the sign, she spent every spare moment reading Macy's newspaper ads—on the subway, during her lunch hour, and at home—and in one week made $14 extra just by spotting mistakes.

When her temporary job with Mr. Byrnes was over Miss Hamburger found, like many of the people who have gone to work there, that she did not want to leave Macy's. Through Mr. Byrnes she got an appointment with William Cozier, then advertising manager, to whom she confidently asserted, "I want to write Macy ads, and *not* make any mistakes!"

Mr. Cozier, a former newspaper man, interrupted his regular perusal of the seventeen daily papers then published in New York to look at her over his glasses. "Oh, you're the girl who's been collecting all the dollars for our mistakes, hey?" he said kindly. "Well, you better see Mrs. Riordan. She's been writing all the ads up to now, and I guess she could use a little help."

Mrs. Riordan thankfully handed her new assistant a stack of memorandums listing the articles of merchandise to be advertised next. The top memo stated: "marabou neckpiece, $2.79."

"Could I see it, please?" asked Miss Hamburger.

"*See* it!" cried Mrs. Riordan, shocked. "Heavens, child, you'd never get through your day's work if you had to *look* at every article you write about."

"But I don't know what marabou *is!*" wailed Miss Hamburger.

In the end, she made a quick and somewhat furtive trip down to the floor where the neckpieces were to be on sale, got a good look at the marabou, and came back and triumphantly wrote an ad featuring "FLUFFY marabou neckpieces at $2.79." It was one of the earliest attempts to woo the prospective customer with words, not statistics. And it was the beginning of a self-imposed schedule that often kept Miss Hamburger working late into the night. Each morning she would tour the store with her pile of memorandums, looking over the merchandise mentioned in them; then, after twenty minutes for lunch, she would return to her office and write the ads, usually about forty a day. The buyers loved her—for the first time, the advertising department was taking a real interest in the merchandise. And Macy's ads not only carried practically no more mistakes, they acquired a new kind of personal appeal.

One morning in the furniture department a joyful reunion took place when Estelle Hamburger noticed a girl pushing desks and chairs around. "Why, if that isn't Mary Lewis!" she exclaimed. She and Mary Lewis had gone to Wadleigh High School in New York together, and both had been on the staff of the school magazine, *The Wadleigh Owl*. After embraces and more exclamations, Miss Hamburger suggested that Miss Lewis quit this furniture-moving and get a job in the advertising department, writing ads about furniture. This, after consultation with Mr. Crozier, Miss Lewis did, later expanding her field to include Macy fashions. In fact, the two girls wrote just about all of Macy's advertising from 1916 to 1920, the overburdened Mrs. Riordan having taken a lengthy and well-deserved leave of absence.

Mary Lewis went on to a remarkable fashion career, at Best's, at Saks Fifth Avenue, and later with her own Fifth Avenue shop. She is now a prosperous fashion consultant. Estelle Hamburger traveled from Macy's to Franklin Simon's and Bonwit Teller, and became executive vice-president of Jay Thorpe. She was known to the trade as "Paprika," in recognition of her spicy qualities. Currently she is merchandising advisor to a large clientele of retail stores, with her own headquarters in Rockefeller Plaza.

Before they progressed to wider fields, Estelle Hamburger and Mary Lewis gave department store advertising much of the spark it had long needed, and even some of the proper organization it had lacked. However, it was not until almost the mid-twenties that humor and exceptionally good writing came into department store ads. In this long step forward, Macy's, under the fierce guidance of Jesse Straus, can truthfully be called a pioneer.

Mr. Jesse had engaged Kenneth Collins, a young Harvard teacher of English, as copy chief in the advertising department because, as he said, "We need somebody to write good English around here." Mr. Collins, who rapidly became advertising manager, now gracefully passes along the accolade. "If I could be remembered for one thing," he says, "I'd like people to remember that I fostered and encouraged a brilliant group of young women at Macy's, and even brought some of them into the store. Stella McClure, book buyer, Mary Murphy, merchandise councilor . . . and in advertising, the copywriters . . . ah, the copywriters! Bernice Fitz-Gibbon, Margaret Fishback, Alice Hughes, Katherine Lowe . . ." Here Mr. Collins blissfully closes his eyes, recalling his little band of golden girls.

"I don't know that we were as brilliant as all that," modestly states Bernice Fitz-Gibbon, who now operates her own agency with offices on Fifth Avenue. "But there was one thing about all of us, including Ken Collins. We *cared* about Words on Paper. You know how it is—either you care about Words on Paper, you have a sort of feeling for them and an affinity with them, or you don't. And we did."

Miss Fitz-Gibbon, who was to invent some of the most memorable advertising slogans of all time, came from a farm in Wisconsin and taught English for a time in Wisconsin schools. She wanted to be a writer, or at least to get a job in a publishing house, so she journeyed to Chicago where, finding editors and publishers both cool toward her ambitions, she went to work at Marshall Field's. Macy's in New York had just organized its Training Squad, recruited largely from college graduates who were to be groomed into executives, and the idea had caught on in other department stores throughout the country, including Marshall Field's. Miss Fitz-Gibbon was placed on the Marshall Field Training Squad where she spent half of each day selling and the other half learning how to be an executive, and she instantly got into trouble. Her first selling job was at the ribbon counter. The rule was that, when you rewound a bolt of ribbon, you wound it counterclockwise, and at the end of a half-hour Miss Fitz-Gibbon was tangled from head to foot in ribbons like a Maypole.

"These ribbons are alive!" she remarked bitterly, and asked to be put to work dealing with larger and less animate objects. She was transferred to the furniture department where she promptly asked for the same commission on sales as the men in the department were getting, and soon she was making $100 a week.

At that time, in the early twenties, Macy's in New York was acquiring fame everywhere as the most "up-and-coming" store in the United States, so Miss Fitz-Gibbon traveled on to New York and applied for an appointment with "Jimmy" Goold, predecessor to Kenneth Collins as advertising manager. When no appointment was forth-coming, she got a job writing advertising copy for Wana-maker's, and speedily became involved in a small war be-tween Wanamaker's and Macy's.

Macy's had been advertising men's shorts which featured something apparently of value called a "banjo-seat." Wana-maker's, advertising similar garments, pointed out in its ads that *its* shorts likewise had "banjo-seats," whereupon Macy's, claiming to have coined the expression, got out a legal injunction restraining Wanamaker's from using it. Wanamaker's next ad, composed by Miss Fitz-Gibbon, was a minor effort in the light of her later achievements, but it was compelling, to say the least. It displayed a fellow perched on a fence, playing a banjo, and dressed as a hill-billy except that he was wearing the famous shorts. The text read:

> Oh, I Come from A-a-alabammy
> With a Banjo on My Knee . . .
>
> NOT ON MY SEAT!

Whether the authorship of this retort came to the ears of Jimmy Goold is not clear, but Miss Fitz-Gibbon soon had her long-awaited interview with him and was engaged as an advertising copywriter at Macy's.

Her most famous contribution to Macy's came about in 1928, after Goold had been succeeded by Kenneth Collins, and after Miss Fitz-Gibbon herself had married Herman Block, an attorney, and had already applied for maternity leave because of the impending birth of her first child.

Walking back from lunch one day, about a month before the baby was due, she was waiting for a green light at Herald Square when her eye fell on a long, shining town car with chauffeur and lady passenger nosing its way into Macy's entrance. This was nothing remarkable; wealthy women from uptown had long since discovered Macy's values and regularly descended on the store in increasing numbers. Miss Fitz-Gibbon viewed the car idly, her thoughts busy with a slogan she had been trying for weeks to devise which would express that very idea—that Macy's, though full of bargains, was no longer just a "cheap" department store. Dimly, she heard a girl next to her on the curb say to her companion, "See that car over there? I happen to know it belongs to John D. Rockefeller Junior, and that's Mrs. Rockefeller on the back seat."

Who can tell what goes on in a copywriter's mind? As Miss Fitz-Gibbon now recalls it, her own thought-processes during the few moments it took her to cross the street, enter the store and go up in the elevator were something like this: "That's a mighty smart turnout, that town car . . . Shopping at Macy's, eh? . . . Well, stop thinking about the rich, Bernice, and concentrate on the problem at hand . . . It's frugal to shop at Macy's . . . I've always heard those Rockefellers were frugal people . . . Frugal . . . frugal . . . Now *there's* an ugly word . . . Besides, who uses it any more? My grand-mother used to use it . . . No, she didn't. Grandmother had a better word . . . She used to say her geraniums were 'thrifty,' meaning 'prosperous' or 'blooming' . . . Why, of course, the word 'thrifty' comes from the word 'thriving' . . . The Rockefellers must be thrifty people, and they certainly are thriving, coming down here in that smart-looking turn-out . . ."

Suddenly the words leaped at her:

IT'S SMART TO BE THRIFTY

There are two versions of what immediately followed. Miss Fitz-Gibbon says that she rushed down the hall to Kenneth Collins's office, shrieking "It's come! It's come! It's HERE!"—meaning the slogan they had all been struggling for, for so many weeks—and that Collins, springing to his doorway, yelled at the gathering crowd, "Don't just stand there! Can't you see Bernice is having her *baby?*"

Collins, perhaps a little embarrassed by this memoir, remembers it differently. He maintains that when he called on Bernice in the hospital the day after her son, Peter, was born, she smiled at him palely and whispered, "Well, I've done it!" He thought she was referring to the miracle of having produced a child, until she slipped a scrap of paper into his hands bearing the magic words of the new slogan.

The Smart-to-be-Thrifty phrase turned out to be the most durable of all Macy slogans, but not even a copywriter knows just what will succeed and what will fail. Most of Miss Fitz-Gibbon's inspirations at Macy's were sure-fire hits, as when she headed an advertisement of the then-new strapless evening gowns with the artless query:

HOW DO YOU KEEP IT UP NIGHT AFTER NIGHT?

which was, of course, followed by the explicit information that Macy's strapless gowns stayed up practically by themselves. But some of Miss Fitz-Gibbon's most cherished wheezes fell with an unaccountable thud. One ad, headed READIN' AND WRITIN' AND THRIFTMETIC passed right over the heads of the public into oblivion, because readers simply read "'rithmetic" for "thriftmetic," and missed the point altogether. The same thing happened with another play on words, DON'T BE AN INCOMEPOOP. People, from force of habit, read "incomepoop" as "nincompoop," and the message failed to get through.

Errors—misquotations, printer's errors, or mistakes in fact—are bound to creep into almost any printed text, especially when the text comes off the presses as fast and furiously as Macy advertisements. Macy's, once terrified of such disasters, had come to treat them blithely. When an advertisement misquoted a passage in *Pickwick Papers,* an apologetic notice from Macy's two days later read:

GREAT SCOTT! WE SLIPPED UP ON OUR DICKENS!

And when another ad, about taffeta dresses, attributed "Rustle of Spring" to the wrong composer Macy's apology (also written by that illustrious pixie, Bernice Fitz-Gibbon) displayed a wild-haired pianist performing amid a storm of grace-notes, over a text which lightheartedly read:

WE MADE A MISTAKE ON THAT SCORE!

In a recent fashion advertisement (the apology continued) . . . we referred to the musical composition

"Rustle of Spring" which we blunderingly attributed to Rubenstein.

. . . Immediately our dear and well informed public pulled us up short—put us in our place. We've been twitted and taunted and scoffed at. Because it seems that Christian Sinding wrote "Rustle of Spring."

You see it was this way. We were thinking of—

da dum de *da* dum de *da* dum de *do* . . .

which any nit-wit ought to know is the Melody in F. What we should have been thinking of was this—

la la la *la* la la *la* le . . .

. . . As we were telling you when the slip occurred, TAFFETA'S BACK. We are sorry that we sinned against Sinding—so now we're rescinding! But the quaint new dresses with the little taffeta capes are as beguiling as if we had made no mistake. Come in and see them— they are in

THE BETTER DRESS SHOP—Third Floor

MACY'S

This ad was a terrific success, mainly because thousands of Macy's dear and well-informed public wrote letters and telephoned to inform them that they had misspelled "Rubinstein." When she is asked today whether it was deliberate, Miss Fitz-Gibbon smiles and says, "Wel-lll . . ."

It also set thousands, or possibly hundreds of thousands, of Macy's well-informed public on the trail of Christian Sinding, whom nobody had ever heard of. On that point, Macy's was strictly accurate. Christian Sinding did write "Rustle of Spring."

Macy's was a great one, in those days, for stimulating the public mind, for leading it up one path and down another and leaving it exhausted, but refreshed.

Jesse Straus turned an indulgent eye on errors in the text of advertisements, for the sound reason that they brought in just such floods of letters and telephone calls from the public, all of which was good for business. It might be wrong to say that Mr. Jesse actually encouraged slip-ups in advertising copy, but he was never unhappy when one occurred that caught public attention and kept on doing it. Mr. Jesse was a man who seldom made mistakes himself, so the advertising department particularly enjoyed a little incident that happened to him one day when he was making one of his occasional tours of the store.

He came upon a stock boy playing with the electric trains in the toy department. Lunch hour was long past, these were working hours, and Mr. Jesse's wrath was majestic.

"You are a stock boy, are you not?" he demanded, eyeing the unmistakable stock boy's jacket the youth wore.

"Yes, sir," murmured the boy.

"How much do you make a week?"

"Eighteen dollars, sir."

Mr. Jesse took eighteen dollars in cash from his pocket, plus thirty-six dollars more as two weeks' severance pay, and handed it to the lad. "You," he informed him icily, "are fired!"

"Thank you, sir," said the boy, and pocketing the money, went back to playing with the trains.

"What's the matter with you? Why don't you *leave?*" thundered Mr. Jesse.

"I guess I should have told you, sir," said the boy, "I'm a stock boy at Gimbel's."

There has been some speculation, it might be inserted here, as to the truth of the terrible "feud" which is alleged to have been going on between Macy's and Gimbel's ever since Gimbel's opened its store across the street from Macy's in 1910. Among the people who ought to know, some insist that it is a true vendetta, others say that it originated as a publicity gag, like the radio "feud" between Jack Benny and Fred Allen, or the "feud" between Bing Crosby and Bob Hope. Still others maintain that Eddie Cantor started it, unbeknownst to either store, when in a comedy skit his stooge urged him to reveal some dark secret or other and he replied with the now famous line, "Does Macy tell Gimbel?"

Macy's public attitude about competition from Gimbel's is somewhat lofty, as if to say, "Who's competing?" Macy's considers itself, accurately, so much bigger in size and scope than Gimbel's that it prefers to regard the other store's rivalry, outwardly at least, as so many pebbles flung against a rock. Gimbel's, questioned about its own feeling in the matter, replies amiably through its president, Bernard F. Gimbel. Mr. Gimbel's words are these:

> We congratulate Macy's on their 100th birthday. (They certainly don't look it). We're only 115. (We certainly don't feel it). Our public recognizes that the "battling for business" in midtown New York, good natured in the main, has helped build the most varied, the most accessible and most patronized shopping area in the greatest city on earth. Sometimes it has been a little rough on the contestants, but it has never been unpopular with the crowd. If the manners look a little better, it does not mean that the battle is less real. (Neither store ever takes its eye off the other. What it sees, it quickly translates into action). This is the kind

of competition the customers love; and we have always
believed that the customer is the boss.

It is certainly true that a rivalry exists, not only because
the two stores are close together geographically and offer
rather similar services to a rather similar clientele, but also
because Gimbel's has lured away some of Macy's best talent
to work under the rival roof. Bernice Fitz-Gibbon was one
Macy star who abandoned the Straus firmament, in 1935,
to go to Gimbel's, where in due time she thought up her
second most famous slogan, one which was to contribute a
fashionable phrase to the American language itself.

Macy's, with its 6% less for cash policy, had long claimed
to undersell all other stores which did not sell exclusively
for cash; what Gimbel's, through Miss Fitz-Gibbon, wanted
to put across to the public was the idea that Gimbel's was,
in truth, equally thrifty. The word "thrifty" now belonged
to Macy's and could not be used, but the general idea was
that Macy's wasn't the *only* low-priced store in the world
whose quality was good. The Fitz-Gibbon stream-of-con-
sciousness began its usual scamper: "Macy's undersells
everybody, or tries to . . . If one store can claim that, why
not another? . . . Maybe no one can undersell *everybody* . . .
No one can undersell Gimbel's . . . Nope, 'no one' is weak . . .
Nobody . . . What was that verse of A. A. Milne's? . . . 'Nobody, my darling' . . ." The verse, a popular one at the time,
came to her slowly:

> The King said,
> "Bother!"
> And then he said,
> "Oh, deary me!"

The King sobbed, "Oh, deary me!"
And went back to bed.

.   .   .   .   .

"Nobody,
My darling,
Could call me
A fussy man—

BUT

"I do like a little bit of butter to my bread!"

" 'Nobody, my darling' . . . Nobody, de da, da . . . Nobody,
but nobody . . ." There it was:

NOBODY, BUT NOBODY, UNDERSELLS GIMBELS

That was about thirteen years ago. Soon junior misses
were exclaiming to patient parents, "Oh, Mother, nobody
but *nobody,* does *that* any more!" or among themselves,
"Nobody, but *nobody,* sends me like Sinatra!" The phrase
became such a fad that many people believed the Gimbel
slogan was founded on it; actually, it was the other way
round. The slogan's fame was established once and for all
when Winston Churchill, on a visit to New York, attended
a dinner party given by his friend, Bernard Baruch.

"Tell me," Mr. Churchill asked his dinner partner, a
lady related by marriage to the Gimbels, "is it really true
that nobody, but nobody, undersells Gimbel's?"

Another of Kenneth Collin's garland of girls who brought
deftness and humor into advertising at Macy's was Margaret
Fishback, who also later became as eminent a writer of light
verse as Dorothy Parker or Ogden Nash. Miss Fishback,

from Washington, D.C. and Goucher College, came to New York in 1926 and got a job with a firm that raised money for charitable organizations. She wanted to be a writer, and verse often bubbled from her in spite of her stern duties at the fund-raisers'. At that time Franklin P. Adams ran a column called "The Conning Tower" in the New York *World* which was the Mecca of all hopeful young writers. F. P. A. didn't pay anything, but if he printed your contribution it had to be good, and to be published in "The Conning Tower" was indeed to be touched with glory. One early April day Miss Fishback sent Adams this couplet:

Can Spring Be Far Behind?

How do I know that winter relents?
Arbutus is down to seventy cents.

Adams printed it, and several others that she submitted, and finally gave her an appointment to come down and see him. Her notion was to get a job on the *World,* but Adams, a brusque but kindly man, discouraged her from the harsh milieu of newspaper work. "The way to learn to write is to *write,*" he told her, voicing one of his favorite aphorisms. Miss Fishback, following his advice, soon had a slim scrapbook of published verse clipped from "The Conning Tower," and various magazines, but her income from these successes was scarcely enough to support her enjoyably, even at the girls' club where she lived. Somebody had given her a letter of introduction to Jack Straus, so she journeyed to Macy's to see him, scrapbook under arm, and Mr. Jack sent her to see Jimmy Goold, then advertising manager. Mr. Goold looked through the scrapbook distrustfully.

"What's verse got to do with writing advertising copy?" he wanted to know.

He was to find out, soon after he gave her a job as copy-writer, when one of "Marnie" Fishback's early ads appeared:

Ode to a Street Car

O matchless Thirty-fourth Street car!
  O fine upstanding trolley!
Your influence is felt afar.
  You traffic not with folly.

Day in and out you sagely dash
  Straight to our doors determined
Upon a program strictly cash
  For both the poor and ermined.

Pay-as-you-enter is the scheme
  That keeps *you* going places.
Pay-as-you-go's the thrifty theme
  That brings the crowd to Macy's.

This ad was favorably received and brought in business, but Miss Fishback promptly proved that she could write prose as well, and that she was complete mistress of the one-line blockbuster. Asked to compose an ad illustrating the fact that Macy trucks, manned by driver and helper, delivered merchandise far and wide, to almost any place the customer desired, Marnie came up with two nice ones. For the first, she had an artist draw a picture of a cannibal and his cannibal wife seated happily by a bubbling cauldron in darkest Africa. A Macy driver's cap lay on the ground beside the cauldron and the cannibal husband, delicately finishing off a bone, was saying to his wife:

"PUT A LITTLE MORE SALT ON THE HELPER, DEAR."

In the other, the illustration depicted a Macy truck loaded with palm trees backing up to the tent of an Arab sheik in the middle of the burning Sahara. The sheik's sentry is calling within:

"SAY, HASSAN—DID YOU ORDER AN OASIS FROM MACY'S?"

All this was a zany approach new to advertising, and Miss Fishback is quick to acknowledge the co-operation of artists who strung along with her, such as Dick Sargent and Jack Skolnick (who was also Macy's assistant art director). Probably no two minds ever mingled more sweetly, though, than when the beloved Helen Hokinson of *New Yorker* fame drew some illustrations for the Fishback text. One of the most popular—and Miss Fishback cannot now remember whether the one-line accompaniment was hers or Miss Hokinson's—showed a typical Hokinson lady riding upward on a Macy escalator, her plump rear firmly presented to the escalator's top, or point of arrival.

"I ALWAYS GO UP BACKWARDS SO AS NOT TO MISS THE VIEW"

she is explaining to a front-facing friend on the step below.

Early in her career at Macy's Margaret Fishback was made a divisional copywriter, which means that she was assigned to write ads for a wildly assorted group of departments including women's accessories, cosmetics, notions (Chronicle of a Notion Voyage), toys, candy, groceries (You May Know Your Groceries—BUT!), sporting goods, silverware, and luggage (The Cows Destined for Macy's Kit Bags Are Not Contented . . . They Are *Thrilled!*). She then became institutional copywriter, meaning that she wrote ads for the whole store, or institution, and also copy chief. A copywriter's life is a drastic one, especially if the copywriter, as in this case, happens to be of a poetic turn of mind. Like a caption-writer, the copywriter must count not only words but letters, and not only letters but the spaces between letters, so as to fit his composition into the exact space allotted him by the make-up department. It is a little like cramming the Muse into a telephone booth and shutting the door.

Miss Fishback and the other copywriters flourished even under these strictures, probably because Macy's advertising department was as lighthearted as its ads. People always seemed to have time to leave little notes in one another's typewriters. Once, there was a spell while Miss Fishback was simmering under two annoyances. First, Macy buyers kept bustling into her office at odd hours, all day long, to discuss the ads concerning their departments; try as she would, she could not organize the buyers' interviews into regular hours, preferably in the afternoon. Second, she kept having a mysterious visitor, a pipe-smoking gent, somebody's friend, who drifted in every day and made himself at home in her office. His name was Powell, or Powel. Miss Fishback had come to be pretty nervous about both interruptions when, one day, the whole ugly mess was solved by a small verse left in her typewriter by Mr. Powell, or Powel. He wrote:

> Buyers and their assistants
> Both business-like and flirty
> Will meet with less resistance
> From two until five-thirty.

Miss Fishback liked this offering, and displayed it prominently, right next to the "Mr. Jesse" sign. The "Mr. Jesse" sign was a Must for all copywriters. The rule was that it be in plain sight at all times. If it ever got lost, or mislaid, or obscured under piles of proof on a copywriter's desk, Mr. Jesse somehow knew about it, and immediately sent down a duplicate from his office. Copywriters were sometimes ankle-deep in "Mr. Jesse" signs.

Mr. Jesse's sign read simply:

AVOID THE USE OF SUPERLATIVES
THEY LEAD TO EXAGGERATION

"It was sound advice," says Miss Fishback now, "even if we did keep losing the signs. If you look back through Macy ads you will notice that we never said anything was the Greatest, or the Most Wonderful. A restriction like that led to more skillful writing, too. Copywriters had to put across the idea that something or other *was* the Greatest and the Most Wonderful, without ever saying so."

The presiding genius of the advertising department was, of course, Kenneth Collins, who had succeeded Jimmy Goold shortly after Miss Fishback went to work at Macy's. Reflecting on Mr. Collins nowadays, Miss Fishback sighs admiringly and says, "He had the most *untrammeled* mind of any man I've ever met."

One day, Mr. Collins was missing from his office for several hours. It turned out that he had been up on Macy's roof with a squad of men he had stationed there with stop watches, field glasses, and a third magical instrument that not even Mr. Collins can remember the name of now. The squad's mission was to clock and enumerate the number of people who entered Macy's that day. Toward dusk he descended wearily to his advertising department and presented a sheet of paper to Miss Fishback.

"Well, here are the figures," he said. "Write an ad about it."

The ad, which appeared in newspapers the following Monday, was headed:

302,928 PEOPLE WERE EXPOSED TO MACY'S LAST SATURDAY

and, Miss Fishback not being one to overlook a dramatic nuance, continued:

Eagle-eyed statisticians, moored to our roof, counted them as they presented themselves at the intersection of Broadway and 34th Street . . .

"I always thought it was pretty honest of Ken," Miss Fishback says now. "After all, Macy's could have printed *any* vast figure—who was going to stand around and check it? But Ken Collins was a man who was interested in finding out the truth, and he always found it out."

Collins, when not passionately dedicated to statistics, was as lighthearted as the rest of his department. It was his inspiration, one summer when Macy's decided on a Saturday closing during July and August, that produced one of the store's most blithesome ads. It displayed Fontaine Fox's Toonerville Trolley, packed to the gunnels with merrymakers, under the carefree announcement:

WE'VE ALL GONE FOR A TROLLEY RIDE

Hearty faith and honest cheer welcome in the sweet o' the year, as the poet said, and the advertising department's unfailing good humor proved contagious even to the august executive precincts where the Strauses reigned and where Edwin Marks, a senior vice-president, had his office. In 1935, Margaret Fishback married Alberto Antolini, Macy's rug buyer, and in a few years had a son, Anthony Frederick. Marnie left Macy's for her maternity leave on a Friday. Her son was born the following Sunday. The next day, Monday, she received a telegram at the hospital from Edwin Marks. She tore it open eagerly, for Mr. Marks was not only a senior vice-president, he was also the executive to whom she (in the trade vernacular) "reported"; he was her supreme boss, even over Kenneth Collins.

WHY ALL THIS LOAFING? (*Mr. Marks had wired*) HERE
IT IS MONDAY AND YOU ARE NOT BACK AT YOUR
DESK YET.

Mrs. Antolini, née Fishback, laughed, but privately decided on a return engagement in the near future. At Macy's,
one good gag deserved another.

When Tony, the baby, was six months old Marnie took
him down to Jack Straus's office and the two of them, with
infant, repaired to Mr. Marks's suite, having ascertained
that Mr. Marks was out to lunch but expected back at any
moment. They placed the infant on the carpet in front of
Mr. Marks's imposing desk and, giggling like fools, hid in
the closet. The idea was to have the great Marks stroll back
from lunch and find his office occupied by a crawling, gur-
gling baby.

Mr. Marks did exactly that. And Jack Straus and the former Miss Fishback stifled in the closet for some twenty minutes while Mr. Marks cordially picked up the baby, sat it on
his knee, and entered upon a long and fascinating game
with it concerning the paperweights on his desk. The plot-
ters in the closet are not sure to this day whether he ever
knew they were there, until they fell out, gasping for air.

"Oh, that's nothing," says Jack Straus nowadays, reminded of this incident. "Marnie was always getting people
into the damndest things. Everybody liked her, you know,
and she had a way of making you want to co-operate with
her. Sometimes, people co-operated too much! Did you ever
hear the story about Marnie Fishback and the night watchman?"

It seems that Miss Fishback, always a great one for flowers,
had many potted plants in her office, arranged along the

window sill. Taking off for a few days' vacation, she thumb-tacked a large sheet of paper to the window frame with the message, "Night Watchman: There is a pitcher of water on the window sill. Would you be good enough to water my plants while I am away?"

She forgot that Macy's vigilance system includes about

one watchman to every office every hour. When she came home from vacation she found her dear plants drowned, and the blank space beneath her note painstakingly filled in with initials and times, like a punch-clock.

> 9:15 P.M. Watered plants. E. C.
> 10:15 P.M. Watered plants. J. W.
> 11:15 P.M. Watered plants. H. J.

and so on, every hour, for about four days. The night watchmen were simply anxious to *oblige* Miss Fishback.

"Marnie is not as helpless as she seems," Jack Straus goes on to say, expressing what everybody knows, that Miss Fishback is a demure blonde from whose pale presence lightning regularly strikes. Sometimes her store experiences exploded into verses published in magazines and books. One mild explosion was entitled:

SALESLADY'S SPRING SONG

and went on to complain:

> Polka dot, polka dot, printed foulard,
> Thirty-five inches is almost a yard.
> If it were wider, a remnant would do;
> Here's the same print in a new shade of blue.
> Wrap it about your anatomy. So . . .
> Youthful, distinctive! You'll love it, I know.
> Polka dot, polka dot, printed foulard,
> Thirty-five inches is almost a yard.
> (Make up your mind, will you, madam, and buy
> Something before you get socked in the eye.)

Here, obviously, was a girl who loved flowers and was skeptical about people. The Strauses cried, "Clever!

Cll.. *evv*.. er!" and Mr. Jesse asked Miss Fishback to compose a poem for the forthcoming Macy Christmas Eve party. Miss Fishback charmingly agreed.

Her poem was nothing sensational. At the Christmas Eve party she simply rose and recited a little thing beginning:

'Twas the night before Christmas, and all through
    the house
Not a creature was stirring, not even a Straus...

Where Margaret Fishback contributed an elfin wit to Macy's new advertising style, and Bernice Fitz-Gibbon gave it its solid brilliance, most of its snob appeal came from Alice Hughes, a New Hampshire girl who had been to Paris and personally knew Chanel, Lanvin, Vionnet, and the other great dressmakers of the day. Miss Hughes, a graduate of the Columbia School of Journalism, had been an editor of *Detective Story Magazine,* and had also written a column for Hearst's *Journal-American* called "Mary Jane's Household Guide"—a collection of recipes, menus, advice on child care, and other hints for the busy wife and mother concerning which Miss Hughes was considered to be something of an expert, although she was still in her early twenties and as yet unmarried. She had traveled on to another job, writing fashion ads for a Fifth Avenue department store, when she wrote Kenneth Collins at Macy's a three-line letter asking for an appointment. Collins chose her letter out of dozens of applications because it was so short. Miss Hughes had a good Paris dress for the interview but no proper hat to go with it, so on the way to Collins's office she stopped at Macy's second-floor budget shop and bought an untrimmed pink felt number for two dollars. "It put me in a rosy frame of mind," she says now, "and I got the job."

The weekly meetings of Collins and his staff were full of laughs, but productive of many good ideas as well. He constantly reminded the girls of the upswing in modern living, and of Macy's corresponding policy of "trading up" and emphasizing chic in addition to value. He gave them his blessing and an expense account and sent them around to lunch and dine at the fashionable places in town where good food and good clothes were to be seen, observed, and carefully noted. And he encouraged and improved the "headline style" in fashion advertising, with one or two attention-getting lines of print surrounded by a good deal of white space.

"The old-time kind of fashion ad, describing every pleat and tuck in small print, was gone forever," Alice Hughes explains now. "Instead, a fashion ad writer had to implant in every woman the *urge* to own a particular dress, and she had to do it in about six well-chosen words."

Collins himself was always on the alert for new ideas and for people who could think them up and execute them. With the encouragement of Oswald Knauth, a member of the Macy top brass in the last half of the 1920's, he engaged a young man whose chief duty was to tour the store daily, throwing out some designs, improving others, and creating new ones. This talented youth was Henry Dreyfus, now the noted industrial designer of Lockheed Aircraft and of the interiors of the S.S. "United States" and the S.S. "Constitution," among other achievements. Not long ago Mr. Dreyfus redecorated the President's airplane, "Columbine," and he has been heard to remark with admiration that Mrs. Dwight D. Eisenhower is probably the least troublesome customer a designer ever had. Asked to suggest some of her preferences, and the President's, she replied, "Oh well, all you really have to remember is that Ike likes green and I hate to sit on leather." End of conference.

Kenneth Collins and his golden girls are widely scattered these days. Collins lives in Chicago, Macy thinks, and travels around a good deal, making speeches that enchant people. Bernice Fitz-Gibbon has her own advertising agency in New York, where she presides with a large and beaming charm. Margaret Fishback, who left Macy's in 1942 but stayed on for a while as an advertising advisor, is a free-lance writer living in New York, and is just as blonde and unpredictable as ever. Her latest despairing remark, when faced with redecorating her apartment, was "I don't see why I just can't throw the *apartment* away!"

Alice Hughes now writes a popular syndicated column for King Features, and is still as slender and chiselled-looking as she was in the Macy days when Bernice Fitz-Gibbon used to try to fatten her up by pressing large tankards of milk on her. "Oh, how I wish I had some of my good Wisconsin dairy cows here," Bernice would murmur, eying the dainty Miss Hughes, "I'd give you one and teach you how to use it."

Of the other girls, Stella McClure and Mary Murphy are dead. Some of the rest have left New York and lost touch with Macy's. Perhaps it doesn't matter.

After all, wherever the girls are, in this world or out of it, they must feel a far-off distant glow when Kenneth Collins sits back and thinks about them.

Wherever he is.

7

D.A., C.T., and V.I.P.

★

THE WEEKLY MEETINGS of Jesse, Percy, and Herbert Straus with Edmond Wise and their other advisors were sacred occasions, immune to interruption from within or without the store. One hot summer day, when the meeting for some reason took place in a second-floor office, all the windows were open when a Salvation Army band struck up in the street below. Mr. Jesse sent a messenger scurrying to ask the musicians to play a little farther away from Macy's. Presently the messenger returned, accompanied by the leader of the band who was evidently a man of initiative and imagination, for he held out his tambourine and said charmingly, "For five dollars in the tambourine, Mr. Straus, we will go across the street and play in front of Gimbel's."

Generally the meetings were held in Mr. Jesse's private office, in the rarefied precincts of the thirteenth, or executive, floor.

"Do not disturb us for any reason," Mr. Jesse always instructed his secretary, "unless the store is on fire. And if the store is on fire, do not disturb us until the smoke begins coming under the door of my office."

One day in 1933 Miss Florence Delehanty, then Mr. Jesse's secretary, received the usual instructions as the door to the private office closed behind her boss and his colleagues. (Promotion from within being a Macy principle, Florence Delehanty is the same Miss Delehanty who is now assistant manager of the personal shopping department.) In the next half-hour, a certain long-distance telephone call moved Miss Delehanty to break the rule against interruptions. Quietly, she entered the inner office and laid a note at Mr. Jesse's elbow. "Governor Roosevelt is on the wire from Albany," it read.

Mr. Jesse treated Miss Delehanty to a firm repetition of the sacred rule while Governor Roosevelt's secretary held the phone. Then he said, "Tell the Governor to call back in an hour." As Miss Delehanty recalls it, it took three telephone calls from the Governor's mansion to capture Mr. Jesse at a receptive moment, and the third time Governor Roosevelt himself was on the phone. This struck Miss Delehanty so forcibly that no summons, however exalted, was ever again permitted to interrupt the weekly meeting.

A little later that same year, another long-distance call came through, from Macy's affiliated store in Toledo, Ohio, while Mr. Jesse was in the weekly conference. Miss Delehanty dealt briskly with Toledo, and so informed Mr. Jesse when his meeting broke up.

"Good lord, why didn't you *tell* me the Toledo store was calling?" cried Mr. Jesse. "That's a six- or seven-dollar call, and *we* have to pay for it!"

The Toledo call, too, turned out to be—indirectly—from Franklin D. Roosevelt, who had recently become President of the United States. What the manager of the Toledo store wanted to know, Mr. Jesse learned when he returned the call, was what Mr. Jesse's instructions were, now that President Roosevelt had closed all the banks.

Mr. Jesse's instructions, like those of other merchants and industrialists throughout the country, were "business as usual." Macy's ran newspaper ads proclaiming its confidence in the government. and set about proving its confidence in Macy customers. Many people still had some cash, and when the customers' cash ran out, Macy's honored their checks and, in some cases, their IOU's. Naturally, business fell off a good deal, but business was falling off everywhere in the thirties, even without the added shove from the bank crisis.

Paradoxically, the lean years were also the years of Macy's greatest opportunity. It would be foolish to say that the store did not suffer from the depression, but perhaps it suffered less than most stores because now, if ever, was the moment to demonstrate the solid truth of the slogan, "It's Smart to be Thrifty." Prosperous persons who had shopped at Macy's as a lark now found, with prosperity gone, that Macy prices were less of a lark than a blessing. The store ran encouraging newspaper advertisements, mostly the work of Margaret Fishback, addressed to this group, whom Miss Fishback called the *nouveau pauvre*. One ad depicted a forlorn gent sitting in his underwear, over the caption:

IF YOU'VE LOST YOUR SHIRT . . .
Don't Give It a Thought

. . . Macy's will replace the shirt at a
price comfortingly low . . .

People Are Finding IT'S FUN TO BE THRIFTY

Another showed Mother in a bathing suit and Dad in overalls pushing their naked kiddies in a soapbox on wheels.

6 Easy Ways to Save Money (*this one read*) . . .

1. Give up wearing clothes. If you don't wear them they won't wear out. Thus you won't need to replace them.
2. Do without shaves and haircuts, finger waves and manicures.
3. Give up eating and drinking.
4. Sell your furniture and stand up.
5. Live in the Park, and save rent altogether.
6. Walk, don't ride.

Take your pick, pals. But if you feel these methods are too rigorous or impractical, there's still another way of conserving cash. That is, shop in the World's Largest Store, and get that very special money's worth for which Macy's is famous. Macy's, thrift specialist of 84 years' standing, provides the things you need at prices you can afford.

Now more than ever
it's smart to be thrifty

A pleasant little Christmas gift from the government to retailers in stores and restaurants everywhere was the repeal, on December 5, 1933, of the prohibition amendment. Repeal Night is still memorable for the crowds who celebrated it, and the stuff they drank. Women who were old enough to drink before Prohibition knew little about drinking, nevertheless, and the younger ones had learned to drink on bootleg hooch. The result, on the night of feasting, was that womanhood in a body clamored for that idiot's delight, "sparkling burgundy." Even men, those connoisseurs, could mostly dream no higher than the ignoble rye-and-ginger ale. A few epicures savored the event delicately, or at least they tried to. But the restaurants had not had time to replace their innocent waitresses by wiser bar waiters, and in at least one establishment this caused embarrassment and financial loss. Early in the evening the management discovered that its newly-opened bar had run completely out of brandy. Investigation showed that the waitresses, taking orders for "brandy in a snifter," had regularly been serving the pleased but astonished patrons with brandy-snifters brimming full.

Repeal Night was a glorious shambles. It was as though the government, having put a ban on all reading for thirteen years, had suddenly required the populace to absorb and digest the *Encyclopaedia Britannica* in one evening.

A year earlier, in 1932, Jesse Straus had summoned William Titon, Macy's buyer of groceries, wines and spirits, who was about to go on a buying trip to Europe. "I feel repeal coming," said Mr. Jesse, who sometimes seemed to have an inside wire to Mr. Roosevelt even though Mr. Roosevelt could not always get through to *him.* "Contact our old friends in Europe." Titon placed orders with the vineyards, distillers and brewers in France, England, and Germany with whom Macy's had done business before Prohibition. The orders were on an "if and when" basis, meaning that they were negotiable only upon the repeal of Prohibition in the United States. The happy outcome was that, with repeal, Macy's orders instantly came through, and at 1932 prices. When Hitler came into absolute power in Germany, in 1934, Macy's canceled the German orders.

The store's liquor license number is L-1 which, according to the New York State Liquor License Bureau, is a nice number but does not necessarily mean that Macy's got the first license after repeal, only that it obtained one of the earliest. A Macy wine and liquor catalogue of 1937, still in existence, runs to thirty pages and lists wines and spirits of as many countries. The champagnes alone number some fourteen brands, including the familiar Bollinger, Mumm's, Heidsieck, and Lanson, and featuring Macy's Own Brand, bottled in France for Macy's and proudly labelled *Etoile Rouge*. *Etoile Rouge* cost $2.49 a quart in 1937. Imported Marceau Triple Star cognac cost $2.69 a bottle, imported English gin $2.49 a fifth, imported Mortlach twelve-year-old Scotch $3.79 a fifth, and gift baskets were available from $2.98 (one York House ruby port, one York House topaz sherry) to $67.75 (champagne, cognac, Scotch, gin, rum, wine, vodka, and other goodies in profusion). "York House" was the Macy brand name for the products of England, Portugal, and Spain; "Old Cobweb," "Old Musket" and "Old Whaler" designated Macy whiskies, bottled domestically under the Macy label.

Before Prohibition, Macy's had operated its own bottling works and were licensed as rectifiers and blenders as well as importers and retailers. The new laws, under repeal, allowed only one license, so Macy's now operates as a retailer. The liquor shop in the store does a healthy business, but its salespeople sometimes wonder if the American drinker has come such a long way, after all, from the confusions of Repeal Night. Not long ago a lady customer firmly requested two bottles of "Pussy-Fussy," and it took something approaching second sight on the part of Miss Kay Alchermes, the salesclerk, to translate this into *"Pouilly-Fuissé."* Another woman, whose culinary skill exceeded her penmanship, wrote in to order "some good brandy to spill on my nice red chairs." Macy's deciphered that one, too, and sent her some good brandy to pour on her cherries *flambées*. Miss Kay has become accustomed to patrons asking for "Triple Sex" and "Grand Manure," and their name for Old Overholt rye whiskey was easy to grasp until, one day, a shopper refused to pay more than half-price for a bottle of it. "Why should I pay more for a whiskey that's just an old something you hold over?" this customer demanded. "Why, it's even *labeled* 'Old Overhold'!"

The liquor store numbers many gentle connoisseurs among its clientele, however. Early one morning, during a liquor shortage in World War II, a clergyman whom we shall call the Reverend Mr. X. turned up at the store to buy his weekly tot of brandy or wine. The doors were not yet open and a line had formed on the sidewalk waiting for opening time. Miss Kay regretfully told Mr. X. that he would have to join the queue. "Heavens, I couldn't do that!" cried the clergyman. "If my bishop happened to pass by and saw me in a liquor line he would defrock me!" At the sound of his voice, a gentleman near the head of the line turned around and bade him a serene good morning. It was the bishop, of course.

Fine wines figured, a couple of years ago, in a stirring rescue at sea achieved by Macy's. Charles Wachsman, manager of the customer relations department, found a letter on his desk one morning from a D.A. customer asking that Macy's deliver twenty splits of champagne to friends sailing August 4 via the Swedish-American Line. Mr. Wachsman glanced at his calendar, groaned, and raced for the desk of Dorothy "Tommy" Thompson, trouble-shooter of the ad-

justment department on the fourteenth floor. "Read this," he said, handing her the letter. "And today is August seventh!"

Miss Thompson made a fast call to personal shopping, who suggested that she call the Maritime Commission for the name of the ship. Maritime Commission told her it was the MS "Stockholm." She then called the Swedish-American

Line, got the assistant passenger traffic manager, and told him the grisly tale with a rider to the effect that not only were his passengers being deprived of substance by this contretemps, but Macy's reputation was at stake. The Swedish-American traffic manager, a Mr. Samuelson, promptly authorized Macy's to radio the order to the "Stockholm" at sea.

The "Stockholm" radioed back that it had no champagne in splits, only Mumm's in quarts. Macy's replied via radio-gram that Mumm's in quarts was okay. That evening, and for the rest of the voyage, the friends of the D.A. customer, unaware of all the excitement, were served a quart of Mumm's in an ice-bucket at dinner, with the compliments of their chum back in New York.

The episode cemented Macy's friendship with the New York *Daily News,* of which the D.A. customer happened to be business manager. When Mr. Wachsman, drawing a long breath after all had been accomplished, telephoned him and explained what had happened, he replied only with grateful praise. But when he found that his D.A. account had been charged only for the twenty splits—*minus tax* because the champagne had been delivered at sea—he called back and said, "Hey! I feel like sending you people a jeroboam of that stuff!"

The first Macy's D.A. account card, issued to Mrs. Isidor Straus in 1901 when the department was established, is now in the Museum of the City of New York. Isidor and Nathan Straus wanted to give customers the convenience of a charge account, and to relieve them of the inconvenience of waiting at home for C.O.D. deliveries; nevertheless, the Strauses declined to buy or sell on credit alone. The Depositor's Account was the solution. As everyone must know by now, a D.A. customer places a sum of money in Macy's Bank—which is an incorporated state bank—and is given a numbered card by which he may charge purchases to the deposit in his account. He receives 1½ per cent interest a year on a minimum semiannual balance between $25 and $500.

The system worked well, and filled all of Macy's and the customers' needs until 1939, when a strange truth became apparent. Automatic washers, refrigerators, and other wares which Macy's sells in quantity became (largely through Macy's own striving for perfection) so highly-styled and so attractive that people who could not afford to pay cash down began buying them on the installment plan—a procedure which, also automatically, removed these people as customers from Macy's.

It was clear that Macy's needed some kind of credit system. Edwin I. Marks, then a vice-president, took the problem to Jack I. Straus, also a vice-president. Together they consulted Beardsley Ruml, later known for his Pay-As-You-Go Tax Plan, who was at that time Macy's treasurer. Among them they thought up C.T., or Cash-Time, which is about as thrifty as a credit plan (or, as the trade terms it, a "revolving credit plan") can well be. C.T. customers are now buying whole kitchens intact at Macy's, and Cash-Time represents the dominant part of the D.A. and C.T. department's business. Charles Wachsman, however, has been with the store thirty-two years and he still enjoys the old-world flavor of a solid D.A. account, as well as the unexpected relationships it gets him into.

One Christmas a D.A. customer ordered a set of doll's furniture for her little girl. The child received a duplicate

set from friends, and the mother called D.A. after the holi-
days and asked Macy's to call for the set she had bought, and
to credit it to her Depositor's Account. The next time Mr.
Wachsman heard from this lady she was laughing so hard
he could barely understand her. Seems a huge Macy furniture van, quilted and padded, had just drawn up to her
door and the driver had inquired, "Where's the furniture
you want returned, lady?"

Another good depositor, a man, came into the store and
ordered a Leg-O-Matic bridge table and four chairs for a
bridge party he was giving. Leg-O-Matics were out of stock
and would not be available in time for the party, but the
clerk conferred with her supervisor and said, "I'll tell you
what we'll do. We will *lend* you a regular bridge table and
chairs for your party. Then, when Leg-O-Matic comes in,
we will deliver it to you and the driver can pick up the borrowed set." The grateful customer agreed, and when Macy's
delivered the Leg-O-Matic set two weeks later, he had the
borrowed set all ready to hand to the driver. The driver refused it. He had no order to pick up anything, he explained,
and couldn't do so without authority from the store. When
he had gone, empty-handed, the customer telephoned
Macy's adjustment bureau where a charming voice said,
"Oh no, sir, you must be mistaken. We *couldn't* have lent
you a bridge table and four chairs, we just don't *do* that.
Are you sure it wasn't another store? . . . No? Well, do you
remember which clerk it was?" No, said the customer, but
he would know the clerk by sight, and would come in next
day and identify her. When he arrived he couldn't find the
clerk or the supervisor, and there was no record of any
transaction except his order for Leg-O-Matics. Macy's began
to eye him indulgently, as a mother regards a child waking

from a bad dream. However, they insisted, the store could not take back the borrowed table and four chairs, since the store had never lent them.

"To this day," muses Mr. Wachsman, "that guy has an extra bridge table and four chairs that belong to Macy's. He knows it, and Macy's knows it, but we can't admit it because there was no record of the loan."

Then there was the young couple from Long Island who went on a winter honeymoon in the North woods. Out snowshoeing, the husband took a spill and never noticed, until he and his bride had trudged back to the little backwoods hamlet where they were staying, that he had dropped his wallet in the snow. Fresh snow had fallen, wiping out all traces of their route, and when he explained that he had lost his wallet the village innkeeper was not too backwoodsy to give him a sophisticated look. The young man wired collect to Macy's D.A. department, where he had an account, urging them to send him some money by wire. The money arrived in a couple of hours, and the honeymoon was a success. Mr. Wachsman heard all about it because, nice as Macy's is to its customers, its customers are also nice enough to come in and say thank you.

Sometimes the store's service is even more poignant. A Mr. G. of Cleveland wrote that he had found, among some papers of his late father, Mr. S. G., a statement from the D.A. department dated twenty-five years earlier and bearing a certain account number, which he enclosed. Was this account still open, he asked, and was any money still on deposit? Macy's replied that the account was long closed, and had been in the name of Mr. *A. G.*, not Mr. S. G. The Cleveland gentleman answered via air mail and with excitement that Mr. A. G. was his older brother, who had disappeared twenty years ago. He then flew to New York and came to Macy's, where he and Mr. Wachsman checked the latest addresses given by A. G. As a result the Cleveland man eventually traced his long-lost brother to a sanatorium in upper New York State.

Human fallibility being what it is, the D.A. department sometimes marches hand in hand with Adjustment Service, as in the case of the "Stockholm" champagne and the case of the borrowed bridge table. For many years one of Adjustment's most colorful workers was Charlotte Smith, now retired and living in Florida. Miss Charlotte, who was plump and merry, sat on a high stood behind a partition separating her from the customers. When an irate lady complained that her package of birdseed, for instance, had not been delivered, Charlotte would say gravely, "Just a moment, madam," slip off her stool, and do the old vaudeville act of appearing to walk downstairs by bending her knees progressively until her head disappeared behind the partition. "Joe!" she would call to a mythical employee below, as she went, "Oh, Joe! Where is this customer's birdseed?" When Charlotte reappeared, simply by turning around and gradually straightening her knees, the customer was always visibly flattered by this prompt attention.

Once, at a sale, a woman bought a canary marked "AS IS." A few days later she indignantly brought the canary back, dead.

"There was no guarantee that it would live," Charlotte reminded her gently.

The canary-buyer refused to be appeased, demanding to see the manager. "I want to speak to someone higher up!" she kept insisting angrily.

ADJUSTMENT   SERVICE

"Madam," said Charlotte, at length, "I suggest you speak to God."

Charlotte, although a sprightly soul, had her moments of tension and one of these occurred when a sale of wardrobe cedar closets in the adjoining department coincided with a particularly trying day in Adjustments. The noisy crowds and the endless complaints at her own desk exhausted even Charlotte's good nature. "I am sick and tired of this whole thing," she finally declared, and getting down from her stool, she went to the nearest cedar closet, got in it (a tight fit), and shut the door behind her. The next ten minutes are hilariously remembered by everyone present. Whenever a customer approached Charlotte's closet and started to open its door to inspect the interior, Charlotte hung on to the doorknob from inside. The customer pulled, Charlotte pulled, and the closet wildly rocked and swayed. Soon the mysterious closet was surrounded by a little knot of puzzled shoppers, and the supervisor was called.

"There's something *in* there!" the customers told him. "It won't let go of the *door!*"

"Let me try," said the supervisor, but he had barely touched the knob when the door popped open and Charlotte stepped out. "Boo!" she said to him pleasantly, and returned to her stool, refreshed.

One of the adjustments her department was called upon to make is comic in retrospect, although it seemed gruesome at the time. A recently bereaved widow placed an order with Macy's gardening department for a large assortment of special shrubs to be planted on and around her husband's grave in Woodlawn. Assured that Macy's would take care of everything, she sailed for Europe. Many months later, on her return, her first pilgrimage was, of course, to her husband's grave. Her second, more violent, excursion was to Macy's. The gardening department had slipped up on its plant-identification, and she had found the resting place of the dear departed richly covered with rhubarb.

All of the Strauses were civic-minded, and three of the family had held government posts: Isidor as a member of the House of Representatives, his brother Nathan as New York City park commissioner and president of the Board of Health, and the third brother, Oscar, as Ambassador to

Turkey, Secretary of Commerce and Labor under Theodore
Roosevelt, and a member of the Permanent Court of Arbitration at The Hague. Early in Franklin D. Roosevelt's administration there was some talk of Jesse Straus, son of Isidor, being appointed Secretary of Commerce. The rumor
never became reality but, in 1933, Roosevelt appointed
Jesse Ambassador to France. Macy executives who worked
with him in the months before the appointment came
through now say that Mr. Jesse's thoughts began to wander
far from Macy's long before he left the store in person. "He
had simply outgrown his work at Macy's, and was ready for
a bigger job," is the opinion of Kenneth Collins, his advertising manager.

One day during this period Collins, who had been toiling
over a four-million-dollar publicity campaign for Macy's
and Bamberger's, brought the budget plan into Mr. Jesse's
office for him to approve it. Mr. Jesse glanced at him ab-
sently, and ignored the thick document Collins laid on his
desk.

"Have you ever read Luigi Facta's *God in Freedom?*" he
asked Collins. When Collins said no, Mr. Jesse embarked
on a description of the book together with many comments
upon its author who, he explained, was Mussolini's predecessor as premier of Italy. After some twenty or thirty minutes Collins mildly reminded him of the problem of the
budget, and Mr. Jesse okayed it after little more than a riffle
of its pages.

Macy buyers remember Mr. Jesse's tenure at the Paris
Embassy with nostalgia and delight. He always had time
for them when they called on him during their buying
trips abroad, and they were always asked to Embassy parties.

"Those parties," recalls Irving Eldredge, "were famous in diplomatic circles as the *only* ones where the champagne *never* gave out." William Titon remembers how the old feudal democracy of Macy's prevailed, even at the Embassy. Mr. Titon, paying a call on his former employer, addressed him as "Your Excellency."

"Mr. Jesse to *you*," said Mr. Jesse graciously.

In the third year of his appointment Mr. Jesse's health had begun to fail, and he was granted a leave of absence from his post because of illness. He died in New York the same year, 1936, at the age of sixty-four. Herbert, the youngest of the three brothers, had died three years earlier, at fifty-two. Percy, the middle brother, lived until 1944, when he was sixty-eight. Percy was president of Macy's for three years after Jesse's death, but his own ill health prevented him from coming to the store every day, and in 1939 Jesse's son, Jack Straus, was appointed president. (Macy's New York was not made a separate operating division, apart from the nation-wide R. H. Macy & Co., until 1949, ten years later.)

Jack's mother, Mrs. Jesse Straus, is now a spirited lady of eighty-three, much given to sea voyages. Her children, grandchildren, and great-grandchildren have an affectionate name for her; they call her The Admiral.

The Straus family tree numbers one hundred and fifty descendants of Lazarus and Sara Straus, and it has acquired several more buds in the form of new great-great-grandchildren since it was last drawn on paper, in 1954. Two years ago Mrs. Alfred Hess, Jack's aunt, held a family reunion at her house, with practically all members attending. Jack Straus is a trim, young-looking man who somewhat resembles Richard Rodgers, and his bearing is usually confident and debonair; but even he wears an expression of awe whenever he thinks of that family gathering.

"There were so many of us," he murmurs, shaking his head, "that we had to wear *identification tags!*"

8

How To Get a Job and Keep Breathing

★

ONE DAY, AROUND 1935, a young man wandered into Macy's in search of a job. Merchandising was not his ambition, but he had been living for weeks on boiled eggs in a hall bedroom, Christmas was coming, and somebody had told him that Macy's always hired extra help at Christmas. His first stop, after passing through the employees' entrance, was a dim, cement-floored room that looked to him like some anteroom to oblivion. A young woman in a booth handed him a card to fill out and he took it to one of the benches along the wall.

Handing back his card, he was taken into a larger, brighter room with cubicles along one side and rows of chairs arranged along the other. Presently an interviewer beckoned him into one of the cubicles. "We will give you an aptitude test," she said, and ushered him into another room where a large piece of metal was placed before him with one hundred holes in it, along with three hundred nails. He had to put three nails in each hole as quickly as

171

possible. The only other contestants were eight girls, who placed the nails accurately and with dispatch, and then sat back and sneered at him while he struggled with his metal block—or mental block. He failed the aptitude test dismally.

"We will give you another test," said the interviewer kindly, and handed him a pile of sales checks which he was required to fill out rapidly with name of customer, address of customer, sales-check number, employee's number, and so on. With the speed of desperation the young man filled out slip after slip and leaned back, panting. Soon the interviewer reappeared.

"I am happy to tell you that you have broken the all-time speed record for *this* test," she informed him, "and we are able to offer you a very good position. In the sub-basement," she added.

When the successful applicant tells this story nowadays his face creases into the grin that has become familiar to theater-goers who saw him in *The Seven Year Itch* and *The Tunnel of Love*. "Macy's was always good to out-of-work actors, and I worked there every Christmas and every Thanksgiving for quite a while," says Tom Ewell.

In the sub-basement, Ewell was put to work sorting packages as they came down the chutes and off the conveyor belt for delivery. "One day the conveyor belt broke, and we were up to our eyebrows in packages," he recalls. "All I could think of was the old gag about the two drowning men up to their chins in water, remember? One of 'em opens his mouth to yell for help, and the other one says 'Sh! Don't make a ripple.' "

Except for the usual rounds of casting directors' offices during his lunch hour, Ewell worked diligently at his Macy job and soon was promoted to the toy department to demonstrate electric trains. After a brief absence the following year, when he got a part in the ill-fated musical version of *Sailor, Beware!*, Ewell was back at Macy's in time to sell electric trains again that Christmas. One day, three friends happened in to the toy department and discovered him at his labors. They were Mary Martin, Bert Wheeler, and Pert Kelton, and they set about helping him so enthusiastically that their combined efforts soon had every train on the table running backwards, to the mystification and delight of the kiddies present. Not long after that Ewell got a call, one lunch hour, from Maxwell Anderson's office, offering him a part in *Key Largo*. "I walked out at one o'clock and never went back," he says. Macy's sent him a check for the full week, and he still doesn't know why. "I guess they didn't miss me," he surmises.

A few years earlier, another youth worked for a week at Macy's, selling ties at the thrift tables on the main floor. He was spared the sub-basement routine because he had been to Amherst College and Macy's considered him possible executive material. (He neglected to tell them in his interview, that his Amherst career had lasted precisely two months.) This was Burgess Meredith, who remembers certain aspects of the dramatic approach to salesmanship that was instilled into him during his short stay at the store. "I was told always to keep the best-looking ties under the others," he says, "so that when a customer was rather dejectedly fumbling through the ties on the top of the pile, I could suddenly reach underneath, whip out this stunner, and spring it on her. Element of surprise, you know."

Meredith quit Macy's to join Eva Le Gallienne's Repertory Theatre almost thirty years ago, but he still has the salesman's knack of displaying a tie the professional way, by flipping it around a couple of fingers and holding it up to view.

Garson Kanin, Philip Faversham, Carol Channing, and Butterfly McQueen all worked at Macy's at one time or another, but future celebrities who kept body and soul together in the lean years by getting a job there were not limited to the theater. The late Mayor James J. Walker, who was notoriously tardy for all appointments, liked to tell how he once toiled as a stock boy in the store during his school days and was fired for failing to report on time. While he was mayor of New York, Macy's invited him to speak at one of the 9 A.M. rallies frequently held on the main floor before the doors open. The mayor arrived at 8:59 and, in his speech, formally requested of Jesse Straus that his record now be cleared.

In the middle 1920's a little French girl, newly arrived in America and looking like a *gamine* off a cover of *La Vie Parisienne,* applied for a job at Macy's and was taken on as a salesgirl in the French millinery department. There, she became deeply irked by the monotonous business of making out sales slips and waiting for customers' change to come back in little metal cylinders. "I wanted to all the time run and sell hots!" she says now, doubling up her fists and pushing them forward in a vigorous gesture. She did so much running and selling hots to newly arrived customers that others, waiting vainly for their parcels and change, began to complain to the supervisor, and he, after several reprimands, finally hollered at her one day. She stared at him.

"How long you been here, Meester?" she inquired.

"Twelve years," the supervisor replied with dignity.

"Ho!" cried the new French girl. "If I was here as long as you, I would *own* the place!"

She resigned then, before he could close his mouth to fire her. And two years later she *did* own her own shop, on Broadway at Seventy-seventh Street, with her name proudly placed above the door: Lilly Daché.

The average new salesclerk's reaction to her first day of selling is best expressed by Birdie Schwartz of the fabrics department, who remembers keenly how she felt the first day she came to work at Macy's, in 1931. "The crowds seemed to move *at* me instead of *with* me," is the way Miss Schwartz puts it. It is no easy matter to handle merchandise, answer questions, make out sales slips (Taken, Sent, C.O.D., Exchanged, D.A., or C.T.), figure sales tax, accept money and return change, have merchandise wrapped and deliver it to customers, and to do all this swiftly, efficiently, and— as Macy's printed instructions to salesclerks insist—to do it *with a smile*. Not all customers are as pleasant as the little old lady who comes into Macy's every week with a box of candy and wanders through the store, offering some to her favorite salespeople. Macy's pamphlet of instruction and suggestion to the sales staff contains the following appraisal of customer types, with a guide as to how to treat each one:

1. Impetuous, nervous, tense.
2. Slow, difficult, hard to satisfy.
3. Decisive, confident, aggressive.
4. Indecisive, wavering, changeable.
5. Friendly, sociable, reasonable.
6. Intelligent, analytical, critical.
7. Quiet, timid, indifferent.

These classifications are kindly, and do not include the downright nasty customer (for whom Macy's has made other arrangements, as will be noted in the next chapter) or the screwball, of whom there are many on the opposite, or buying, side of the counter. One elderly patron invited a pleasant saleswoman to spend the following month with her at her mansion in Florida, and, concluding their amiable chat, borrowed fifteen cents from the saleswoman for carfare. Miss Theodora Smith, of cotton fabrics, remembers a lady who asked for one yard each of seven different cotton prints, to make pajamas. As she fingered the bolts of material she picked up each one, held it beneath her side of the counter and murmured, "Does mother's angel-pie like this one?" When the purchase was completed the lady once more addressed the tot at her side, saying "Now we will go home and make angel-pie's itsy 'jammies," and taking her package, she rose and strolled away with a Chihuahua in ermine sweater and diamond collar trotting at her side.

The training of a new employee at Macy's varies according to the newcomer's eligibility to an executive position or to a career of straight selling. Executive prospects, mostly college graduates, are interviewed at their colleges by scouts from Macy's personnel division or, if they apply at the store, by Miss Virginia Carlin, a former lieutenant commander in the WAVES and now director of executive placement. Macy's interviews about one thousand young people every year for executive training. The recruit is then placed on the Training Squad for a period lasting from four and a half to six months which he spends in selling, merchandising assignments, and classroom instruction. At the end of his training period, he becomes a junior assistant buyer. In another year, if all goes well, he is promoted to sales manager in one of the branch stores, then home to Thirty-fourth Street as a senior assistant buyer. With his next promotion, to buyer (or department manager), he becomes a senior executive, ranking just below merchandise administrators, vice-presidents, and president. It takes a bright boy or girl an average of four and a half to five years to advance from junior assistant buyer to buyer.

During this period regular reports of his progress are filled out by his superiors on printed forms and submitted to the personnel department, which records each report as an indication of the employee's progress, or otherwise. The reports list such qualities as Character, Job Knowledge, Dependability, Expression, Leadership, Personal Appearance and so on, and a printed form reads, in part:

> CHARACTER—Is he intellectually honest and loyal? Is he a person of high principles? Will he defend what he thinks is right?

> (with the following answers, one of which the superior checks):

> Devious. Lacks courage. Easily swayed. Not above chiselling.
> Does not always tell whole truth. Will cut corners.
> Questionable loyalty. Gives in too easily.
> Truthful. Loyal. Usually defends his position.
> High personal standards. Has courage of his convictions.
> Has unquestionable honesty and integrity. Firmly defends what he thinks is right.

> EXPRESSION—Does he use good English? Can he express himself in a clear, concise manner?

Hesitant, unable to present his thoughts in a simple, direct manner. Careless diction. Verbose.

Forceful, talks well. Sometimes confusing. Average command of language, wordy.

Exceptional command of English. Superior ability to express himself in clear, concise manner.

Uses poor English, vague and incoherent. Inarticulate or garrulous.

Uses effective English, gets his ideas across in a simple, straightforward manner.

The straight-selling employee goes through much the same interview and aptitude tests as Tom Ewell did. Interviews are conducted by a staff of nine people under Mrs. Margaret Gafill, a pretty, silver-haired woman who reversed the usual order of things by coming to Macy's from Gimbel's some years ago. If the applicant is hired, he is taken to training class and is then given selling experience out on the floor under the guidance of a "sponsor" (the experienced salesperson who wears a red carnation) until he is able to operate on his own. Anita Duehren of the training department remembers holding classes for a group of deaf-mutes being groomed as merchandise checkers. "What impressed me most was their wonderful manners," she says. "I couldn't erase the blackboard or open the classroom door—everything was done for me. And they were so appreciative, and so anxious to learn. When we practiced the various wraps they would help their neighbors by nudging them or slapping them, sometimes real hard, and anybody who was doing something wrong was shown—by force, in some cases —how to do it better."

The regular staff of Macy's New York numbers 11,391

employees, including those at the Herald Square store, at the Long Island warehouse, and in the five local branches at Roosevelt Field, Parkchester, Jamaica, Flatbush, and White Plains. In addition, there are 2,261 employees (known as "Saturday Onlies") who work only on Saturdays or on nights when the store is open late. The minimum wage for regular employees is $42 for a forty-hour week, with the usual "fringe" benefits such as pension plan, group insurance, unemployment and health insurance. The store's only major strike occurred last year when 8,500 workers walked out. Even this unpleasantness inspired the old Macy spirit of co-operation, for junior executives, senior executives, and even vice-presidents quickly manned the counters and all pitched in and helped. There were mishaps, of course. A woman supervisor, assigned to the lowly task of sending packages down a chute to the basement for sorting and delivery, sent them all into the incinerator instead. She was replaced by a stock boy who surpassed even her efforts. *He* leaned over too far and sent himself down the chute along with the packages. When he was picked up in the cellar ten stories below, he made one simple statement. "I hurt my finger," he said.

The only professional chute-rider at Macy's is Mike Reynolds, who has been riding the chute from the nineteenth floor to the basement every working day for thirty-six years. Mike's mission is to see that no packages get stuck in the chute. He wears out a pair of coveralls every six weeks and figures that he slides about two miles per week. Now that conveyor belts have taken over a large part of package delivery to the basement, Mike's duties are less rigorous than they were. He is not required to ride the conveyor

belts, which are enclosed and comparatively narrow, and he feels that this is fortunate. "I'd never fit in wan of dem t'ings," says Mike, a hefty man.

Other tasks, other talents, and Macy's sales staff numbers several hundred people who, among them, can speak nineteen foreign languages, including Arabic, Dutch, Gaelic, and Greek as well as the usual French, German, and Italian. This comes in handy, but not even Macy's cosmopolitan approach can please everyone. Elsie Curtin remembers one customer, an Irishman, who accosted her in the furniture department, saying indignantly that he had heard that Macy's had just "laid off two hundred good Irish Catholic employees." Miss Curtin answered him sweetly in her own Irish brogue.

"Well, now," she said, "do you see that man over there looking like the Alderman himself? That's Jim Gorman. And do you see that other man, talking to a customer? That's Mr. Hanlon. My name is Curtin—a good Irish name. Mr. Shaughnessy, the head of the department, is on vacation. If you don't believe me, talk to Miss Kelly, his secretary, and she'll give you a few more names. And besides, if you go around saying things like that you'll likely get us all fired."

"Maybe you're right, at that," said the customer. "Now, what have you got in a good three-piece parlor suite?"

Miss Curtin might also have mentioned Tom Maloney, one of Macy's porters and a man with the shamrock in every syllable. Once, when the store had just opened a new *boutique* featuring a special display of summer draperies, a male customer stopped Tom and asked, "Can you direct me to the Chintz Room?"

"That I can," said Tom, and personally escorted him to the Gent's Room.

Tom was a good-natured man, but he could be severe in the interest of Macy's. At one time a familiar nuisance in the store was a woman who came in only, it seemed, to use the writing room on the eleventh floor. She never bought anything, and she was always accompanied by two bad-tempered dogs on a leash who growled and snapped at salespeople and at paying customers too. When the floor manager remonstrated with her gently about the dogs, she and the dogs both snapped at him and kept on coming. "I'll fix her," said Tom. One day while she was writing at her usual desk Tom filled the inkwells and deliberately let fall a drop

of ink on the carpet beside her. Briskly, he fetched a mop
and a pail of water and, having cleaned the spot, squeezed
the mop over it until the water formed a small puddle.
"There, now! This is the limit!" he exclaimed so loudly that
the lady was forced to look up from her writing. "Lady, you
cannot brings dogs into Macy's that ain't housebroke!"
Madam Deadbeat and her snarling pets swept out and were
not seen again.

Regional patois naturally extends to some of Macy's customers as well as to some of its staff. One patron of the millinery department whose accent was strictly upper Manhattan was having trouble finding a hat to suit her. She tried
on and rejected every hat Miss Jagoda, the saleswoman,
offered. It is not easy to ruffle a Macy saleswoman's com-
posure, but when at length the customer bounced around
in her chair and made plain her desires, Miss Jagoda had to
retire briefly to the stockroom.

"I vont a sailor vot should lay flat on me," the lady stated.

Sometimes plain English is confusing enough. There was
the shopper who announced clearly to an impressed staff
that she wished to buy a Rembrandt, and was directed to
the art department five times before it was discovered that
what she wanted was a "remnant." And there was the
browser seen peering into the depths of a cedar chest who,
when a salesclerk asked "May I help you?" replied, "Yes,
please, I am looking for my daughter." (Only after peering
into the chest with her did the clerk realize that she was
looking at cedar chests for her daughter.)

Often, a customer really *is* looking for her daughter, since
small children love to roam around a big store and easily
get lost. One four-year-old, excitedly reported missing by

her mother, was located strolling peacefully along an aisle in the company of two nuns.

"I do hope she hasn't bothered you," the mother apologized.

"Not at all, we've had a nice chat," said one of the sisters. "She thought we were penguins."

Children love Macy's, and Macy's loves children, in spite of everything. Two little boys, one closing time, fulfilled every small boy's dream by hiding in a bin in the toy department at the Parkchester store and spending a glorious night with the toys before they were discovered in the morning, curled up and sound asleep on a carrousel. When Macy's New York featured a fishpond with live fish, one Christmas, the kids adopted the fish as their personal pets, scooping them out of the pond with both hands, patting and hugging them, and, on their demise, laying them to rest in unexpected places. More than one salesclerk got home at night that week and found two or more dead fish in his coat pocket.

The Macy staff suffereth long and is kind. A few years ago, during a sale of two-piece wool bathing suits, two customers were trying on bathing suits in adjoining booths. The trouble was, they were both trying on the same suit; one had the top, the other the pants, and neither would relinquish her half. It was the last suit of its kind left in the sale. Catcalls increased in volume over the partition, the saleswoman rushed beseechingly from booth to booth, and at last the section manager was summoned. No use. The lady with the top demanded the pants, and the lady with the pants demanded the top. Furthermore, both Mrs. Top and Mrs. Pants declined to remove the portion of the suit she was wearing. Hastily, the section manager ordered the clerk to cover the two ladies with beach robes snatched from a rack, and he took them to the superintendent's office where the whole scene was repeated. It was then about five o'clock. The superintendent telephoned the manufacturer, who happened to have one other similar suit on hand in the right size. A Macy messenger was dispatched to fetch it, and by six o'clock both customers had the complete bathing suits of their combined choice.

"If either one of them had decided not to buy it at that point, we would have all dropped dead," sighs Evadne Rodriguez, who was present at the fracas.

It takes time to learn these nuances of service, and veterans among the Macy staff look indulgently upon greenhorn clerks who make mistakes. They were once new to the whole thing too, they remember. They treasure their pet jokes, like the one about the new clerk in the gardening department who, when a customer asked for peat moss, seriously replied "Pete Moss? I'm afraid I don't know him, but I'm new here"; or about the other novice who had never heard of "Mrs. Coates." In the days before cash registers were installed, when a customer's change was obtained by shooting the money in a carrier through metal tubes, the tube system caused many casualties among the newer hands. Once, when a customer complained that she could have cooked and served a seven-course dinner in the time she had spent waiting for her change, investigation proved that a new clerk had simply thrown her money down the tube without the precaution of putting it in a carrier.

A clerk sent money up or down the tubes, depending on where she was in relation to the tube room, which handled the change. Miss Ulla Kimball, now a department supervisor on the third floor, remembers a new employee reporting to her that the change from a certain transaction was too slow in returning.

"Call up," Miss Kimball advised briefly, and the new clerk did exactly that. Standing on tiptoes, she opened the flap and hollered up the tube. This was too delicious for her experienced colleagues to resist and they gathered round her, urging her to yell louder. "You've got to simply *scream*, or the tube room won't hear you," they kept telling her, while another clerk privately called up the tube room on the telephone and adjusted the matter in hand. Finally the new clerk staggered away from the tube, exhausted.

"I'm going to make a suggestion to the management," she muttered hoarsely, "to bring the flap of the tube lower down so we don't have to stretch so high when we call up the tube room."

The tube system was abandoned in favor of cash registers when sharp-eyed executives observed that customers had developed the patient habit of handing over their money and then going out for a cup of coffee, or a manicure, or a shave, before returning to pick up their change.

In contrast to the tyro clerks there are staff members like Miss Greenwood, also known as "Barbara Woods, silver consultant," who has been at Macy's twenty-six years and keeps a file of all her customers' purchases during that time. Miss Greenwood's mental file of her clientele is so accurate that she scarcely needs to consult the records. When a long-time customer comes in and orders a pair of silver candelabra, say, to give to a friend who is another old-time customer, Miss Greenwood says immediately, "You can't give her candelabra, she got a pair three years ago." Many jewelers' shops offer the same service, but with them it is usually a temporary record per customer, that is, a list of most-wanted and nonduplicate gifts for one wedding, or one anniversary. Miss Greenwood is different. Miss Greenwood knows everything everybody wants, has had, or has not had, for the past twenty-six years.

Although life holds few surprises for a specialist like Miss Greenwood, other Macy employees sometimes find their eyebrows rising into their hair. One night, a crew of painters was doing a job in the store after hours when one of them accidentally broke a slat on a crate of canaries containing two or three hundred birds. Amid a welter of wings the men managed to catch the birds and put them back, nailing up the broken slat. But when they knocked off work at 1 A.M., the eye of the staff official who was supervising them was caught by the somewhat odd appearance of one departing painter, who was clad in overalls and a derby hat. "You there, just a minute," said the supervisor, and stepping up to the man, he removed the derby. Two tired canaries flew out. "I was just taking them home to the kiddies," the painter explained.

Surprises occasionally lie in wait for customers, too. Some years ago, Macy's converted an empty salesroom on the main floor into a small shoe shop with an entrance on Thirty-fourth Street. A little old lady came in one morning and, glancing around her, asked a clerk if this was Macy's. The clerk answered that yes, indeed it was Macy's, and the little old lady shook her head sadly. "My goodness," she murmured, "I remember when Macy's was a *big* store."

Many Macy customers have their pet salespeople, and always send them Christmas cards and birth announcements and even sometimes leave them money in their wills. "You seem almost like one of our own family" such a customer once wrote to Miss Wallace of ladies' coats and dresses, and

went on to relate how she had bought a dress from another saleswoman during Miss Wallace's vacation and had modeled it at home for her husband that evening. The husband viewed it without pleasure. "Miss Wallace never sold you *that* dress," he averred. However, Macy's mail is not all bouquets. One woman wrote angrily that she had ordered a box of Macy cleansing tissues advertised as containing 1,000 sheets, and that the box she received contained only 999 sheets. Macy's sent her three two-cent stamps, a generous estimate of the value of the missing sheet, with a polite note hoping that she had not been too greatly inconvenienced by the shortage. Another customer—not angry, just confused—flicked the firm slightly on the raw by addressing his order for a set of dominoes to:

> Parker Brother
> Game Manufactures (sic)
> c/o Macy's
> near Gimbel's, I think 23rd
> New York.

Neither rain, snow, heat, or gloom of night stayed this message from its swift arrival at Macy's games department.

One of the most unusual letters in the store's files came to the book department, and read:

> Dear Sirs:
>   Do you have a catalogue of all the different kinds of Bibles that you have? If you have, I would like one, also Bible stories.
>   I would like to know if you could help a couple that are thirty years old each procure some very small children. They have a childless home, and love children. They have a nice home and a job that pays well. Husband works, wife is a good housekeeper. Child would have a lovely home.

Paul Schack, manager of the book department, replied with the information about Bibles and Bible stories, and went on to thank the customer for his confidence in Macy's.

He suggested, however, that the customer consult a recognized adoption service or an orphanage in his own
locality.

Child placement is not the only rare service Macy's is
called on to perform. A patron in Tupper Lake, New York,
wrote:

> Gentlemen:
> Will you kindly advise me if you have any dead
> horses for sale . . . Please quote me your lowest price,
> on receipt of which I will send you my check and give
> you shipping instructions.

This request came to the attention of Delos Walker, a
vice-president at the time, and it was enough to give any
vice-president food for thought. Mr. Walker knew that
Macy's last delivery horse had been retired to Camp Isida
in 1925, when the delivery service was completely mechan-
ized. The horse was old then—so old, in fact, that it kept
lying down, and Percy Straus, an animal lover, had devised
a kind of sling for its hindquarters to help it stand up at
least long enough to graze a bit. This horse was now dead,
all right, but it had long since been given proper burial.
Mr. Walker wrote to the horse-applicant saying as much,
and added:

> We are consumed with curiosity as to just what you
> expected to do with a dead horse. Wonders never cease
> in this business, and new demands from customers do
> occasionally arise . . . Our limited knowledge would
> lead us to believe that the prospect of a dead horse is
> much greater at Tupper Lake than it is at Broadway
> and 34th Street.
> Kindly advise us if we can be of further service.

Apparently Macy's could be of further service, for the customer replied:

> I note that you take my inquiry as a humor. I assure you that I did not intend to inflict you with anything but a serious inquiry.
>
> . . . I have been fishing here without success, and I thought if I could sink a dead horse in shallow water I could at least get some eels and catfish. If you know where I could get a dead horse I would consider it a favor to have the information.
>
> P.S. A dead pony would of course be as good as a dead horse.

"Macy's basement" long ago became almost a part of the American language, a phrase generally used to express derision. "I'd rather work in Macy's basement!" meant "I'd rather die!"—but all that has changed. The transformation actually began thirty years ago, when a young man named Elliot Walter went to work there as assistant buyer. The basement then was a jumble of pots and pans and other houseware, a labyrinth of counters untidily piled with unrelated gadgets. Its lighting was poor, and its whole aspect unattractive.

Mr. Walter started his improvements by assembling all related merchandise in groups, each on its own counter. Everything for preparing food was at one counter, everything for cooking it at another, everything for house cleaning at still another, and so on. The new system was convenient to customers and profitable to Macy's, since a housewife buying a new egg beater is apt to buy other related implements if they are right there before her eyes. When Walter was promoted to merchandising manager he introduced the small sideshows known as "demonstrations" in which the clerk shows the customer exactly how to bake a pie, or roast a chicken, or clean a spot off the rug. These were so successful that they led to even greater rapport between customer and store. One girl confided to a bakery demonstrator that she would like to learn how to make a lemon pie, her boy friend's favorite. The demonstrator showed her how, and a few days later the girl returned, beaming. "He proposed!" she told the demonstrator, who shook her warmly by the hand and wished her well.

Walter is also credited with the improvement which Macy's instigated and called Color in the Kitchen. Until then, all kitchen tools were manufactured only in black or white or natural shades. One day Walter entered the office of Kenneth Collins, then director of sales promotion, with a yellow enameled teapot newly arrived from Europe. "Why can't we get some color into the kitchen?" he demanded. The result was a whole new line of inexpensive chinaware in butter-yellow, Delft blue, apple green, and other alluring shades. When housewives complained that their old dustpans and broom handles didn't match their new dishes and cooky-jars, dustpans and broom handles also burst into brilliant scarlet and jade. Macy's even went through a period of polka-dotted kitchenware because Joseph Mayer, an executive who knew what he liked, was crazy about polka dots. In one year the basement's business showed a sharp increase, and Macy people attribute it mainly to the newfangled idea of Color in the Kitchen.

Elliot Walter, a large, pleasant, pink-cheeked man, is now president of Macy's New York, but his heart is still, partially anyway, with the basement. He likes to wander through its aisles whenever he has time, and his progress is something like that of a popular host at a crowded party. "Hi, Joe! Don't let that thing get away from you!" he will say to an old friend demonstrating a slicing machine, while across the aisle a clerk will be calling "Mr. Walter! *Hello, there!*" Now that he is president the basement calls him "Mr. Walter," but its people know that he is not really as far away from them as his grand office on the thirteenth floor might indicate. "The basement is his baby," one clerk said fondly, not long ago, as she watched him visit along the aisle.

Last Christmas Mr. Walter, on behalf of Macy's, sent four hundred gifts to retired employees and pensioners. Among all the thank-you letters he received, he treasures one from a Jerry Stone with the closing salutation, "All but six, my friend!" This cryptic phrase, Mr. Walter explains with chuckles, refers to the days when he and Jerry Stone worked side by side at a basement counter. Watching the crowds being eased out by guards at closing time after a long, harassing day, one or the other of them would wearily express his true feelings. "The hell with 'em, all but six," he would say, "and we'll use those for pallbearers."

Macy's basement, improving steadily over the years, was completely redecorated in 1955, at a cost of $700,000. It is now fluorescent-lighted, trimly disposed, full of color, and *toujours gai.* Its gaiety stems partly from its new decor, partly from its present senior operating assistant, Leo Adams—a man as pleasant and pink-cheeked as Elliot Walter, although shorter and rounder—and perhaps chiefly from the fact that so many of its staff, including Mr. Adams, are people who used to work in show business. There is something about show folks that lights up any place, even an improved basement.

Leo Adams, who has been twenty-seven years at Macy's, was once assistant manager of a Balaban and Katz theater in Chicago, and also worked for the William Fox theaters in New York. He enjoys knowing that so large a number of his salespeople were formerly in show business. "It takes showmanship to be successful in Macy's basement," he says. "Look at Max Weiner," he continues, pointing out Max Weiner. "Max used to tell fortunes on the Boardwalk at Atlantic City. Listen to him *now!*"

Max Weiner is worth listening to. He demonstrates and sells cabbage-shredders and apple-corers with the speed of light. A typical exchange between Max and a customer goes something like this:

"What's that gadget?"

"That's a precidulator."

"What's *that?*"

"That is thirty-nine cents, thank you madam, you will find your change at the end of the counter."

Charlotte Brunelle, a basement demonstrator of cleaning supplies, was a vaudeville performer billed as "Lottie Gardner, the Little Girl with the Big Voice." Her hit number, which she sang at Hammerstein's Victoria among other theaters, was a song called "Oh, Frenchie!" and she still has the twinkling eye and the flirty manner that go with high kicks and froufrou; but Lottie is modest about her vaudeville career. "I always followed the seals," she admits.

Miss Brunelle often works on Thursday nights when the store stays open until nine, and it is her opinion that night-blooming shoppers somehow require more explanations about household gadgets than daytime customers do. "You find yourself saying over and over 'No, hon, not *that* way, *this* way . . . Look, dearie, let me show you again,' " she says. For that reason Miss Brunelle and the rest of the basement refer to Thursday nights as "hon-and-dearie nights."

Ethel Rickard (stage name Ethel Gray), who demonstrates Mothine and other insect repellents, not only played the Keith-Orpheum and Pantages circuits with an all-girl trumpet band, her mother is now head of a five-piece woman's orchestra called "Lillian Sydney and Her Sailorettes" which plays for parties in and around Baldwin, Long Island. Ethel could perform on the mellophone, xylophone, and chimes as well as on the trumpet, and, dressed in gold kid boots and a lot of yellow pompons, she appeared just about everywhere, from Columbia Burlesque to the Palace Theatre. She remembers as her worst moment on the stage a night on tour in a small-town burlesque theater somewhere in the middle-West. Her mother, who traveled with her and stage-managed the act, nodded a frantic cue from the wings to the orchestra leader in the pit to give out with the fanfare required at that moment. The orchestra leader was inexperienced, and he had had almost no rehearsal with the act. In the hush that followed, he nodded cordially back at Ethel's mother.

"How do you do?" he said, clearly.

Bert Gilbert, emcee of the electrical counter, has worked in night clubs and was in a Shubert musical with Billy B. Van, Winnie Lightner, and Jack Haley in 1925. "Unctuousness comes easily to demonstrators because of their theater training," he explains, "but audience attention here in the basement is not always all that could be desired. For instance, say I'm demonstrating a coffee percolator and giving it all its *punch*"—and here Mr. Gilbert pounds his fist into his palm for emphasis—"and right next to me some customer is talking away about some complaint or other. Well, it distracts from the act."

Paul Marin, demonstrator of furniture-cleaners, started in show business when he was twelve, after seeing an *Out of the Inkwell* cartoon in the movies. Billed as "The Chatterbox Cartoonist" he toured with his own novelty cartooning act, appearing at Leon and Eddie's, N. T. G.'s, and other night clubs, and putting on bond shows and camp shows for Special Services during the second World War. He left the formal entertainment world for Macy's twelve years ago, when he married a girl from Macon, Georgia, and, as he describes it, "She said to me in her inimitable Southern drawl, 'Honey, we-all got to settle down and get us some *security.*'"

Rohna Leigh (stage name Rohna Fray) of aluminum cooking-utensils acted in *Arabesque,* a Norman Bel Geddes spectacle in which she had three speaking lines and understudied two character parts. She was also with Christopher Morley's famed stock company in Hoboken, and played Julie in the touring company of *Counsellor-at-Law.*

Andrew Thurston, who demonstrates hardware, was a machinist from Canada when John Charles Thomas heard him sing at some gathering and introduced him to a voice teacher in Chicago. Thurston later sang in the chorus of one of the innumerable companies of *The Student Prince,* in a couple of other musicals, and with a glee club at Radio City Music Hall. Like the other show folk in Macy's basement, he spends no time regretting bygone glamour but lives intensely for the moment. For a long time after he went to Macy's nine years ago his main ambition was to be transferred from chromium bar-fittings, where he was assigned, to power tools, which he felt he knew something about. He credits the attainment of his goal entirely to Elliot Walter who, as merchandise manager of the basement, knew the background of his employees. Passing by the bar-fittings counter one day, Walter said to Thurston, "What are you doing here? You ought to be in power tools." Thurston was transferred the next day.

Probably the youngest ex-actor in Macy's basement is Ward Bumgarner, purveyor of floor mats and window-ventilators, and he can scarcely be called an ex-actor since he plans to go back to the theater any day. Although he has been at Macy's over five years, he still belongs more to the Tom Ewell-Burgess Meredith group of stage-struck youths who like to pick up a little eating money while waiting for the big break. Ward even looks like a young Burgess Meredith, tousle-haired and eager. He was in Major Melvyn Douglas's Special Service outfit during the war, doing shows throughout India and Burma, and after the war studied at the American Theatre Wing, under the GI bill, until Douglas called him one day and told him he could get a part in *Call Me Mister*. Ward played the youthful general in that show for its two-year run, and then did a summer tour with *A Connecticut Yankee*, playing the dual role of Sir Launcelot and Sir Gerald. He has also studied ballet with Hanya Holm and Katherine Dunham, and danced for a while at the College Inn of the Hotel Sherman in Chicago. Melvyn Douglas, who takes an interest in him, has fought a losing battle to get Ward to shorten his last name to "Garner," but so far Mr. Bumgarner has resisted. "Did Tallulah change *her* name?" he inquires.

The personnel of Macy's basement, teeming with talent as it is, is often called upon to perform at staff parties and annual banquets, and even to stage and produce whole shows for special employee occasions. They are willing enough to perform (Lottie Gardner does a monkey act that has everybody on the floor), but they are reluctant to stage an entire show, and Leo Adams has an explanation for that. "They're professionals, after all," he says, "and you know how it is. A real pro doesn't like to work for nothing, unless it's a benefit. It's in the blood."

Macy's has many inner organizations, such as the Twenty-Five-Year Club, the Fifty-Year Club, and the Friendly Forty, and they give at least one grand party a year, in addition to the continual bride's showers and stork showers for employees who are getting married or having babies. The Twenty-Five-Year Club, consisting of employees and executives who have been with Macy's twenty-five years or longer (and over one thousand of its members are still active in the store) holds an annual dinner in the grand ballroom of the Hotel Statler with an orchestra and professional entertainers such as Herb Sheldon and Red Buttons. There are songs and speeches, and sometimes a lively added attraction as when, one year, Jimmie Woods propelled onto the ballroom floor an original Macy delivery cart from the Fourteenth Street days atop of which proudly rode Miss Lena Rabenau, a veteran of over forty years' service at Macy's.

The Fifty-Year Club is made up mainly of retired employees excepting William Titon who, after sixty-one years at Macy's, is still as active as a ping-pong ball. The Fifty-Year Club has its big parties too, but its members gather more often and more informally every Tuesday in the eighth-floor restaurant for tea and a movie and a good reminiscent chat. Sometimes, over the tea table, a mild rivalry springs up, owing to the human perversity which makes all people subtract a few years from their ages at forty or fifty, but insist on adding a few once they are over seventy. "I worked at Macy's fifty years, and I'll soon be seventy-seven" says Margaret Murray, who remembers silk at one cent a yard in a price war at the old Fourteenth Street store. "Ah, now, you can't be a day over seventy-five!" objects Edward Vause. "Now, *I'm* eighty-one . . ."

They wear their Fifty-Year pins proudly, these veterans, and when they meet on Tuesdays the room is filled with the comfortable laughter of lively people who can, at last, take it a little easy.

Not all of Macy's inner groups are social and one of them, the Flying Squad, even has a kind of the-Marines-have-landed air of derring-do about it. The Flying Squad, managed by Elizabeth "Betty" Hoffman, is a team of trouble-shooters sent to help out any overburdened department when the rush of customers gets too heavy for the ordinary staff to handle.

In 1940, on his fortieth birthday, Jack Straus founded the organization called the Friendly Forty, "to promote friendliness in the store." Its forty members are chosen on the basis of their records and ratings and now number many more than forty, but they have kept the name. Under the direction of Birdie Schwartz, who last year succeeded May Hale as president, the Friendly Forty helps solve employees' problems, distribute Christmas gifts, run charity drives for the Red Cross, and assist new employees to find their way among such mazes as the rows of lockers on the balcony. Greeting a new employee, a Friendly Forty wears a lapel pin reading WELCOME! with the newcomer's name written underneath and FRIENDLY FORTY inscribed across the bottom.

The department of Employees' Services in general is managed by Helen Hyde, and both Miss Hyde and Miss Schwartz find their tasks rewarding, although there are awkward moments. One girl came to them in tears, complaining that her supervisor had switched her day off from Friday to Saturday. Smiles replaced the tears when it turned out that the switch was for one Friday only, because her department was giving her a surprise birthday party after closing and wanted her in the store on Friday, her birthday.

Smiles alternating with tears are the regular emotions of Joe Cooper and Ben Myers, the men who operate the two executive elevators just inside the Macy entrance at 151 West Thirty-fourth Street. At least, this is true during the baseball season. Joe, who has been seventeen years at Macy's, is a Dodgers fan. Ben, a Macy man for twenty-six years, roots for the Giants. Jack Straus, another Giants rooter, has a standing bet of one nickel with Joe every season, and in 1951 this brought about not only tears, but a state of full mourning.

On August 11, that year, Brooklyn was leading in the pennant race by thirteen and a half games, and Joe Cooper was ecstatic. Then the Giants began to win and the Dodgers to lose, and it took Jackie Robinson's heroic play in the dusk of the final day of the season to save a tie in the pennant race for the Dodgers. In the play-off, the Giants won the first game and the Dodgers won the second, bringing the play-off also to a tie. In the third, deciding game, with the Dodgers ahead 4-2 in the last of the ninth inning and Giants on second and third base, the Dodgers' Ralph Branca was called in from the bullpen to pitch to the Giants' Bobby Thomson. Thomson hit Branca's second pitch into the left-field stands for a home run, winning the pennant for the Giants.

When Joe Cooper dragged himself to work the next morning he found that kind friends in the store had draped his elevator from top to bottom in mourning bands of mauve and black, with a funeral wreath here and there. As he viewed the obsequies through brimming eyes, another colleague tapped him on the shoulder and handed him a crying-towel, thoughtfully provided by the linen department.

9

Protection Will Protect the
Working Girl

★

EVERY DEPARTMENT STORE has its occasional ugly customer—a woman, or quite possibly a man—who for
some reason feels free to abuse the salesclerks with threats
and nasty language. What this character does not know is
that, at Macy's, the clerks are as fully protected as though
each one had a police escort. The clerks do, in fact, have a
police escort. Some are in uniform, some in plain clothes,
and there are enough of them in the store to police a city
of three hundred thousand inhabitants. These members of
the Protection Squad are never very far away from any
counter, and a single nod or slight gesture from the salesclerk is sufficient to bring one or two of them, not on the
run, but at a deadly saunter.

The Protection Squad consists of Gray Guards (the men
in uniform) and of plain-clothes detectives (men and
women) who watch out for troublemakers and shoplifters
inside the store, and it also has a squad of "outside investigators" who concern themselves with such misdemeanors

as bad checks from customers and, sad to say, the peccadil-
loes of a dishonest employee now and then. The security
department, or "Protection" as it is called by everyone in
the store, is headed by Francis X. Fay, a former FBI
agent, whose office in a hidden corner of the balcony is
equipped with as many businesslike iron bars, double
gratings, and alarm signals as any bank vault or peni-
tentiary. Mr. Fay was a special agent assigned to the New
York office of the FBI in 1935 when John O'Gara,
Macy's general manager, asked a friend at the FBI to
suggest someone to reorganize the store's security system.
The friend suggested Fay who, after consulting with J.
Edgar Hoover in Washington, got the boss's permission to
give the new job a try.

Fay started out at Macy's by enlarging the security system to include squads of investigators assigned to survey
what were known as "sick" departments—departments
which suffered from chronic ailments such as inventory
shortages and the like. He also formed classes in judo and
classes in the handling of firearms, with regular target
practice on the roof. The Protection Squad does not shoot
shoplifters, but Fay likes his staff to be ready for anything.
In 1942, when the organization was running sweetly, Fay
left Macy's to join the Air Force. He returned after the
war to find that most of his best men were gone, some
into the Army, others to the New York police and fire
departments. "We had to start all over again," he says
now.

Probably the meanest shoplifter Macy's ever had was a
man, later found to be a narcotics addict, who used his
own children as camouflage. He had trained the little ones
to cluster round, jump up and down, emit squeals of joy,

and display other cute tricks to distract attention from him while he snaffled some item off a counter. Protection finally caught him and rushed him off to Fay's office, leaving the kids in the temporary care of a store matron. In Fay's office, the shoplifter broke away from the Gray Guards and took a running dive out of the window, landing on a metal awning just below. He was hauled back, and ended up in jail, but Mr. Fay's windows have all been reinforced by heavy screens since that episode.

The doubtful prestige of Most Ingenious Shoplifter could be awarded to any one of several crooks. The lady who wears outsize bloomers and manages to stuff stolen goodies into them is pretty old hat now, and so is the one who uses the dangling umbrella as a receptacle, or the one who hangs her treasures on a belt studded with hooks and worn inside her coat. But there is always the malefactor with the large, inventive approach. Two men dressed as Macy porters recently got away with a canoe from the sporting goods department, carrying it calmly down an escalator and out of the store in full view of several thousand spectators. They were later apprehended, but not (as some wags like to suggest) because they couldn't resist coming back for the paddles.

Shoplifting is an ever-present evil in department stores, but sometimes it seems even worse than usual, as though a steady wave of pilfering had set in. During one of these spells at Macy's a section manager who had been alerted to keep a special eye out for thieves was obliged to turn his back on his department briefly when he noticed an elderly woman struggling to maneuver a baby carriage through the crowded aisle. Always courteous, he hurried to help her with the carriage and pushed it as far as the elevator for her, returning to find his department in a state of excitement. "Somebody just stole a baby carriage!" the clerks informed him.

Stealing from Macy's staff itself is a refinement of shoplifting that does not always bring the expected rewards. A woman buyer, pausing on her way to lunch to speak to a salesclerk, laid a brown-paper parcel she was carrying on the counter for a moment. When she turned to pick it up, it was gone. After searching the counter and the floor beneath, she called Protection, and with a woman detective made for the nearest ladies' room. The ladies' room is a favorite refuge of shoplifters, affording the privacy of booths where the marauder can inspect her loot at leisure and perhaps dispose it more cunningly about her person.

This time, one of the booths was locked and the matron opened it with a key. There, slumped in a corner in a dead faint, lay the shoplifter, the opened parcel on the floor beside her. It contained the body of the buyer's pet cat which had died at home early that morning, and which she was taking, suitably wrapped, to the A.S.P.C.A. for proper disposal.

Macy clerks leave the problem of shoplifting pretty much to the store detectives, but in the case of troublemakers, or ugly customers, the clerks generally like to handle them alone as far as possible, without calling on Protection unless it is absolutely necessary. Not long ago a drunk weaved into the leather department where a young man from the Training Squad was getting his experience as a salesman.

"Wanna buy a desh shet," he announced.

"A desk set? Yes, sir," said the salesman, and laid out an array of desk sets on the counter.

"Wassamatta, ya stoopid or sumpin? I wanna *good* desh

shet, none o' thishere junk!" said the customer, and with a gesture he swept all the desk sets from the counter to the floor. "As fer *you*," he added, breathing heavily on the young salesman, "I like ta punch you in the nose."

"Nothing would give me greater pleasure than to afford you the opportunity," said the young salesman, a former light-heavyweight boxer at Yale, as he stepped briskly from behind the counter.

It was without a doubt the first time the Protection Squad was ever called upon to protect a customer from a clerk. The clerk, having been cautioned that kind words are better than a right cross, is now a happy junior executive. But Macy's still remembers with a certain twinge how the drunken customer paid his bail in night court with a wad of money amounting to eighty dollars, and mournfully remarked, "There goes the money I meant to spend at Macy's."

A customer's threat to punch a clerk in the nose is not enough to warrant the Protection Squad laying hands on him—he must actually hit somebody. In the incident of the desk set, the drunk swung wildly and landed a clumsy blow on the arm of an arriving Gray Guard while other guards were restraining the young salesman. The blow, though harmless, was technically sufficient to get the drunk hustled out of the store and booked in night court on charges of disorderly conduct and simple assault.

Equally, a store detective does not arrest a shoplifter in the store; he waits until the shoplifter has left the premises with his haul, and is outside in the street with it. The guilty party, once detained, is then taken to the office of Protection. In the case of habitual offenders, known to the store, Protection calls the police and prefers charges. Sometimes, however, if the shoplifter is a first offender, or possibly a helpless kleptomaniac, Macy's simply takes back the stolen merchandise and does not press any charges. As in any problem related to human beings, there are a hundred nuances of decision, judgment, and penalty.

Sinister doings at Macy's are not limited to shoplifters and troublemakers. One year, salespeople in the ready-to-wear department began to find all the clothes hanging on racks mysteriously slashed to pieces. Presently the luggage department reported slashes in its suitcases and other leather goods, obviously made with some sharp instrument, and the furniture department reported deep gashes ripped through upholstered sofas and chairs. There were no clues, and all that Fay and his staff could surmise was that the Slasher might be anyone, from a deranged customer to a disgruntled employee. Fay's first move was to ask the New York police if there had been any recent similar cases in the city. The police sent out a call for information, and learned that the New Haven Railroad had been finding its seats slashed lately, and that several New York hotels, buses, and taxicabs had been having the same trouble.

Railroads, hotels, and bus companies were alerted to be on the lookout, and the police ordered every New York cab driver to get out and inspect the interior of his cab each time he dropped a passenger. It was a New York taxi driver who finally caught up with the Slasher.

He had taken a fare from the Statler Hotel to the Astor, this driver reported, and on getting out to inspect the cab, had found the seat slashed. He called the cop on the beat, took him into the Astor, and recognized his fare sitting at the Astor bar. He was a nice-looking elderly man, well-dressed and mild-mannered.

Arrested and taken to court, he was released on bail for further hearing, and he promptly disappeared. He had a gift for disappearing, it seemed. Located after many months of search in a mental hospital on the West Coast, he escaped from there, too. Eventually he was trailed to Boston, where he had developed a new hobby. He was busy writing scurrilous anonymous letters to the Board of Directors of The First Church of Christ, Scientist, and distributing by mail pamphlets attacking Christian Science. This time, it was the pamphlets that undid him.

Police discovered that the pamphlets were printed in New York City, and quietly picked the man up the next time he called at the printing shop for a new batch. He was sent to prison and died there, declaring his innocence to the end. Fay, who had become horridly fascinated by this character, found that he had held a good job with a packing house concern and had retired, some years earlier, with a comfortable income and the respect and good wishes of all his co-workers.

The Mad Bomber, arrested in New York last year, included Macy's among the places he was going to blow up, but he was not the first incendiary to threaten the store. In the late thirties, when Percy Straus was president, Mr. Percy began getting anonymous letters demanding money and promising, unless the stated amount was forthcoming, to set off a bomb in the store. The letters started arriving just before Christmas, at the beginning of the rush season. Fay and his Protection Squad took over Mr. Percy's office, and Mr. Percy. Detectives answered all telephone calls, hoping for one from the extortionist, and finally it came. The bomber, thinking he was talking to Percy Straus, instructed a detective to put the money in a package and take it to a designated place by a certain route—say, walk to Thirty-fourth Street and Seventh Avenue, then three blocks north, take a cab to the Union Square subway station, put the package in a locker there, and tape the locker key to the underside of the shelf in a telephone booth in a theater lobby on the lower East Side. (Real criminals often talk just like the cops-and-robbers types in the movies, Fay says.)

Pausing only long enough to double the squad assigned to keep watch in the store, Protection sent a detective to the assignation with a dummy package—money on top, torn newspapers underneath—and covered him while he followed the instructions. In spite of a twenty-four-hour wait, the bomber never showed up. In a day or so another telephone call came, and Fay had a woman detective answer it. The bomber made the same appointment with her, except that the route was different and the locker key was to be left in a telephone booth in another theater. A series of dud assignations followed, with no bomber, but apparently he was watching the woman detective for he finally telephoned again and, after telling her pleasantly that she wasn't a bad-looking chick, made a definite appointment for the money to be left in still another locker and the locker key to be taped under the shelf in yet another telephone booth.

For this rendezvous Fay, as usual, surrounded the telephone booth with a casual-seeming group of plain-clothes men; one was reading a newspaper, another apparently waiting for a date, a third gandering the billboards outside the theater. A few New York City detectives, alerted to the capture, also loitered nearby. Fay rigged the locker key this time so that a small flashlight, visible to the watching detectives, would go out when the key was taken.

On schedule, the woman detective placed the package in

the subway locker, proceeded to the theater, and went through the motions of taping the locker key to the shelf in the telephone booth. A duplicate key was, of course, already there and connected to the flashlight.

A few minutes after the woman detective left the booth a man entered it. The flashlight went out, and the Macy men and the city detectives closed in on the bomber. He turned out to be a boy of sixteen or seventeen, with a long record of juvenile delinquency.

"The whole business, until we nabbed him, took about three weeks—from the middle of December to the first part of January" Fay relates. "It was not exactly a merry Yuletide season for any of us."

In 1952, Protection made its most colorful gesture by installing the famous Macy dogs, which patrol the store at night. Watchdogs had been tried at Macy's before, as early as the 1920's, but the innovation did not work out well because the dogs, longhaired German shepherds, suffered too much from the heat and humidity of the summer months.

Francis Fay, an Air Force security officer during the war, had been impressed by the work of the K-9 Corps, the Army dog patrols which were made up largely of Doberman pinschers, so when he returned to civilian life and to Macy's he suggested Doberman pinschers. Macy's was all too willing to try the experiment. In the past five months up to that point their Gray Guards had caught fifteen prowlers, and there was no telling how many others had escaped—including one gang that got away with twelve thousand dollars' worth of fur coats stolen from the racks at night.

Macy's started out with four trained Dobermans at a cost

of one thousand dollars each, including training, and named them appropriately Cash, Red Star, Suzy (the brand name of a Macy perfume), and Mom (short for Macy's Own Make). Suzy has been twice a mother since then, one litter being sired by Red Star and the second by Champion Dobe Storm, and six of the pups are now big enough to work right along with their elders on the dog patrol. The dogs receive their basic training at John M. "Mike" Behan's Canine College in Connecticut, and are kept in trim by regular drills with their handlers on the Macy roof where their kennels are located. The handlers, who accompany them on their nightly rounds, are uniformed guards specially assigned to work with the dogs only. Macy Dobermans at drill are a lovely sight to see, jumping hurdles, climbing ladders, and leaping through hoops like so many streaks of black lightning.

"They look so *peaceful!*" a lady visitor remarked recently to Francis Kilmartin of Protection, as she watched the dogs perform on the roof outside a twentieth-floor window. "They don't seem ferocious or bad-tempered at *all.*"

"Oh," said Mr. Kilmartin, shocked, "Dobermans are not bad-tempered dogs! They're very peace-loving animals."

"Well then, how can they be useful as watchdogs? What do they *do?*" the lady asked.

"They just eat people," Mr. Kilmartin told her, peacefully.

That is, of course, not strictly true. A Macy Doberman will not eat anybody, except on command.

The Macy Dobermans' working day begins at nightfall, when the store is emptied of customers and clerks, showcases are shrouded, and all the vast stretches of counters and aisles are silent and in darkness except for a dim night light here and there. The silence is not broken even when the handlers start out on their rounds with the Dobermans on long leashes, for the handlers wear rubber-soled shoes and the dogs' nails are kept filed short so that no scratching sound on bare floors may warn an intruder of their approach. The routine tour of a Macy guard with a Macy dog is as still as death, and just as deadly.

At designated areas the handler-guard unleashes his dog and gives him the command to "Search!" The dog takes off at a run, first inspecting in one direction, then in another. If he finds anything suspicious, he barks to summon his handler-guard. If there *is* a prowler the guard commands the dog to "Watch!" which means that the dog is to keep the prowler motionless until the guard decides what to do next. In the case of a single prowler the guard will probably handle him alone, marching him down to a certain Macy entrance where a special officer is on constant duty. If the intruders number more than a man and a dog can easily take care of, the guard uses his two-way radio to notify the special officer and ask for help.

An intruder confronted by a Macy dog who has been given the command to "Watch!" might as well be handcuffed, bound, and gagged for all he can do about it. The dog just sits there, looking at him. He will not attack, except under two conditions, both of which he is trained to know. For attack, he must be given the command "Get him!" or he must detect, on his own, some slight movement on the part of the man he is watching. Let a prowler being watched by a Macy dog take one half-step, or even lift a little finger, and the dog is on him in a flash, closing his teeth unerringly on the right, or weapon, arm, and hanging on, no matter how desperately the man tries to shake him off. A full-grown

Doberman weighs ninety pounds and his jaws exert a pressure of about fifty pounds to a square inch, so the prowler really hasn't got a chance.

Both former and would-be prowlers seem to be aware of this fact. The Dobermans have caught one or two since they went to work at Macy's, but most nighttime pilferers have been scared off simply by hearing about the Macy dogs.

The Dobermans generally work two hours at a stretch, on alternating shifts from dusk to dawn. Sometimes they even work alone, when a guard attaches a dog by a twelve-foot leash to a stanchion in some part of the store while he attends to required duties elsewhere. The guard knows that the dog will summon him by barking if anything funny happens even remotely near the stanchion. There is an undoubted rapport between the dogs and the men who handle them, but the Dobermans, though fond of their handlers, have a nice sense of proportion about it, and a lack of sentimentality. A Macy dog will attack his own handler, if another handler gives him the command. That is why, in the practice drills frequently held to keep the dogs in top form, the handler who plays the part of the prowler always wears a padded suit.

Catching thieves is only part of a Macy dog's duties. The dogs also spot any smell of smoke, or of escaping steam from a faulty pipe which might ruin thousands of dollars' worth of merchandise, and they even bark insistently at a window left open which ought to be closed. One Saturday night, a Doberman stopped stiff-legged in front of an automatic computing machine, covered for the weekend, in the controller's office. No commands from his handler would persuade him to move on. Finally the handler impatiently snatched the cover off the machine and discovered that it had been left running and was red-hot to the touch. If the machine had been allowed to run throughout Sunday, it would have cost Macy's hundreds of dollars, and worse, could have started a serious fire.

The Macy dogs don't get any cash bonus for such services, but they have their own rewards. All dogs love to ride in automobiles, and few travel so grandly as Macy's Dobermans. Often, they are recruited to ride, along with the other guards, in the front seat of a delivery car carrying payrolls, furs, or jewels. And such is their training that they sit front-faced and dignified, and never sprawl beamishly out of the windows as ordinary dogs do.

They are trained, as well, to eat only in their penthouse kennels on Macy's twentieth floor. This is a precaution against the dogs' accepting any bribes of juicy morsels, or possibly poisoned meat, from prowlers or other people who are up to no good in the store. The handlers are in favor of all forms of training, but they consider the meat-bribe an unlikely possibility. "Listen," one of them said not long ago, "if you saw the good food these dogs get at Macy's you'd know that not even a tenderloin steak would be apt to tempt them, from a stranger."

"Not unless they could eat the guy first, as an appetizer," added another.

However, Macy dogs are really peace-loving creatures, as Mr. Kilmartin said, and indeed as any law-enforcement officer must fundamentally be. And only a short time ago the dogs had a chance to perform a gentle act of mercy. Two teen-age girls ran away from home together and were reported missing by their frantic parents, who finally telephoned the police around midnight. The police traced the girls to Macy's, where they had last been seen, but in the vast and darkened spaces of the empty store it was impossible to guess where they might be hiding, if they were still there. Only the dogs could find them, Protection decided, and the dogs were given the command: "Search!"

The dogs nosed out the girls in a corner of a balcony stairway. They started to bark, and the girls, seeing themselves pursued by dogs, naturally started to scream. But before the guards could arrive on the scene the screams stopped.

"Nobody will ever know what those dogs did to keep those girls from being frightened," says one handler, who was present at the capture. "When we got there, the dogs were in their trained position of 'Watch!' and they would never have let the girls make a run for it. But what beats me is that those girls were screaming one minute, and the next minute they weren't frightened at all."

One of the teen-agers, restored to her grateful family, tried to explain it. She said that the biggest, most ferocious-looking dog of all had come up to her and licked her hand.

"That's nonsense" says the handler. "No Macy dog would lick a stranger's hand."

"However," he adds thoughtfully, "I must say that one of 'em, that night, looked as though he'd *like* to!"

A Macy rule, instituted by the controller's office but highly approved by Protection, explicitly states that no ladders are to be carried on escalators. This law derives from the unhappy day when a porter rode up an escalator with a twelve-foot ladder and set it down, near the top, to get a better grip on it. The ladder caught on the top step and somehow broke a connection with a two-inch pipe that supplies water, at a pressure of two hundred and fifty pounds, to the fire-sprinkler system. A mighty jet of water shot out of the pipe and knocked eighteen people on the escalator across a whole floor and into the bridal salon.

The victims, including several drenched brides-to-be, were rushed to the store hospital on the nineteenth floor, treated for shock, and supplied with dry clothes on the house. Only one of them sued Macy's—for damage to her fur coat. But the lawsuit came to nothing after Macy's Bureau of Standards examined the coat, appraised it as a twenty-year-old rag worth about nine dollars and a half, and was upheld by the court in its honest opinion.

Escalator incidents are not always so violent, but are often colorful. A memsahib from India, wearing the sari which consists only of yards of material wound around the body and mysteriously tucked in with no hook or zipper anywhere, was rather grandly riding upward on an escalator one day when an assistant buyer, glancing idly in her direction, noted with horror that the sari had caught in an escalator step and the Indian lady was being slowly unwound. The assistant buyer dashed to shut off the power, and racing up the steps, gallantly covered the lady with his coat. The sari was retrieved, almost intact, by reversing the machinery, and no hospital care was required beyond a small whiff of smelling salts administered to the assistant buyer.

Macy's hospital is a bright apartment presided over by Dr. Michael Lake, medical director, Miss Marie L. Troup, R.N., an assistant medical director, four part-time doctors, two visiting nurses, a physiotherapist, and a chiropodist. (A chiropodist is a felt want when a girl has been standing on her feet from nine until six.) Fainting spells and minor abrasions, among both staff and customers, are treated on the spot, and sometimes they can be gory. When metal became once more available after World War II Macy's advertised a limited supply of roller skates. The customers knocked each other down to get into the store—literally, in at least one case. A fat lady, flying up the aisle to get her skates, collided with a small man who had already bought his skates and was leaving with them. Brushing him aside with a powerful arm, she knocked him clean through a glass showcase, and kept right on going. Horrified clerks dug the small gent out of the showcase and found that he was so badly cut and bleeding so profusely that they called for a wheel chair and took him to the hospital on the nine-

teenth floor. The small gent spoke only four words while his wounds were being treated, but he spoke them over and over again.

"Where are my *skates?*" he kept asking.

In any case of acute illness the Macy hospital applies first-aid treatment until an ambulance can be called, and the patient transferred to a city hospital. In such emergencies, the Macy hospital staff works quietly and with speed. One late-working Saturday night last year an elderly male customer in the basement keeled over with an apparent heart attack at five minutes past six. A clerk summoned a porter with a wheel chair and Leo Adams, the basement executive, called a staff doctor and cleared an express elevator. At 6:12 the staff doctor arrived and the customer was taken via wheel chair and express elevator to the nineteenth-floor hospital. There, the staff doctor advised his removal to a city hospital and an assistant called police to send a city ambulance while Adams alerted the elevator operator to stay on duty, and also telephoned a report to Protection in case the man died. At 6:15 two policemen, alerted by their radio, arrived at Macy's in a patrol car and hurried to the nineteenth floor with a portable oxygen tank. At 6:30 the ambulance arrived, and at 6:40—thirty-five minutes after his seizure—the patient was on his way to the city hospital.

A week later, he came back to Macy's and tried to express his thanks. He was a Cuban who knew very little English. Through a Macy interpreter he explained that he was subject to heart attacks, but never—*never,* he insisted with tears and gestures—had he received such prompt and wonderful care.

Macy's speedy and efficient attention to stricken customers became at one point almost too perfect for the store's

own good. Six years ago a pregnant shopper was taken with
pains and rushed to the Macy hospital, where she gave birth
to a baby girl. The store's promotion department, embrac-
ing the story with glad cries, gave it to the newspapers, most
of which considered it worth a spot on page one, or a human
interest column on page three. Macy's and the baby, chris-
tened Ann Macy Hertrich, got so much publicity that many
another expectant mother decided that Macy's was as good
a place to have her baby as any hospital, the service being
so fine, and free to boot.

"I swear they would count their pains and then go shopping" one overworked hospital assistant recalls, wearily.

Six-year-old Ann Macy Hertrich pays frequent visits to
Macy's, where she is regaled with candy and sodas, and
spends a pleasant hour chatting with her friends in the store.
"We all feel like her godmothers," says Catherine Yanez,
who was among those present at the birth.

Little Ann has also appeared on the television show, "I've
Got a Secret," where her secret won her eighty dollars and
a carton of Winston cigarettes.

Ann's mother is only one of the grateful Macy patrons
who declare that Macy's hospital rates right along with the
best hospitals in the city.

"Eez as goot as the Miracle Center!" one foreign-born ad-
mirer has stated enthusiastically.

10

Some Corner of a Foreign Field
That Is Forever Macy's

★

MACY'S OPENED its first foreign office in 1885, a tiny one-
room establishment in Belfast, Ireland, to take care
of the Irish linens and laces that Macy's had begun to import
to its New York store. The second foreign office followed in
Paris, in 1893, more or less as a gamble since the average
Macy customer of that era was not exactly Parisian-minded.
Women like novelty, however, and French imports of
chinaware, lace, and gloves were so successful that the store
went on to expand its foreign activity. It now has importing
offices in eight foreign cities: Belfast, Ireland; Brussels, Belgium; Florence, Italy; Frankfurt, Germany; Zurich, Switzerland; Osaka, Japan; and, of course, London and Paris.

This empire is largely ruled by Leo Martinuzzi, head of
Macy's Foreign Office with headquarters on the eleventh
floor which he rarely has time to visit, being bound to spend
most of his time traveling. He likes keeping on the move,
and he has a favorite saying that he likes to quote: "Travel
faster than the sun—and you will always see it rise." Born in

Venice and educated in Switzerland, Mr. Martinuzzi is a slight, suave man with the *politesse* of a diplomat, the sure taste of an artist, a merchant's knack of quick decisions, and a gift of prophecy about merchandising trends that his colleagues often speak of as "weird."

Martinuzzi's career literally started off with a bang. During World War I, when he was still in his teens, his mother brought him from his Swiss school home to Venice, where he soon got a dollar-a-day job with the then American consul, B. Harvey Carroll, Jr. Carroll was the adventurous type and kept dashing off to the front, or as near as he could get to it, in an automobile, taking young Martinuzzi with him every time. The consul seemed to woo the idea of getting shot for the greater glory of the American Consulate or something, and Martinuzzi, who definitely did not want to get shot, was dragged along anyway, sometimes dodging bullets like a wild thing. Finally the war ended, and the youthful Martinuzzi heaved a sigh of relief when the next problem confronting the Consulate proved to be one concerning only propaganda and diplomacy.

Both Italy and the United States, its ally in World War I, wanted to emphasize the goodwill between the two countries after the war, and a great fuss was made over the launching, in 1918, of the U.S. Shipping Board vessel "Piave." The American Consulate in Venice got the idea of having Gabriele d'Annunzio compose a salutation to be cabled to the United States in time for the launching ceremony. D'Annunzio formally vouchsafed a message which read, in part, in a free translation by Mr. Martinuzzi:

> The fighting soul of Italy is today across the ocean
> while the great redeeming people inscribe on the prow

of their robust ship the Italian name of that glorious
river which spread the victory to all the waters of the
Adriatic . . . Let the war cry which resounded in the
sky of Vienna strongly echo across the ocean. In the
name of the Union it was repeated with a raised arm
by all the aviators, all the sailors, all the infantrymen
of Italy . . . Let it now be repeated by all our glorious
American allies aboard the *Piave:*
> *Eia, Eia, Alala!*

The final phrase, a Greek war cry, was obviously too
much for the Italian telegraph operator who handled the
message, and he substituted a patriotic hail of his own.
D'Annunzio's deathless words were transmitted to America
and printed in the Venice newspapers the same day, in
Italian and English, with the following stirring finish:

> . . . In the name of the Union it was repeated with a
> raised arm by all the aviators, all the sailors, all the in-
> fantrymen of Italy . . . Let it now be repeated by all our
> glorious American allies aboard the *Piave:*
> *Hurray, hurray, for Italy!*

Mr. Martinuzzi still wryly cherishes the letter he got from
d'Annunzio. Dated September 8, 1918, it reads, rather
mildly and again in translation:

> My dear Martinuzzi:
> It is deplorable that my good-will should be so badly
> rewarded. Attention is a form of courtesy.
> Now my very clear text is *spoiled* in the print of the
> *Gazetta di Venezia.*
> I cannot but be pained.
> > Yours,
> > (signed) Gabriele d'Annunzio.

Martinuzzi, who speaks five languages and knows everybody everywhere, had become acquainted with many Americans in Venice, and in 1925 he came to America and went
to work for the Treasury Department. In 1930, once more
in Italy and living in Florence, he met Alberto Antolini who
was about to open a Macy branch in Florence. Antolini
wanted to buy Martinuzzi's car, a lavish Packard he had
brought back from the States, for use as the official car of the
Florence office, but said he would have to consult his boss
first. His boss, Jesse Straus, met Antolini and Martinuzzi by
appointment at the American Consulate, where they
showed Mr. Jesse the car.

"Magnificent," said Mr. Jesse, "but not appropriate to
Macy's."

Martinuzzi himself, however, turned out to be wholly
appropriate to Macy's in Mr. Jesse's opinion, and he soon
went to work in Macy's Florence office. From there he went
to London, as manager of the London office, and stayed
there until World War II broke out in 1939, when he found
himself again dodging bullets almost as literally as in World
War I. After a brief trip to New York headquarters (where
Macy's quickly made him a sort of vice-president in charge
of Big Trouble), he spent the first year of the war visiting
Macy offices in Holland, Belgium, and as many other countries as he could get to, always traveling one jump ahead of
the invading Germans. His first concern was to see that the
foreign staffs were assured of some kind of safety, or to ar-
range their evacuation if safety was out of the question; his
secondary mission was to keep merchandise coming to
America, mostly through neutral Spain.

The London office, of course, stayed open throughout the
war, and even though England had more immediate tasks

on its mind, managed to get a good deal of merchandise to America under convoy. The Paris office kept on running too, although after Occupation its communication with New York was cut off. The Paris office puzzled the Nazis who came to take it over; there wasn't a sign of equipment anywhere, not even a filing-cabinet or a typewriter. The Nazis naturally guessed that the staff had hidden the office equipment and files somewhere, but they never found the hiding place, and on Liberation Day the staff triumphantly carried everything back and set up in real business again.

During the war Macy's did its bit with bond drives, blood banks, and Red Cross units among its employees, and most of all with its long list of other employees wounded or killed after America entered the war. But World War II, though horrible everywhere, touched America less than it did Europe. Macy's, along with other American industries, still had time to think of the American consumer as its prime responsibility.

After the war, Macy's found itself with a new, and graver, responsibility. The rehabilitation of Europe and Japan depended largely on trade with America, and if any American firm was already in business with Europe and Japan, Macy's was.

Macy's itself would gag at the notion that renewed trade with foreign countries was pure philanthropy on the part of the store; any merchant worth his salt wants something in return for what he gives. Europe was more than willing to give that something but, after the earth-shaking shock of the war, was not quite sure what it was that America wanted. It was as though an elderly lady, giving tea to a friend, were suddenly interrupted by the explosion of her stove. "Oh,"

she would manage to say, picking up the pieces, "now, what *was* it you wanted, cream or lemon?"

The man who had the answer was Leo Martinuzzi. In 1944 a British government official (who was no slouch, either) called on Martinuzzi in Macy's London office to ask him what the American market would be wanting from England after the war. Martinuzzi asked for a day or two to think it over.

"I couldn't tell Sheffield how to make steel or Manchester how to make cotton, and besides many of the plants there had been bombed out," he says now. "I decided that if I could tell the British what the United States would want in, say, 1948, they could gear their production to 1948. The only question in my mind after that was: What will the United States want in 1948?"

It was one of the crises that bring out the prophet in Mr. Martinuzzi. The trend in American homes was one of space and comfort. Martinuzzi, recalling his Swiss school days, thought about the snowy spaces of the Alps and the comfortable Tyrolean cottages scattered among them. Tyrolean furniture might catch on in America, he thought, and instantly answered himself with a loud "No! Tyrolean furniture would be too rustic, too *hick,* for Americans. What we need is a *sophisticated* Tyrolean style."

When the British official returned, Martinuzzi was ready for him.

"What America will want in 1948 is French Provincial," he said. "Tie in your products with French Provincial, and America will use them in 1948."

England promptly assembled all the French Provincial furniture it had on hand or could get out of France, and adroitly adapted its cottons, silverware, and other manufactured products to the French Provincial style. Things came to pass exactly as Mr. Martinuzzi had foretold, and that, according to everyone in the trade, is how "French Provincial" became the American housewives' dream.

A letter in the Foreign Office files, dated 1948 from Hay Robertson Ltd. of St. Margaret's Works, Drumferline, Scotland, speaks awesomely of Martinuzzi's 1944 advice concerning French Provincial, "which (the letter reads) in view of the coming vogue takes the semblance of a prophetic utterance."

After D-Day and the actual end of the war in Europe, Italy was the first country to ask merchandising counsel, as England had done, and Martinuzzi applied his usual psychological approach to the problem. It is an approach which often, at first, does not seem to concern the country in question at all. Martinuzzi has the true cosmopolitan mind.

"Just to buy something and then sell it is of little value to foreign trade. There must be a *thought* behind it," he explains. Sitting back in his chair and making a steeple out of his fingers, he continues dreamily:

"For instance, in medieval times kings and knights and common men led strenuous, intensely physical lives. They spent their days fighting, jousting, eating, and drinking, and when they came home at night they were physically tired and wanted physical comfort."

Here, Mr. Martinuzzi leans forward earnestly and plants his hands on his desk. "Modern man is different," he says. "Today, men come home not physically but *mentally* tired, and what they want is *mental* relaxation."

Reminded of the Italian problem, Martinuzzi transports his listener instantly to Paris. "Once, in the window of an art shop in the rue de l'Opéra, I saw three prints—by

Gauguin, Van Gogh, and Matisse. The Gauguin and the
Van Gogh were not restful—but the Matisse *was*. Do you
know why? It was because Matisse never really finished
anything. He always painted a picture with a lot of space
in it, something a tired man could look at in complete relaxation, filling in his own details."

But the Italian problem?

At this point Mr. Martinuzzi regards his questioner
kindly, realizing that it is not always easy for the novice at
merchandising philosophy to follow the Martinuzzi train
of thought.

"The Italian Fair at Macy's in 1951," he says, "embodied
everything I found in that Matisse picture in the Paris window; space, beauty, and relaxation. There was the noble
sweep of Italian sculpture and even furniture, the beauty
of Italian paintings and Venetian glass, and the utter relaxation and *fun* implied in the Italian sportswear, beach-
bags, play-shoes, and so on. It was an expression of the true
Italy which is still, after all, the cradle of art and the home
of festivity. Why, even your English word 'regatta,' meaning a holiday boat race with crowds laughing and cheering,
was originally a gondola race in Venice. The Italian Fair
was a great success," Mr. Martinuzzi concludes briskly. "It
was copied all over the United States and Europe, and also
in Australia and New Zealand, and Mr. Jack Straus and I
were decorated by the Italian Government for our part
in it."

There is little doubt that the Italian Fair encouraged the
popularity in America of Italian styles, which all but un-
seated France as the undisputed queen of fashion.

American women will remember, around 1953, a wave
of Indian saris, Indian scarves, and lovely full skirts heavily

embroidered with Indian gold and gems. These confections were largely the result of the young Indian Republic consulting with Mr. Martinuzzi. Martinuzzi is so well-known in nearly all foreign countries that a foreigner, coming to see him in his office at Macy's, sometimes stops short and says "I didn't realize you worked for Macy's!" Nobody minds this, including the foreigner, Mr. Martinuzzi, or Macy's.

Probably the greatest postwar challenge Martinuzzi and Macy's faced was the problem of Japan. For years, even before the war, the label "made in Japan" was a synonym for shoddiness. Housewives shrank from it and comedians made jokes about it. The sad truth was that they were right. Articles "made in Japan" usually fell apart at a touch, and were not worth a nickel.

Japan, after the war, naturally wanted to resume its trade with Macy's, but Macy's, through its Foreign Office, laid it on the line to Japan. "We want to help you rebuild your trade," the Foreign Office said, in effect, "but we are not about to handle any more of that junk."

Constructive advice being needed as well, Martinuzzi traveled to Japan. On the way, he considered the problem psychologically. The American trend was for spacious living, after so many American families being shut up in Quonset huts during the war. The Japanese knew how to create an illusion of space, in their decoration and their art, because so many of them had lived for centuries cramped into tiny paper houses. "Space" was Martinuzzi's key word as he stepped onto Japanese soil.

He began by ordering a set of chinaware in which the conventional Japanese trees were, at his request, painted in a three-dimensional, *trompe-l'œil* effect that gave anyone who picked up a dish the feeling that he was looking *through* the trees at a far horizon. A feeling of *space*, in fact. The Japanese at first thought Martinuzzi was crazy, but when they saw the *trompe-l'œil* plates they admitted that he might have something. The chinaware is still on sale at Macy's, and selling very well.

When he felt that he had won their confidence, Mr. Martinuzzi called a meeting of Japanese manufacturers and once more told them the facts of life. The label "made in Japan" was absolute death, he explained to them, and he was there to tell them how they could retrieve Japan's reputation, or at least better it. Only two men walked out, he remembers; the others stayed to listen.

"The two who walked out aren't doing business any more, even in Japan," Martinuzzi now says sadly.

Martinuzzi's work with the Japanese manufacturers produced some really good Japanese imports, and culminated in a visit to Japan by a delegation of European department store executives. A reporter asked a British member of this group why he had come to Japan. "Really, I don't know," the Englishman replied, "except that I never truly believed that Japan could produce any distinguished merchandise until I was told so by Leo Martinuzzi of Macy's. . . . You know Macy's," he added impatiently, "the New York emporium."

Robert Gutter, a Foreign Office buyer, has had his own experiences with the Japanese. Once, calling on a Japanese manufacturer in his New York hotel room, Gutter put his hat on a hall table and felt something soft under the hat.

"What is *this?*" he cried, pulling it out. (All buyers, feeling something saleable to the touch, always pull it out and cry "What is *this?*")

It proved to be the Japanese manufacturer's sweater,

made in Japan out of Japanese cashmere. "Japanese cashmere" is a contradiction in terms, since true cashmere is said
to come from the British Isles and originally derives from
the goats of Kashmir in the Himalayan mountains. For a
moment Mr. Gutter felt confused. But then he examined
the sweater.

"It was simply wonderful cashmere," he has since declared. "My host told me it came from a hidden cache the
Japanese had kept buried in oil during the war."

Macy's now has the Japanese cashmere sweaters for sale.
They are cheaper than British or Scottish cashmere and customers, shown the once-fatal label "made in Japan," vow
that they cannot tell the difference. Mr. Gutter has traveled
in Japan and enjoys dealing with its people, although he
admits that their passion for politeness sometimes lends an
air of wild unreality to even the most concise of business
conversations.

"A Japanese businessman likes to agree with everybody
for the sake of good manners," he explains. "Nothing hurts
him more than to have to say 'No.' On the other hand, he is
a good trader and nothing is going to stampede him into
saying 'Yes.' To solve this problem the Japanese have perfected a kind of 'Yes-Yes' and 'Yes-No,' each with its own
shades of meaning. 'Yes-Yes' means 'maybe.' 'Yes-No' means
'probably not.' If they ever say 'Maybe' it means a one per
cent chance of concluding the deal. And they have one
other little phrase that's a real masterpiece. When they actually conclude a deal—or so you might think—they smile and
bow, and hand you the decisive statement. The decisive
statement consists of the words, 'Yes! Maybe!' "

Mr. Gutter relates this without rancor, indeed with affection. Macy's treasures its relations with Japan and feels a

touch of pride that it has helped the country to free itself from the longtime derision caused by the label "made in Japan." The Foreign Office has taught Japanese manufacturers things like "full fashioning," which they had not heard of, and the importance of keeping to their native designs and not trying to copy Western art. Japan is grateful to Macy's, and Macy's cherishes the bond for reasons of amity, commerce, world trade and, indirectly, world peace itself.

"Don't get me wrong," said an executive recently, "Macy's doesn't set itself up to preach about world problems. World problems are more complicated now than they were in the days of Isidor and Nathan Straus, when everybody knew right from wrong. But," this man went on to say, "world trade is a part of world peace. If you are not at peace with the world, you cannot trade with the world. I guess Macy's idea is just to be at peace with the world, and maybe not for business reasons only. Hell, even if it *was* only for business reasons, it's still a good idea."

Martinuzzi the philosopher and student marches hand in hand with Martinuzzi the merchant, and he is always delighted when he can discover in some ancient custom a true sense of solid sales-appeal. "Take the Chinese," he says. "For centuries, most of the Chinese people have not had enough to eat. So what do they do? Instead of putting everything they *have* got onto one plate, as Western countries too often do, they dispose it daintily in a number of small bowls so that it offers variety and looks like more. And then, instead of using a knife and fork, or a spoon, they use chopsticks, which actually oblige them to savor each morsel at a time.

"Take the illusion of coolness," says Mr. Martinuzzi, warming to his subject. "The Orientals, Chinese and Jap-

anese alike, live in climates which are often insufferably
hot. Again, what do they do? They have the charming custom of hanging tiny bells over their doors and windows,
with long strips of colored paper attached to their clappers.
The slightest current of air starts the paper strips blowing,
which in turn causes the clapper to strike against the bell,
thus pleasantly announcing that a breeze has sprung up.
This is pure artistry, and in a way, pure salesmanship," Mr.
Martinuzzi adds, "because the *sensation* of being told that
there is a breeze is often greater than the breeze itself."

To illustrate this point further, Martinuzzi likes to tell
a true story about an air-conditioned American aircraft
plant where the workers began to complain of the heat,
even though temperature and humidity had been scientifi-
cally tested and recorded as ideal. Some genius at the plant
got the idea of tying ribbons to the grilles of the air ducts.
Workers the next morning saw the ribbons fluttering, and
with one voice proclaimed, "Now, *that's* more *like* it!" And
they went happily and comfortably to work, even though
the temperature and humidity remained the same as it
had always been.

In spite of his fascination with Oriental *trompe-l'œil,* or
possibly *trompe-tout,* effects, the last thing in the world that
Martinuzzi wants to do is to "fool" the Macy customer. He
simply wants to guide the customer along the pleasantest
path to the most attractive purchase. As he has solidly said,
"Man has no other direct way of judging merchandise than
through his senses. It follows that the more senses any given
goods will satisfy, the greater pleasure they will give."

Appeal to the senses must not, however, be confused with
the magic quality called "taste," Martinuzzi points out. A
customer may demand a red couch, because red appeals to

her color sense, when it is all wrong for the rest of her color scheme. Another may order a sweet wine to serve with a roast of beef, because she likes sweet wine even if it doesn't go with roast beef. Martinuzzi is all for individuality, but at examples like these, he draws the line. And he places the responsibility, not upon the customer, but squarely on the shoulders of the salesman. Salesclerks, he declares, must know everything about the wares they are selling, and when they think they know everything, they must start all over and learn some more. They must know so much, in fact, that some of the knowledge brushes off, unobtrusively, onto any customer who seems to need it.

In a speech to Macy's Training Squad not long ago, Martinuzzi posed to the class the following questions, which he called "elementary":

Can you tell the difference between a block, screen, and roller printed cloth?

Could you distinguish a moulded from a half-cut or cut glass?

Do you know whether low-end double damask is better than the same count single damask, or if

There is any obvious difference between hand-loomed and power-loomed tweeds?

Is it always possible to differentiate a hand-painted decor on earthenware or china from a good lithograph?

How would you recognize a blown glass from a moulded one, a masterpiece from a perfect reproduction?

Should handmade articles be more expensive than machine-made ones, and if so, is it because they are better made? Does handmaking improve their appearance?

"Ignorance of these facts is very serious" said Mr. Martinuzzi in conclusion, and retired to stunned applause.

Martinuzzi's conviction that good taste is not something we are born with, but a quality which must be cultivated through complete knowledge, has a staunch supporter in William Titon, Macy's wine and food buyer, who also spends much time abroad. "Titon the Taster," as he is called, believes that you must sell the customer what he wants, the earthbound staples like ham, cheese, and so on, but that you must also widen his scope to include frivolities like capers and truffles.

"There was a time when people wouldn't even buy *pâté de foie gras*," says Mr. Titon, "and when they saw the truffle in it, they screamed. Thought it was some kind of dirt got in there. Nowadays," Mr. Titon adds complacently, "they won't buy *pâté de foie gras* UNLESS it's got the truffle in it. It's a matter of slow infiltration, you might say."

Mr. Titon had his own experience of slow infiltration when he first started traveling extensively in England and on the Continent as food and wine buyer for Macy's. Everybody was nice to him, but he felt that he was not getting the full attention that a great store like Macy's should command. Somehow, he had the feeling that the red carpet was not fully unfurled. Finally, he told his troubles to a friendly merchant in England.

"My dear man," said the friendly merchant, "you invented the tea bag, did you not?"

This was quite true. Sometime before World War I,

Titon had thought up the idea of the tea bag, and Macy's had been the first store to publicize it. Titon admitted as much to the Englishman, not without a glow of pride.

"My dear fella," said the Englishman, "what you don't understand is that we English prefer our tea without cheese-cloth."

Titon fled to France, like Mary Queen of Scots in search of haven, and was again met with a request to wait in line, or words to that effect. Again he unburdened himself, this time to a French merchant.

"But, see you, *mon ami*," said the French merchant, "we have many large stores that we supply in the United States. How can we drop all that to attend to the wants of this medium-sized grocery store that you call Macy's?"

"*Grocery* store!" hollered Mr. Titon.

"But of course. You buy nothing but groceries, how could Macy's be something else than a grocery store?"

To his dismay, Mr. Titon found this opinion unanimous in Europe. Macy's, the Europeans thought quite simply, was a grocery store.

The next time Titon went to Europe on a buying trip, he carried an extra satchel. In it was a large photograph of Macy's imposing building on Herald Square, a catalogue of some of the thousands of articles the store carried at the time, and a brief run-down of the store's gross earnings in the year just past.

"That red carpet came out quicker than a snake's tongue," Mr. Titon says now.

Macy's has long carried on a love affair with Europe, all misunderstandings forgotten. Martinuzzi and Titon both like to remember Louis Sipp, for instance, a vintner in Alsace-Lorraine. Macy's had ordered thirty-seven cases of Alsatian wine from Louis Sipp. In World War II, the Nazis, streaming through France and Alsace-Lorraine, marched on Louis Sipp's town. Louis fled with his wife and children, his cow and goat and the family pet dog, *and* with the thirty-seven cases of wine.

The Nazis killed Louis. But six years later Macy's received the thirty-seven cases of wine from his widow, with a letter saying, "Here are your wines. We are sorry for the delay."

There is a kind of *tendresse*, too, between Macy's and Latin America that goes beyond mere shopkeeping. In 1954, Macy's devised a gesture to South America that caused Ed Sullivan, division superintendent of the fourth and fifth floors, to make the trip of his life. Mr. Sullivan still speaks of it with emotion.

"I was walking along, minding my business, when out of a clear blue sky," he says, paraphrasing a popular song, "WHAM! BANG! A publicity gal came along and told me I had to be Santa Claus for our South American neighbors."

Almost before Sullivan could catch his breath he was outfitted with a Santa Claus costume, including a beard made of Tibetan yak-hair, handed an inexhaustible sack of toys, and put aboard a Panagra plane bound for a fast three-day tour of Panama, Quito (Ecuador), Cali (Columbia), Guayaquil (Ecuador), Talara and Lima (Peru), and Santiago (Chile). His mission was to bound from the plane at each stop, cry "Merry Christmas!" in Spanish to the children gathered at the airport, distribute toys, and explain, also in Spanish, that he was traveling by plane because his reindeer were at home getting ready for the North American Christmas.

It was easy, except for a few hitches. There were plenty of children at every airport, hundreds in fact. But what Macy's had overlooked is that Santa Claus does not exist in Spanish-speaking countries, which celebrate Christmas quite differently; and that, although there is a Spanish word for reindeer, it is as unfamiliar to Latin-American children as a "Tibetan yak" is to North American children. Mr. Sullivan, sweating in his hot Santa Claus costume and beard, was reduced to greeting the kids at each stop by shouting, "¿Cómo se han portado?" which amounts to a fairly formal inquiry, "How are you enjoying yourselves?" He gave up entirely any idea of explaining about the reindeer.

But children are wonderful. They knew right away that this grotesque figure in a red suit and white beard meant well, and somehow signified a festivity. Besides, they could hardly ignore his bag of toys. Soon, some intelligent child called out "Papa Noël!" and Sullivan remained "Papa Noël" for the rest of the tour.

In Guayaquil, one little boy was so fascinated by Papa Noël's big silver belt buckle that he crept behind him and slit his belt with a sharp knife. Papa Noël finished that distribution of gifts with one hand, while he held up his pants with the other. Sullivan's command of Spanish faltered then, and he will never forget the Guayaquil emcee who saved the day by smoothly addressing the crowd over the loud-speaker.

"And now," this blessed emcee announced, "as a special treat, Papa Noël will say a few words to you all in *English!*"

Mr. Sullivan remembers the trip with pleasure and a

certain amount of philosophy. "Maybe my mistakes were as valuable as my successes," he says now. "Of course, the whole thing was a promotion stunt, a tie-up with Macy's and Panagra Airlines, everybody knows that. But you know something? When I saw those kids I didn't *feel* like part of a publicity campaign, I damn near felt like Santa Claus! Probably that's why I nearly lost my pants and did lose my Spanish. But I can't think that those things are important. The important thing was goodwill, and goodwill was simply oozing out of all of us.

"After all," says Mr. Sullivan, smiling, "no South American people can watch Santa Claus make a fool of himself without feeling a little affection for the old boy, and the country he came from."

11

The Well-Adjusted Customer

★

O<small>N A HOT JULY DAY</small> last summer a customer entered
Macy's basement on a business errand. She wished to
return a paper of pins she had bought there in 1927. No,
there was nothing the matter with the pins, she said, it was
simply that her eyesight was not as good as it had been and
she was obliged to give up most of the dressmaking and fine
sewing she had been accustomed to do thirty years earlier.
Therefore, she obviously did not need the pins, and she
would please like to have back the nine cents she had paid
for them. The startled clerk consulted Leo Adams, management executive of the basement, and Macy's took back the
pins and graciously refunded the lady's nine cents.

Incredible as this little episode seems to the layman,
nothing about it really surprised Macy's. Things like that
happen often. In 1946 a customer mailed in a credit voucher
for eleven cents, dated 1922, with a note inquiring whether
this sum had accrued any interest in the twenty-four years
between. Macy's replied, Sorry, no accrued interest, but sent
her eleven cents in stamps. In 1952 a humorous gentleman
in Wisconsin mailed back *his* credit voucher for twenty

cents, dated 1921, with a letter saying that he had observed Macy's notice on the face of the voucher to the effect that it was acceptable for credit or merchandise in exchange. "I thought perhaps we might be able to compromise," the sprightly fellow continued, "by my accepting merchandise instead. So, if agreeable to you, you may send me parcel post one suit of clothes, three neckties, one pair of drawers, and one pair of sox, any size." Macy's, deadpan, thanked him for his suggestion and refunded his twenty cents, in stamps.

Sometimes the system works in reverse. Eight years ago the store received a letter from a Brooklyn woman admitting that, twenty years earlier, she had bought six pairs of stockings at seventy-six or eighty-one cents a pair at a Macy sale, and had been charged for only three pairs. She did not report the mistake at the time, she said, because a friend had told her that, if she did, the clerk responsible for the error would surely be fired, and she didn't want to be the cause of anyone losing a job. However, her conscience had bothered her for twenty years, so would Macy's (she concluded) "be kind enough to let me know how I can pay what I owe, and take a load off my mind." Miss Lillian Beyer, associate manager of Adjustment Service, replied that the records for the transaction were long closed and that the lady need not pay anything further, and must not worry unduly about Macy clerks being fired. "We, at Macy's," Miss Beyer's letter went on to say, "readily recognize the margin for error which exists in any large, human operation. I do not wish to convey the impression that we condone a clerical error, but I do want you to know that the clerk is given every opportunity to explain and correct the error whenever possible."

Macy's Adjustment Service has been handsomely stream-lined since the days when it was called "The Complaint Department" and when Charlotte Smith, sitting on her high stool behind a railing, almost single-handedly took on any and all complainers. Nowadays, a customer who goes to the store in person to return an article for credit, refund, or exchange, takes it straight to the department where she bought it. There, a supervisor handles the matter on the spot. If there is any complication, a quick telephone call to Adjustment Service on the fourteenth floor generally straightens it out. Some departments have their own small adjustment desks on the premises, but these, like all other details of the adjustment system, are controlled from the fourteenth floor headquarters, whose motto is: DON'T LOSE A CUSTOMER, MAKE A FRIEND.

Macy's has been known to refund cash for a pair of shoes obviously worn for months rather than antagonize a customer. However, neither the store nor its Adjustment Service is softheaded about the thing. While legitimate beefs, and some not so legitimate, are promptly honored, Macy's knows that there exists a type of woman who apparently has nothing else to do in life but take back to the store the merchandise she bought there yesterday. These "old offenders" at complaining are as well known to Macy's as are the "old offenders" at shoplifting. The staff calls them "bad complainers" and, after a reasonable length of time, quietly enters their names on a certain private black list . . . not a long list, but a lethal one. After that, although the service is courteous as always, it is cooler, and Mrs. Bad Complainer finds that she has somehow lost the ever-ready shoulder that was hers to weep on, the listening ear so patiently tuned in to her troubles. Puzzled and saddened, she generally mends her ways and is received back into the fold as unobtrusively as she was banished.

Complaints and adjustments by telephone or letter are handled on the fourteenth floor, where the main switchboard and the mail room are located. These departments also handle telephoned or written orders for merchandise, since "adjustments," though often colorful, constitute a very small part of Macy's business compared to the orders that pour in daily. The switchboard is called "the order board" because its principal activity is taking orders directly from customers who call in. If you, the customer, see an ad in the morning paper for something you want at Macy's, and you call Lackawanna 4-6000 to order it, you are connected with an operator who is sitting at a long double switchboard in a long line of other operators. Directly in front of this operator is an upright rod with a light that flashes green when she is talking, and in turn lights up a number on a huge indicator, something like a scoreboard, at the end of the room. The purpose of the indicator is to show how many customers are calling in at any given moment, and—at *any* given moment—it is lit up like a Hollywood première. Also in front of the operator are mimeographed copies of all the store's newspaper ads for the day, a stack of order-slips, and a conveyor belt.

You, the customer, say, for example, "I'd like to order that Acrilan blanket for twelve ninety-five that you advertise in the *Times* this morning."

The operator flips her mimeographed pages to "B" for Blanket, notes down on her order-slip the department number and other vital statistics, plus your personal order with name, address, manner of payment (C.O.D., D.A., or C.T.), specified quantity, color, and size, and drops the order-slip into the conveyor belt. The conveyor belt delivers it to a bin from where it is channeled to the correct department. In that way the transaction is completed by customer and operator alone, without any tiresome switching around. In cases where the customer wants extra, or special, information, the operator may plug in a salesclerk in the designated department and clerk, customer, and operator can have a cosy three-way chat, if everybody's time permits.

The order board needs to be omniscient about more things than just the store's daily newspaper ads. One of the less endearing traits of the Great American Customer is that she invariably wants her fur coat out of storage *immediately* on the first cool day of autumn, and wants electric fans or an air-conditioning unit delivered *immediately* on the first warm day of summer. Adjustment Service keeps in close touch with the weather bureau so that its order board may be more or less prepared for these urgent demands, and not swamped at any time by the seasonal avalanche. Operators are also briefed on forthcoming Macy sales to enable them to suggest further items to customers after the original order is taken. Each girl gets a 2 per cent commission on all sales made in this way, and a bonus of stockings, lingerie, or $10 worth of groceries if she makes a special sale such as $25 worth of ham sold over the telephone around Easter time.

It is no coincidence that Macy's telephone-order and mail-order departments are grouped together, on the fourteenth floor, with its "complaint" and "adjustment" system. Without orders, there would be no complaints, and vice versa. Or, as the poet once remarked:

Hope is unto doom a brother,
Neither lives without the other

and Macy's order board receives and relays complaints as calmly and as swiftly as it executes orders—except that if the customer gets excited or unpleasant, a supervisor usually plugs in and takes over the call. Complaints generally fall into one of the following categories: nondelivery, claims credit (wrong sales tax or wrong addition), wrong merchandise, merchandise damaged in delivery, unsatisfactory quality (a dress shrank, or the seams split after wearing), shortage (customer ordered a dozen, received only eleven), or service (Macy's man was supposed to come and measure for slip covers, hasn't showed up). The operator writes down the details and sends the complaint-slip to the proper department via conveyor belt and appropriate bin. To the customer she says (if, say, the complaint is one of nondelivery), "You will either receive your merchandise or hear from Macy's within three days."

This promise is made good, for a couple of practical reasons above and beyond the store's everlasting desire to please the customers. First, Macy's naturally would rather give good service than have its service complained about; and it would rather not have its merchandise rejected or returned, either by the customer in person or by "pick-up" from the store itself, at the customer's request. It costs Macy's fifty-five cents to "pick up" an unsatisfactory article even as small as an ash tray, therefore the store sensibly prefers to get the transaction right the first time. Second, and perhaps more potent, is Macy's written "adjustment policy," a law as immutable as its 6 per cent policy and regularly distributed in mimeographed sheets to all the staff as a constant reminder.

> The future of our business depends upon customer satisfaction in all their relations with us (this policy memorandum reads, in part) . . . When a customer is dissatisfied with the performance of our merchandise, it is our policy to satisfy the customer. If we agree with her claim, we make the adjustment promptly. If we feel that the claim is unwarranted we can attempt to convince the customer of our position, but if we are unsuccessful, we will make an adjustment to her complete satisfaction. An adjustment may at times be made by a compromise allowance, provided this is satisfactory to the customer . . .
>
> We expend considerable money and effort to attract customers to Macy's. Acting on the assumption that most customers are honest, we would be shortsighted to incur the risk of offending a customer for a relatively small amount. Even if we are convinced that our position is right, if the customer does not agree and thinks otherwise, we are apt to lose her good-will and future patronage by refusing an adjustment.

How could any store, one wonders, go further in pampering Madame?

Adjustment Service reports monthly to the store's top executives its complaint statistics, not against last month's record, but against an established goal of perfection. When the number of complaints in a month is below the number considered permissible according to the established goal, Lillian Beyer and her colleagues of the adjustment department go around beaming for days. This is one corner of a big department store where a low score, as in golf, is the highest accolade.

Until about two years ago Macy's main switchboard, or order board, at Lackawanna 4-6000 handled all calls to and from the store's executive offices as well as all customer calls. To relieve the pressure, Macy's installed in an adjoining room a smaller switchboard with its own number, Oxford 5-4400. This PBX (private branch extension) switchboard now takes care of the calls concerning the more than six hundred executive extension lines in the Herald Square store alone. Its operators, like those at the order board, are chosen for their tact and patience as well as for their skill, and at least one of them has an added distinction. Operator 10, her fellow workers will tell you proudly, is Mrs. Italiano, the mother of Anne Bancroft, a successful young actress. Mrs. Italiano enjoys her work, and has no wish to quit Macy's just to loll around being an actress's mother.

In the mail room, a bright, many-windowed apartment along the hall, one hundred women channel incoming mail, both orders and complaints, to various departments at the rate of ten thousand pieces a day. Among these toilers are several unsung wits and balladeers who have the knack of answering a letter in the spirit in which it was written. Thus, if a customer writes a humorous complaint Macy's, through these gifted girls, replies in kind; if another customer is moved to address the store in verse, Macy's is able to respond in rhyme. Not all of Macy's spirited answers to its customers are written in the mail room. Sometimes a department manager or a stenographer or a vice-president gets an inspiration and composes a reply to some particularly striking communication from a customer. Sometimes nobody gets an inspiration, in which case the striking communication is sent to its proper department with the despairing penciled scrawl, "Have you got a genius in your outfit who can answer this?"

All customer letters are answered appropriately, and the correspondence files of Adjustment Service are as rewarding as those of the D.A. department. A lady in Hasbrouck Heights, New Jersey, sent Macy's this melancholy plaint:

> I think that I shall never see
> A bra that's fashioned just for me;
> I thought that I should order "C",
> Surveyed again, and ordered "B";
> "B" is too large, to my dismay,
> And yet *I* am too big for "A".
> Poems are made by fools like me;
> I guess my bras will have to be.
>
> The gist of this is just to say,
> Please come and take the bra away.

Macy's took thought, and replied to the customer, in verse slightly looser than her own:

> We read your poem and do agree
> You have a problem 'twixt A & B.
> Our heads went together, our minds were knit;
> The solution to your enigma is "custom fit".
>
> So, to our shop on the second floor
> We suggest you come at least once more;
> You'll see our clerks and then the fitter,
> And after that, you *can't* be bitter.
>
>> Yours very truly,
>> MACY'S

Customer complaints are not always so good-natured. An indignant family living on a Jersey farm reported that Macy's driver never delivered their purchases to them directly but always left them at a house down the road. It turned out, on investigation, that the Jersey farm was a nudist colony and the driver, a family man himself, had had no orders from Macy's to strip before delivering his packages. Then, there was the outraged New York housewife who demanded:

For God's sake, while there are still some children alive in this city, get after the manufacturers to make underwear that is *wearable in the Winter*.

We do not live in the tropics.

Little girls are forced to go around absolutely naked to the navel because of a few crazy people who like to feast their eyes on bareness and nakedness.

I speak for thousands of mothers—*this is absolutely known to me as an unquestionable fact.*

Macy's replies to these wails are not on record. Generally, though, the tone of customer letters is one of humorous desperation. Shortly after the release of *Miracle on Thirty-fourth Street,* a movie whose action took place largely in Macy's, a gentleman on Long Island wrote to the store wistfully asking for yet another miracle, this time on behalf of the silver baby cup, a Macy item, presented to his son on the occasion of his birth nearly a year before.

We returned the cup to Macy's for initialing (this father wrote). The baby's initials were to go on the piece. But your craftsmen made it come out "X.Y.Z." or something. Of course, we could have changed our name and the baby's. But that would have brought about complications, such as having all the deeds to our home and other chattels changed to conform. So we sent the cup back with a request that the initials be rectified.

That was nearly a year ago. Since then there has been much correspondence, but no cup. About a month ago, we were informed that the vessel would be ready on June 4. We had a party to celebrate, and my wife insisted that I call in person for the cup. I might mention here that she swears by Macy's. Macy's is to her what Mecca is to the Moslem.

En route from my office to the train, I stepped blithely into your store bubbling with confidence and immediately ran into a run-around. The postcard we got from Macy's announced that the cup would be on the 6th floor. I found blankets there. The blanket man said "maybe in the monogram dept." I found that pillow slips and stuff were being monogrammed there. No silver. A young lady with freckles and a Brooklyn accent, plus a kind heart, took a look at the card. "That," she announced enthusiastically, "is the 9th floor."

After escalating some more, I was told the department I sought was removed to the ground floor the previous week. Back to the ground floor, and then to the balcony where a Romeo-less Juliet told me "This ain't our department. Whyncha try the 5th?"

I did, bleating "Heigh-ho, Silver." No success. By then it was train time and I had to flee.

Now, this whole business may be the fell work of a Gimbel gremlin. But why pick on my little boy? He wants his cup to drink from, but it looks as if he will get it in time to use for a shaving mug.

Macy's response to this gentle gripe was wholehearted. With the family's permission, the store ran a full-page newspaper ad headed:

HOW LITTLE —— —— —— FINALLY GOT HIS SILVER
CUP FROM MACY'S—WITH THE RIGHT INITIALS ON IT

The ad, recounting the father's sad tale, was illustrated with pictures of the baby playing with his dog, staring at a flower, and so on, and it concluded:

> Obviously, there was nothing left for us to do but deliver the cup in person, on a silken pillow, with our most abject apologies. We took along a photographer just in case. As you can see, we got pictures of the Baby and the Tulip, the Baby and the Pup, the Baby and the Macy Stroller, but no Baby and the Cup.
>
> He didn't like it. He fwowed it in the rosebushes.

The complaint with the friendly approach, tinged with sorrow, is naturally more successful with Macy's than the angry explosion—although the store dutifully takes care of both. One woman wrote simply:

> I bought my television set at Macy's because I knew it was a store I could trust for quality and rely on for service. At the time, I signed the usual contract with the television repair service recommended by Macy's. This television repair man has now failed to show up for three appointments in succession, and my feeling is not one of anger, but one of sadness that Macy's has finally let me down.

The television repair man was at her apartment less than an hour after the letter was delivered to Macy's.

The Korean War interfered for a time with a Macy refund to a dissatisfied customer. In 1953, Melbourne G. Slade Junior, a captain in the United States Army, wrote to Macy's from Fort Bragg, North Carolina:

Gentlemen:

Enclosed is a check for the amount of $1.61 that was drawn against your account with the Chase National Bank of the City of New York, and made out in favor of Mrs. ——, Shanghai, China.

There is a bit of a story behind my coming into possession of the draft:

I was in Korea during the initial days of the conflict and had the good fortune to be one of those who got very near the Yalu River prior to the intervention of the Chinese Communist Forces, commonly known as the Chinese Peoples Army. I was with the 1st Cavalry Division, the first UN Force to enter the capital of North Korea, Pyongyang.

It was at Pyongyang that I found this check. I found it in the basement of a Presbyterian School. The building had been badly damaged by gunfire and the basement was flooded by several broken water mains. While searching out the building for hidden enemy and booby traps I happened upon the basement which was littered with what apparently was several bags of mail that had been stolen in Seoul, South Korea, and removed to North Korea. The bags of mail were recovered and turned over to the proper military authorities. However a few days later when the water had receded in the basement, I found a letter that had come apart due to the soaking in the water: it still contained the check.

I dried out the check and had in mind at the first opportunity to mail it to you. Well, due to the rapid change in events my attention was diverted to other tasks at hand, mainly fighting back at the Chinese

Communist Armies. In the course of events I was ro-
tated back to the States and had completely forgot
about the check which had been placed in an old
wallet that I was carrying at that time—until this
evening.

This evening I was watching television when Faye
Emerson came on, and interviewed a member of your
firm, the head of the complaint department. At the
mention of your store, I instantly remembered the
check, whereupon after the program I began searching
for my old wallet and for the check that you have found
enclosed herein.

I realize that I'm about three years late in forwarding
the check to you so that you may credit the rightful
owner.

Again I apologize for being so slow to perform my
intentions.

Sincerely,
Melbourne G. Slade, Jr.
Captain
Army United States

Macy's, much moved by this missive, wrote Captain Slade
its heartfelt thanks, adding, "This is the first time we have
ever made a refund with the aid of the United States Army,
and we are most appreciative of the trouble you have taken
to help us." The firm then wrote out a new check for a
dollar sixty-one and sent it, along with a copy of Captain
Slade's letter, to the lady customer who, it developed, was
by that time living in New York City. Her emotions upon
learning that a little thing like a battle against the Chinese
Communists had prevented Captain Slade from returning

her dollar sixty-one sooner are, unfortunately, not included in Macy's files.

Customer letters are often rather long, the patron apparently being moved to pour out his heart to Macy's, but occasionally one comes along which is terse and to the point, like this bulletin from a book-purchaser:

> Dear Macy's,
>
> On November 27 I paid $1.24 for a book called *Crime File #1*, and ordered it sent to the above address.
>
> Saturday your driver delivered a copy of the Holy Bible—price $2.34.
>
> I am deeply touched by the missionary spirit which prompted a clerk to make such a substitution. On the other hand I feel I must tell you about it, for I am almost certain that Macy's would rather see me go to Hell for $1.24 than attain salvation without paying the $1.10 difference.

Other compelling "shorties" on file include letters from: The plaintive matron who wrote:

> As far as exchanges go, you are not as courteous as some other department stores. I returned a pantie (silk) that split at the seams. One of your Section Managers, a (lady?) asked me to try them on and bend over, as she doubted my word about the size. Do you think this is a proper way to treat an honest customer?

The young mother whose note enclosed the printed announcement of her daughter's recent birth containing the arch words, "Mommy bought her at Macy's on Monday, February 20, 1939, at 4:02 A.M.," and went on to suggest,

AND THE PRICE IS RIGHT

"Any compensation that I may receive, you may rest assured, will be fully appreciated." (Thanks for the ad, but no compensation, was Macy's reply.)

The unmarried lady who confessed:

> As this is too embarrassing to buy verbally, I am writing to you. I would like a chair too large for one and too small for two.

The rural dweller who wrote:

> It is the desire to obtain these butiful radio which she is picktured as per like the newspipper ad it is the honor to send by me. the low Macy price *what it is please* to send per the train for milk.
>
> Can the oil burner by the Honeewell regilator be affiliated so as to *remote control of the radio from the privy.*

(Macy's treasures this letter as a perfect example of the marriage of the machine age and the primitive life.)

The New England customer, wearied by nondelivery of a lamp base, who wrote:

> I should like the above mentioned lamp base sent to me at the above address, provided your Salesman Number One can identify it and send me the one I ordered. If this is impossible, perhaps you can ship me your Salesman Number One and I can use *him* for a lamp base . . . He ought to be a better lamp base than he was a salesman.

Macy's answered:

> Having examined our Number One salesman with great care and from all angles, we have decided not to

ship him to you for use as a lamp base, as we believe
he makes a better salesman than a lamp base.

We have decided, after a good mull over the matter,
to send you a duplicate lamp base. The original one
was sent out on January 27th, parcel post. If it finally
reaches you, we would appreciate having it returned to
us, as we are a little short of salesmen now, and might
have to use it in a pinch.

The harried mother and dog-owner who complained,
more in bewilderment than anger:

I purchased two boxes of dog biscuits @ .27 for Judy, the book *Citadel* for Elizabeth, a pair of woollen gloves for Mac, a box of books named, I believe, *Nursery Jingles* for Barbara, a box of four books containing *Red Riding Hood, The Three Pigs,* etc. for Mary Lou, and a large box of tea napkins for $1.00.

Instead, you shipped me an ironing board and some mops with handles.

(Macy's agreed that the children in particular would be disappointed "unless mops were fairy wands," and promised to rectify the order, which had been confused with that of another customer of the same name.)

The highly amused patron who availed herself of a typographical error in a Macy ad which caused it to read:

IT'S A SELLOUT OF MACY'S LUXURY FUR COATS AND SCARVES
$179
Macy's Usual Prices Would Be $2.19 to $2.77

She would like a natural platina fox jacket and a four-skin natural baum marten scarf, this lady hilariously wrote, "not at the sale price of $179, but at the usual prices as listed of either $2.19 or $2.77."

Macy's replied:

We wish to congratulate you on your perspicacity as a shopper in *not* taking advantage of the dramatic values offered in our advertisement of furs. We can readily understand your reluctance to make your selection until these furs are being sold for $2.19 and $2.77 ... but we would earnestly advise you against waiting so long.

The world traveler who wrote "a serious complaint" to the store because a pair of five-dollar Macy shoes she had bought for her husband thirteen years earlier had traveled 300,000 miles through Europe, Africa, Australia, and New Zealand without showing any signs of wearing out, and she was "sick and tired of packing, unpacking, and repacking them." This communication led to another full-page Macy newspaper ad, with pictures of the couple (shoe-wearer and shoe-packer) snapped in various parts of the globe.

A lengthier lament came from a Manhattan bridegroom of one year, who wrote, in part:

> Gentlemen:
>
> It is now almost a year since the very charming Miss Adelaide Neuburger became my wife—a year replete with the first awakening and full flowering of marital bliss—a year of the subtle blending of two distinct personalities into one harmonious partnership—a year of happiness, inspiration, and joy.
>
> I am happy to say that the adjustments which generally make the first year of marriage difficult have, for the most part, been successfully achieved. The two principals, their fond parents, their relatives and friends, her disappointed suitors, and his scorned women all presented certain difficult problems but, intricate as they were, the problems have now been solved.
>
> Only Macy's remains unreconciled . . . It wasn't that we failed to observe the courtesies. The formal announcements were duly mailed to relatives, friends, and business acquaintances, of course. Naturally, however, special announcements went to those arbiters of the

modern world, the Post Office Department, the Income Tax Bureau, and Macy's.

The Post Office graciously responded by forwarding our mail to our new address. The Income Tax Bureau, not to be undone, came forward with the magnificent gift of $1500, expressed in the form of increased personal exemption. Only Macy's refuses to be convinced.

It isn't really that we expected a gift from you . . . But how many times have we written you, how many times have we told salespeople, section managers, and those super-efficient officials of the D.A. division that we really are married, that it's legal, and wonderful, and everything, and please believe us. Always they say politely that yes, they will believe us, but they never do anything about it.

"Yes, you are married now," they say, "and Miss Adelaide Neuburger, D.A. #217591, formerly at —— East —— Street, is now Mrs. Richard B. Leavy, same D.A. number, at —— East —— Street. Yes, we'll make a note of it."

Please, R. H., what do you do with all those notes you've taken? . . . You won't change the name, you won't change the address, and the most that you will concede is that Miss Adelaide Neuburger has become Mrs. Adelaide Neuburger.

Well, she isn't Mrs. Adelaide Neuburger any more than she is Mrs. R. H. Macy. . . . When Miss Adelaide Neuburger married me she became Mrs. Richard B. Leavy, and please get over your silly idea that she became Mrs. Adelaide Neuburger.

Then there's this business about the address. —— East —— Street is where my wife used to live before she married me and became Mrs. Richard B. Leavy. She lived with her mother then, and that was all right as long as she was single, but then when we married we decided we ought to have a home of our own. We don't believe that young marrieds should live with their in-laws if they can help it. My wife moved to our new home right after we were married, and believe me when I tell you that a young girl these days has plenty of things to be moved.

As far as you're concerned, all our efforts in moving have been in vain. You still have us living with our in-laws when, as a matter of fact, we have a very charming apartment of our own, small, but we think it's nice, at the address we keep trying to give you.

Now that our first anniversary is near, don't you think it would be gracious of you to . . . recognize our marriage?

Macy's recognized Mrs. Leavy's marriage, with fond hand-clasps all round, immediately on receipt of her husband's mild but arresting letter. But sometimes the *rapprochement* between customer and store wears thin, in spite of every-thing. A lady wrote in, asking advice about a permanent wave in Macy's beauty salon, and confessing that her hair was "very fine, and decidedly turning white." Through some mix-up in letters she received the following reply from Macy's:

Dear Madam:
    Since we have no facilities for making repairs of the type you requested we are not able, unfortunately, to help you in this instance.

Dear Sirs: *(the lady wrote back with some heat)*
There is a decided difference between *promptness* and *haste*. . . . Some other customer may have gotten the information that I requested.

Macy's was back at the old stand, exuding charm, when an angry matron wrote to say that she had bought some small pillows at the store and her son had found a dead mouse in one of them. If Macy's didn't believe her, she added, she was saving the mouse, and Macy's could send their man up to see it.

Shocked, Macy's nevertheless managed to reply winningly:

We learned with distress of your son's remarkable discovery. We have no professional mouse-inspector in the organization and would not want to send up an amateur to investigate so technical a problem. In fact, we confess quite frankly that the situation you report is new to us. We once had a request to quote our best price on dead horses, but we have had no experience with mice in a business way.

If you will bring this letter in to Mr. Golding, Superintendent of our 7th floor, he will be very glad to assist you in selecting a new, mouseless pillow to replace the old one.

It was then that Macy's learned that the borderline between lightheartedness and flippancy is indeed a delicate one, and that too much charm can irritate a customer. The mouse-holder indignantly returned Macy's letter with one of her own, saying:

So *this* is the answer I get! This is the reply I received which I think is certainly uncalled for, I think this is no reply to make, which I have purchase a good deal from you people and spoke very highly of. . . . And that's the answer I got!

This letter reached the rajahs on the thirteenth floor, who considered it justified, and they took steps to curb somewhat the literary flights of those who answered customer complaints. Letters should be friendly, even humorous, they stated in a memorandum to the Adjustment Service and allied authors, but they must never fail to deal with the problem clearly and succinctly, in a manner both comprehensible and satisfactory to the customer. As a further reminder, the Macy bosses distributed a kind of humorous letter of their own, in the form of mimeographed copies of this anecdote, clipped from a trade journal:

Some letter writers appear to agree with the oft-quoted statement of Samuel Johnson that "words were invented to conceal thought."

As an example, let's review the experience of the plumber who wrote to the National Bureau of Standards. He said he found that hydrochloric acid opens plugged pipes quickly, and asked whether it was a good thing for a plumber to use.

A scientist at the Bureau replied as follows:

"The uncertain reactive processes of hydrochloric acid place pipe in jeopardy when alkalinity is involved. The efficiency of the solution is indisputable, but the corrosive residue is incompatible with metallic permanence."

The plumber wrote back, thanking the Bureau for

telling him that this method was all right. The scientist was disturbed about the misunderstanding, and showed the correspondence to his boss—another scientist—who immediately wrote the plumber:

"Hydrochloric acid generates a toxic and noxious residue which will produce submuriate invalidating reactions. Consequently, some alternative procedure is preferable."

The plumber wrote back and said he agreed with the Bureau—hydrochloric acid works just fine. Greatly disturbed, the two scientists took their problem to the top boss. The next day the plumber received this telegram:

"Don't use hydrochloric acid. It eats hell out of the pipes."

Thereafter, Macy's replies to customer complaints were as friendly as ever, but simpler somehow.

The other day a Macy customer who had been complaining about nondelivery of a table happened to lunch with a friend who works at Macy's. She picked up her friend at the store and they walked past the delivery entrance on Thirty-fifth Street—properly known as "the entrance to the receiving platform" although it also channels outgoing merchandise. Loaded trucks were backing in and pulling out, and men in oxford-gray jackets with MACY'S in red letters on their caps were heaving heavy crates and packages around. The girls had to wait until the passage was clear enough for them to cross.

"What are they *doing*, cluttering up the sidewalk like this?" muttered the Macy customer, impatiently.

"Well, for one thing, they're getting your famous table to you that you made such a stinking fuss about," replied her friend, the Macy employee.

The other woman was silent until after they had crossed the passageway and were sitting over their blue-plate specials in a favorite Eighth Avenue beanery. "You know, I never thought of it that way," she said pensively, then. "I mean, about how packages and things are delivered. I guess I just thought that when you bought something and ordered it sent, somebody just pushed a button and, lo, the package appeared magically on your doorstep. What *does* happen, anyway?"

"You really want to know?" asked her friend. "Okay. It's fast and fairly simple. Your purchase is put into a paper bag, and then into an individual canvas bag with the sales check. The canvas bag is put into the SENT department and taken by hourly pick-up to the packing-center—there's one to a floor. In the packing-center the merchandise is wrapped, the part of the sales check with the address is affixed, and the other part kept as a record. The package is then sent to the sub-sub-basement by conveyor belt or hand-truck and delivered to the United Parcel division where a record is made of receipt. The package is then sorted into the proper address area, placed on a truck, and delivered. United Parcel measures and weighs each package and charges Macy's accordingly."

"My!" said the Macy customer admiringly, "With a system like that, you'd think I would have gotten my table long before this."

"Your table," replied her friend coldly, "was probably sent direct from Macy's Long Island warehouse, which has its own admirable system. Now that's enough shoptalk. You having dessert?"

Walking back from lunch and passing the busy trade-entrance again, the Macy employee shook her head. "The only sad thing, to me," she said, "is to think of all this work and effort going into the delivery of a package that some dizzy dame like yourself will no doubt return promptly the next morning because she's changed her mind, or something."

"Oh, well, that's the spirit of commerce, isn't it?" argued the Macy customer consolingly. "Merchandise going out, and merchandise coming back in again . . . *I* think it's very stimulating."

On one historic occasion the mere act of going out and coming back in again proved to be almost impossible, only in this case it was a question of coming in and going back out again, and it involved, not merchandise, but a newly employed young salesman. Adjustment Service cherishes this anecdote, although it was in no way concerned, because it goes to show that Adjustment Service is not the only section of Macy's that can, at rare intervals, resemble the department of utter confusion.

Some years ago, and for various technical and disciplinary reasons, the store made a rule that no employee could enter or leave the premises unless he was wearing a hat. The new salesman, a young man who never wore a hat and didn't know about the rule, had quite a lot of trouble getting into the store on his first morning and, on being finally admitted, was warned that he must have a hat. He immediately procured an employee's shopping-card and bought a hat which he took, still in its paper bag, to the package-room on the balcony and checked, accepting a slip in receipt.

That evening, when he presented the slip for his package, the package-clerk eyed him with distrust.

> PACKAGE-CLERK: You can't get your package till you're ready to go home.
>
> NEW EMPLOYEE: But I *am* ready to go home.
>
> P.C.: Then get your hat.
>
> N.E.: That's what I'm here to get.
>
> P.C.: Look, friend. You have to have your hat on before you can get your package.
>
> N.E.: But that's my hat in the package.
>
> P.C.: Listen, chum. The rule *is,* you have to have a hat *on* before you can get any packages.

At this point somebody in the impatient line that had formed behind the hapless (and hatless) new employee suggested that he take his problem to the Protection Bureau. There, he was given a slip authorizing the release of the package. "However," Protection told him, "don't open your package in the corridor. Take it into the locker room and put your hat on there."

Clasping his package, the new employee hurried to the locker room. At the entrance to the locker room he encountered a guard.

> GUARD: Here, you can't take any packages into your locker.
>
> N.E.: I've got a slip signed by the Protection Bureau . . .
>
> GUARD: I don't care what kind of a slip you've got, you can't go in there with any packages.
>
> N.E. (*desperately*): Is there any known way of getting out of this building?

GUARD (*relenting*): Okay, I'll tell you what I'll do. I'll hold your package while you go in and get your hat.

It is said around the store that this new employee, as he became an old employee, developed a sort of hat-fetish which caused him to fall into a state of nerves whenever he was without his hat. Ironically, by the time he had acquired this attachment, Macy's had decided that the hat rule was too much trouble for everybody, and abolished it.

12

Moon Over Macy's

★

Rowland macy, who always liked to flabbergast the customers, would have enjoyed the gesture his store made one spring day five years ago. With no advance publicity and with every element of lovely surprise, Macy's opened its doors on a Monday morning in May to reveal an entire ground floor that had, apparently overnight, burst into fragrant blossom. Hydrangeas, blue and lilac-tinted, azaleas, rhododendron, tulips of every color, cherry-blossoms, morning-glories, and roses crowned the partitions between counters and garlanded the walls and pillars; rock gardens with little pools and fountains sparkled in the aisles; flower-laden arbors and trellises filled every corner, and carnations, camellias, and lilies of the valley scented the astonished air. This was the first of Macy's famous flower shows, which have since become an annual spring event, opening on the Monday before Mother's Day and lasting throughout the week.

The flower show originated with Macy's California, in its San Francisco store when Wheelock H. Bingham (now president of the R. H. Macy Corporation) was its president.

Mr. Bingham brought the idea East with him when he became president of Macy's New York in 1952, and the show's impact on the citizens of New York was sensational. Around luncheon tables at "21" and the Stork Club the topic buzzed steadily: "My dear, have you seen *Macy's* this week? . . . Well, get *down* there right away!" Macy's archrival, Gimbel's, was so overcome with admiration that it ran a newspaper ad which was headed:

DOES GIMBEL'S TELL MACY'S?
NO, GIMBEL'S TELLS THE WORLD!

and continued breathlessly:

> . . . Gimbel's is telling the world (that remote corner of the world which hasn't heard) that the most glorious department store flower show in all the world is happening in miracle-crazy 34th Street at Macy's (just a block from Gimbel's doors). *Nobody, but nobody,* sold Gimbel's these raves . . . At the stroke of 9:45 Monday, Gimbel's' big brass marched to Macy's with confident competitive step. Have we seen Gimbel's' big wheels since? Not on your life. Our Mr. E. was reported up to his neck in anemones, our Mr. M. was swooping low over a spray of lily-of-the-valley, our Miss F. was languishing in the hydrangeas. Even our great Mr. G. himself was transfigured in the tuberous begonias. Gimbel's tells Macy's that Macy's flower show is the greatest miracle to hit 34th Street since 34th Street and miracles (and Gimbel's and Macy's) were invented. Gimbel's tells New York that the competitive spirit (for the moment) can go hang. Gimbel's tells the world that it's

just plain silly if it doesn't get to Macy's for the greatest
flower show 34th Street has ever known!

(signed) GIMBEL'S.

The flower show is directed by John R. Foley, Macy's display manager, a smiling man surrounded by sketches and
models of contraptions designed to dazzle the customers five
or six months from now. (On the most stifling day of last
July, Mr. Foley's twelfth-floor offices were filled with the
hot scarlet and gold of Christmas angels and other Yuletide
decorations.) Every winter, around February, Mr. Foley flies
to San Francisco to consult with Mr. Ed Goeppner, the head
of Podesta & Baldocchi, florists, on the design and arrangement of the spring flower show. Between them, Foley and
the florists decide on the most feasible plants to use, and
make a few test shipments by air to see which flowers best
weather the transportation. Comparatively few of the flowers come from California, however, since Foley (an East-
erner) has discovered that nearly all of the plants he requires
can be found in nurseries in Connecticut, New Jersey, and
New York State.

Once chosen, the flowers, plants, and shrubs are shipped
from all points with their roots covered in burlap, arriving
at Macy's on the Saturday before the Monday opening, and
are then placed about the ground floor in pans of water
only three inches deep. This is sufficient, because a special
crew of workmen waters them nightly and picks off any dead
leaves or blossoms. Most of the flowers last throughout the
show, but the window displays and outside decorations must
generally be replaced once during the week on account of
the sun and heat.

Seven o'clock on the Saturday evening before the show is

a time of high excitement around Macy's. Ninety trucks bring the flowers from nurseries and from the airport, and the New York Police Department works along with Macy's Protection Bureau to clear the streets for the trucks' arrival and unloading. A crew of about a hundred and ten people then toils at arranging the flowers from 7 P.M. Saturday until 1 or 2 A.M. Sunday, pauses for a nap and a bite of food, and returns to work again until five o'clock Sunday afternoon. This crew includes fourteen men flown from California by Podesta & Baldocchi, numerous local florists and nurserymen, Macy's own display artists, Macy carpenters, electricians, plumbers, machinists, and porters, and—last year—sixteen students from the School of Horticulture at Rutgers University. The Rutgers boys got paid for the job, but undertook it more in the spirit of learning than earning. Macy's, too, approaches the whole event on a high plane of thought, although aware that it is worth millions in publicity value.

Mother Nature, that ornery dame, does not always collaborate sweetly concerning Mother's Day. Weather can be freakish, a season too retarded or too far advanced. On that account Mr. Foley, for all his careful planning, never knows precisely what color his flowers will be until they arrive. Sometimes another color has bloomed better than the one he selected, and in that case the entire decor must be rearranged at the last moment. Last year, Macy's imported 480 white birch trees, all of which collapsed on arrival because the season was so far ahead of itself. A local nursery had to rush out and cut another 480 white birches in a big hurry.

Azaleas and rhododendron, being hardy, are generally used as the basis of the show, and some huge azalea plants are indeed so tough that they have weathered several seasons of display at Macy's, being kept in cold storage in between. The strong and colorful tulip is another blessing, and Macy's has flown as many as twenty thousand cut tulips from Holland, timed to arrive at La Guardia Airport on the Friday morning before the show. After being cleared at Customs for insects, they are put into deep cold water at a florist shop on Twenty-eighth Street until Sunday, when they are brought into the store and, as Mr. Foley puts it, "arranged for their debut on Monday morning." Mr. Foley often talks about his flowers like that, as though they were lovely young girls being presented to society. "Well, they *are!*" he says with some heat, when accused of this fondness.

Exotic blooms such as orchids are flown from Hawaii for the show, and camellias from the South for Macy's famous camellia hedge. Camellias and tuberous begonias are so fragile that their blossoms frequently fall, or are bruised, during shipment, but Macy's solves that problem with ease. Fresh sprays of camellia-blossoms and begonia-blossoms arrive by air daily during the show, and are neatly tied on to hedge and plant to replace their fallen sisters. Mr. Foley's one regret is that the California viola, a flower he dearly loves, is too delicate to be shipped at all.

The flower show is only one facet of the job that occupies Mr. Foley, who has been at Macy's twenty-five years. As display manager, he is also responsible for the design and decoration of the store's forty-five display windows. A flower-lover by nature, he has come to revere flowers professionally for the elegance and beauty they add to a furniture show, for example, or a window display. Last year, along with the flower show, six of Macy's windows presented tableaux posed by mannequins in richly-flowered settings and depicting "The Flowers in Your Life." The tableaux ranged from "The Memory of Your First Gardenia" and "The Excitement of Your First Orchid" through "Your Joy When Daisies Gave Their Answer True," "Your Wedding Day," "The Sweet Sentiment of Your Mother's Day Bouquet," and "The Delight of Your Birthday Bouquet," the last one showing a charming silver-haired lady receiving a posy from her grandchildren.

"This Is Your Life," pensively murmured an acquaintance of Mr. Foley's, surveying the long row of floral highlights. "I'm glad you left out the funeral."

"We discussed it," replied Mr. Foley, calmly. "At one point I thought we might have a seventh window and just leave it empty, except for a big placard reading: PLEASE OMIT."

The scented purlieus of Macy's-in-the-Spring encourage romantic thoughts, but springtime is not the only season that finds romance afoot in Macy's. All year round, the men and women, and boys and girls, who work in the store meet, fall in love, and get married. In many cases both continue to work at Macy's, and often their children come to work there, too.

"I first met my wife when I noticed that she was doing a lot of errands in my section that she didn't strictly *have* to do," says Dennis Mulhearn of Delivery and Trim-Waste. (Trim-Waste is the department which, among other duties, puts signs on the paper-towel rollers reading: One Dries Nicely, Why Use Twicely?) "I was a service man in groceries then, and she was a clerk at the superintendent's desk on the same floor. We got married on a Saturday and went dancing at the Astor that night, and Vincent Lopez had his orchestra do a big fanfare and announced, 'We have with us a brand-new bride and groom from Macy's!' Somebody must have tipped him off, not me. Then he played *our* song, 'Stardust,' and he gave us a little piano for a wedding present, which we still have. We still kiss each other whenever we hear 'Stardust,' too," says Mr. Mulhearn. "It was a great evening, and a great weekend. We were both," he adds with a sigh, "back at work Monday morning."

The rigors of life sometimes affect a marriage as much as the exigencies of work. Fred Acito of the receiving department married Wynn Bartley, an operating supervisor, in 1941, a couple of days after he had received his induction notice into the United States Navy. "I didn't tell her till after the honeymoon," says Mr. Acito, looking back on it, "and she took it well. After all, we were married on May 16, and I didn't have to report till June 9, so that gave us over three weeks together. In those days, three whole weeks together was so much velvet." Mrs. Acito kept on working at Macy's until her husband was sent to the Navy Training School at Memphis, where she joined him as a Navy wife. She has not returned to the store, being busy at home nowadays with their four children.

"My husband sent me twenty-five gifts in eight hours, from all over the store, the day after I told him we were going to have a baby," relates the former Florence Krage, now Mrs. Paul Cole, speaking for the distaff side. As Miss Krage, Mrs. Cole was a junior executive in Curtains, and also won a staff beauty contest which established her as "Miss Macy's." She has been married eighteen years to Mr. Cole, a seventh-floor service manager who is now a vice-president of Macy's Kansas City store. The son whose birth was heralded by the flood of gifts often comes to New

York, and always pays a call on his parents' old friends at Macy's. "I'm a-goin' daown-east to visit the old cross-roads emporium and sundry-shop," is how he puts it, on leaving Kansas City.

"I lost a bet on the World Series and won my husband," says Grace Pitta, a supervisor in Handbags. "Tony worked in the kitchen furniture department, and for some reason, I can't think why, I never wanted to go out with him when he asked me. Everybody used to tease me about it, and try to get me to date him. They even plotted to bring us together. When one of the boys in Department 116 was sick in the hospital the other employees chipped in to buy him a gift, and decided that Tony and I were the ones to take it to him, so they fixed it with the supervisor to give us the same day off. I couldn't refuse, and that's when we made the bet on the World Series—if I lost, I had to date Tony again. . . . We've been married ten years and have a lovely four-year-old daughter, and I honestly don't know what I was fighting against all that time!"

Supervisors and co-workers may plot away, but Macy's real matchmakers are the elevator men. Hardly anything escapes an elevator operator, even in his limited travels, and the lift men at Macy's love to give Cupid a slight shove in the right direction. Their methods are swift, sure, and unobtrusive, a beautiful thing to see. An operator will gently bar an anxious-looking young man from alighting at the sixth floor while he breathes in his ear, "Uh-uh. She got off on the eighth." Or he will say to another, "You know that new girl you were talking to in the car yesterday? I hear she's been transferred to Better Millinery on the second."

This gossamer filament of romance, wielded so deftly in the hands of the elevator men, binds maidens and swains

together throughout the store as surely as the magic thread bound Theseus to Ariadne in the Labyrinth.

"My wife and I fell in love in Department 129, in 1941 when I was a stock clerk and she was a saleswoman," says Joseph Petruzzelli, "and do you know, we were considered to be excellent workers until this occurred. After that, we both went around in a daze until finally Miss Dooner, our boss, called us into her office and told us we'd better get on the ball. We figured the best way to pull ourselves together was to get married, so we did. Now, my wife is a service manager, I am in the rug department, we live on Staten Island, and we have two daughters. Marriage is a great thing, and good for your business career, too."

"I was a Blue Flower at the adjustment desk in the stationery department," Helen Strapka recalls, "and Herman Wacker was an executive in the department. We danced together at a few Macy parties, and then we planned our vacation together and Herman took me to visit his parents in Lincoln, Nebraska. We were married there, and our vacation became a honeymoon. Herman left Macy's in 1954 to work for a plastics concern," Mrs. Wacker adds, "but I'm still at the store, at the adjustment desk in the men's department."

"I met Agnes in the umbrella department on a very rainy day," says Chester Clolery, assistant buyer of umbrellas. "She was a saleswoman there and Mr. Palmer, the buyer, sent me down to show her how to operate folding umbrellas. Well, I folded and unfolded one for her, and then I held it over us, right there in the store, and I looked at her and said, 'You are going to marry me.' She thought I was crazy, but she married me all right, seven months later."

"One wonderful spring day," Bill Dugan remembers, "an attractive young lady was browsing through the Oriental rug department, where I was a salesman. I asked if I could assist her, and the result is that I am now assisting her through life. She was Dorothy Van Beurden, in charge of the lending library that Macy's then operated in the book department. Naturally, I did a good deal of return browsing among the books during my lunch hour, and then she let me take her out for an evening of dinner and dancing, and finally she said 'yes.' All I can say is, God bless Macy's."

Once, Cupid's busy little bow shot an arrow right out of Macy's and halfway down the block, where it scored a direct hit upon Harold Young at his sidewalk newsstand. On a morning in 1929, a young woman emerged from a Macy entrance and asked the doorman where she could buy a pair of eyeglasses for her eighty-four-year-old grandmother. For some reason she had not been able to find what she wanted in Macy's. The doorman shook his head, and referred her to Harold, whose newsstand was nearby. Harold, having been at this stand since 1906, is a pretty complete authority on everything that goes on in Thirty-fourth Street between Seventh Avenue and Herald Square. Hearing the young lady's dilemma, Harold took her down the block to an oculist friend, and on the way she introduced herself as Lucienne Schamberschère, an employee of the New York Telephone Company. The oculist, on the strength of Harold's introduction, let her take six pairs of eyeglasses for her grandmother to choose from.

Miss Schamberschère was so impressed by these courtesies that, when she returned the extra eyeglasses, she stopped at Harold's stand to thank him once more. "That was the beginning of our romance," says Harold. "We were married the same year."

Mrs. Young went to work at Macy's in 1941, and is still happily employed there. "She is a member of the third-floor contingent, that's something like the Flying Squad," her husband explains, "and she does fine sewing in different departments."

The Youngs' working hours conflict in the mornings. Harold has to be at his newsstand between 6:45 and 7:45 for the early editions, and his wife doesn't come to work until nine o'clock. "But we haven't missed a night going home to St. Albans together in twenty-nine years," says Harold, firmly.

Tradition is as active as romance at Macy's, and many of the store's employees have children, and even grandchildren, who work there too, in some cases all at the same time. A few of them are:

Mary Ruggiero of the Tea Room, her son Jerry of the Photo Studio, and Jerry's daughter, Carol, of the chief cashier's office.

Anthony Guarino of the tenth-floor receiving department, his son, Anthony Junior, a junior assistant, daughter Rosalie of third-floor receiving, and daughter Gloria of the controller's office.

Joseph McPherson, sub-sub-basement machinist, son Mike of Corporate Control, and daughter Mary of the second-floor Flying Squad.

Bernard Kean of Little Shop of Shoes, and son Howard, of Small Leather Goods.

William Neville of escalator maintenance, and daughter Mary, of personnel.

Mary Turner, cook for executive dining room, and daughter Elaine who sells Candies.

Catherine Murray of Sales Audit and her daughter, Barbara Coons, of the D.A. department.

Joseph Sabatini, superintendent of men's wear alterations, and son Joseph Ralph of the grocery department.

Alex La Joie of Screen Doors and Windows, and his son Ray, assistant divisional superintendent of the seventh floor.

Harry Friedman of Rug Sales and son Max, manager of Shop at Home.

There are many others, at Macy's Herald Square, at the Long Island warehouse, and at the branch stores; there are sisters, brothers, and cousins all working for Macy's, as well as mothers and fathers and their children. But one thing comes clear:

In almost every case, the children hold a better job than their parents.

And that is exactly the way the parents want it to be.

"Romance?" said Dorothy Cavanaugh, manager of Macy's Brides' Shop, the other day. "Well, we're in favor of it, as you can see. Just take a look around."

Mrs. Cavanaugh was right. Soft music wafted through the Brides' Shop, and the backs of the pink-upholstered chairs along the wall were molded in the shape of pink-upholstered hearts. The air was hushed, and full of tulle and lace and white satin, with a whisper of lily of the valley . . .

Suddenly there was a shriek from a messenger-girl who had lifted the curtain of a fitting-room and started to enter. The messenger-girl fell back, and was caught by a saleswoman.

"I wouldn't go in there just now," the saleswoman told her kindly. "A bride has fainted."

The lifted curtain had revealed a limp figure supported by two chairs—her head on one chair, feet on the other. Her face was turned away, her arms hung awkwardly, and her bridal finery trailed dismally on the floor.

"It's just a show-window dummy we're dismantling," said Mrs. Cavanaugh, leading the way to her office. "But it does look lifelike, doesn't it? The girls have scared three or four people with it this morning—not customers, of course—and I figure they might as well have their fun, as long as it doesn't interfere with their work."

Mrs. Cavanaugh, a serious-looking woman whose face suddenly lights into laughter, is full of news about modern brides. For one thing, she says, girls have gotten over the notion that a wedding gown must be a dress that the bride can wear "later," as an evening gown or dance frock. There was a time, perhaps a result of the depression of the 1930's, when American womanhood, including brides and their mothers, decided that all dresses should be "practical," meaning usable on more than one occasion. This was the era when an office frock could be "dressed up" by the addition of a sequined bib and "dressed down" by its removal. No longer, at least not in the department of wedding dresses. A girl may only once in her life wear a white wedding dress, and brides and mothers—to Macy's vast approval —have finally come round to the romantic, and therefore proper, point of view that the bride's garments should, on this unique occasion, be equally unique.

"Besides, pity the poor bride," says Mrs. Cavanaugh. "Her wedding dress is the only thing she can actually *see* before the wedding. She can't see the ceremony, or the reception, or even the wedding cake—she can only visualize them. But her wedding gown is something she can see, and touch, and feel, for as long as she likes before the great event."

That is, Mrs. Cavanaugh piously adds, the bride can see and touch and feel the gown for as long as she likes beforehand according to the mercy of Providence and the parcel post. Macy's gets orders for wedding dresses and bridesmaids' gowns from all over the United States, as well as from Europe, South America, and other foreign lands, and although the store is careful to ship the merchandise well in advance, floods, hurricanes, and other acts of God sometimes prevent its prompt delivery. If a wedding outfit fails to arrive at the specified time, Macy's must duplicate the whole order on short notice and rush the duplicates by air express, or whatever speedy transportation is available. Occasionally even this gigantic effort is almost not enough.

One Connecticut bride ordered the wedding wardrobe— wedding dress and veil, shoes, bridesmaids' dresses and hats —to be delivered one month before the wedding date. Less than two weeks before the ceremony the bride's frantic mother telephoned Macy's that nothing had arrived. Macy's flew around duplicating bridesmaids' costumes and retinting shoes, and put in a hurry call to the manufacturer who had made the wedding gown and veil, who, as luck would would have it, was a California manufacturer. The California man cut and made a duplicate of the wedding outfit in twenty-four hours, and rushed it to Macy's via air mail. That was where the act of God intervened in this instance. Halfway to New York the plane carrying the wedding gown was forced down because of engine trouble, weather conditions, or whatever.

After anguished hours, Macy's Brides' Shop received a telephone call saying that the plane had finally arrived at La Guardia Airport, and that the wedding dress was intact and ready, if Macy's would pick it up. Macy's winged a special messenger by taxi to La Guardia, to get the precious package.

At Fifth Avenue and Thirty-fourth Street the taxi came to a halt, and could go no further. It was Columbus Day, and the Columbus Day Parade had merrily stopped all crosstown traffic.

The Connecticut bride got everything in good time, however, and so did another girl, in North Dakota, who received her order in what can only be called full measure. In this instance of unavoidable delay Macy's, as always, rushed duplicates of every item in plenty of time for the wedding. The duplicates arrived on the same day, and at the same hour, as the originals. The North Dakota bride was one bride who assuredly had two of everything.

"I wish I could keep all of these lovely things," wrote the bride's mother, returning one set to Macy's, "but, unfortunately, my second daughter is only four years old."

"P.S. Perhaps we ought to order the four-year-old's wedding dress *now*, at that," nastily added the bride's father, a naturally overwrought man at the time.

Customers of the Brides' Shop are practically never unpleasant about the rare, accidental delay, although they may become understandably edgy, and Mrs. Cavanaugh has an explanation for their serene acceptance of the facts. "We know how nervous a bride and her family must be, if a shipment is delayed," she says, "so we take care *never* to let them know, or even think, that we may be nervous about it too. Actually, we have never failed a wedding yet. So we are able, in the Brides' Shop, to remain calm, peaceful, and reassuring." At this point, Mrs. Cavanaugh leans back looking slightly breathless, and fans herself a little with her hand.

"This is a *happy* business to be in, on the whole," she goes on to say. "The Brides' Shop is one department where the customers are already happy when they get here. And it isn't really difficult for us to keep up the mood. Oh, we get a few complaints of course, usually from some bridesmaid who doesn't like the color of the dress the bride has chosen for her attendants, or the shape of the bridesmaids' hats, or something. But we just take the cross bridesmaid quietly aside and say, 'Look, on *your* wedding day you can have everything the way *you* want it. Right now, let's do it the way *this* bride wants it. Okay?' It always works."

Most Macy girls who get engaged buy their wedding gowns at the Brides' Shop, at the usual employees' discount. Without discount, a Macy wedding dress can cost as little as $49 or as much as $700 or $800 . . . the high-priced numbers generally being one-of-a-kind dreams in white panne velvet or satin, embroidered with seed pearls or tiny feathers, designed by Mrs. Cavanaugh and made in Macy's own workrooms. Last summer, some of the most expensive took on an "heirloom" look, with leg-o'-mutton sleeves and cape shoulders, so that any wedding guest might be excused for thinking that the bride's dress had been handed down from her great-grandmother.

Located cosily next-door to the Brides' Shop, yet not close enough to be blunt, is Macy's Maternity Shop, and from there, for the young married woman, it is all downhill and shady all the way. Throughout the store she can buy suits and socks and ties for her husband, guns and fishing rods, or slippers and pipes; she can clothe her children from infancy through their college years; she can buy everything for her home, from refrigerators and fireplaces to gadgets and sundries. (The difference between gadgets and sundries is that gadgets are contrivances or devices, and sundries are just miscellaneous articles.) She can, in fact, procure at Macy's everything that a family might possibly require, except a house and lot, and an automobile.

And, if she is of a reflective turn of mind, she may pause in the handsome chinaware department on the eighth floor and muse that this department, as a basement china-and-glass concession leased to L. Straus & Sons eighty-four years ago, was the tiny seed from which Macy's, the great department store, has grown.

Not long ago, a customer musing thus, but over a sweater for her daughter on the fourth floor, was astonished to hear a whirring sound and, on looking up, to behold a small parakeet perched on a dress-rack and cocking its little head at her. "You know the old saying about your 'thoughts taking wing'? For a mad moment I thought it had happened to *me*," the customer said, later.

"Oh, yes indeed," says Dorothy Bader, manager of the Pet Shop on the fourth, "quite often some child will open the door of a cage and the bird will get out and fly around the store for hours. Why, one time, a pair of lovebirds flew all the way down the stairs and right to the Brides' Shop on the third. Don't ask *me* why they went there! We don't worry about them, they can't do any harm and they always come back. Like all pets, they know where their food is."

Children love the Pet Shop, which specializes in birds and fish, and so do young lovers, who like to stand arm-in-arm and watch the lovebirds. Frequently, a young swain will adopt the charming practice of sending a pair of lovebirds to the lady of his heart. Miss Bader takes a personal interest in customers of all ages, and they often assail her with heart-rending problems. One woman rushed in with her parakeet in its cage in one hand and a handful of its tail-feathers in the other. In trying to catch the bird to put it back in the cage, she hysterically explained, she had accidentally grabbed it by the tail and all of the feathers came off in her hand. "Please, *please*, put them back on!" she begged. Miss Bader calmly assured her that a bird's feathers grow back in a fairly short time, just like a person's fingernails. Another customer arrived in tears, bearing a droopy-looking cockateel (a small variety of cockatoo) which seemed to be suffering from acute indigestion.

"What have you been feeding him?" asked Miss Bader.

"Not a thing except his favorite foods!" the lady declared. "He just *loves* chocolate kisses and doughnuts dunked in coffee!"

Both male and female parakeets and myna birds can be taught to speak, says Miss Bader, adding that sometimes they say the darnedest things. Miss Bader ought to know. One day, she was showing off Charlie the Myna, who is one of the Pet Shop's star attractions, to a Macy top executive (no longer with the store) who was about the only truly pompous executive Macy's ever had. Charlie has a vocabulary of seventy-five words, plus a ribald wolf-whistle, but on this occasion he turned his back squarely on the top executive and refused to say anything at all. The executive, as long-winded as he was pompous, delivered himself of several thousand words to Miss Bader on the care and training of birds, and as he was nearing his conclusion, Charlie, his back still turned, glanced at him darkly over his shoulder.

"Ah-h-h, shedd up," growled Charlie—the first and last time he has ever been known to speak those words.

Two Macy customers, Alexander Clark, the actor, and his actress-wife, Frances Tannehill, can testify to the uncanny gift of some birds for injecting panic into any conversation. Merlin, their parakeet, has a wide assortment of remarks, mostly culled from the classics and including: "To be, or not to be"; "Lay on, Macduff!"; "Elementary, my dear Watson"; "Doctor Livingstone, I presume"; and (again from Shakespeare, once more *Macbeth*) "Out, damned spot!" The last quotation, "Out, damned spot!" is one of his favorites.

Sometimes Merlin gets his phrases mixed, and offers a combination like, "Lay on, Doctor Livingstone!" But he always pulls himself together and, after a pause for refreshment, generally delivers another favorite announcement:

"And now . . ." (says Merlin) "a word from our sponsor."

One day, the Clarks were entertaining a potential television sponsor who had indicated that he might, just possibly, sign them both to do an important TV show. At the back of their minds the Clarks rather hoped that Merlin might oblige with the "word from our sponsor" bit—it would be cute, and sort of winning—but Merlin was strangely silent that afternoon until, in a lull during the business talk, he hopped to the front of his cage and spoke. His utterance rang clearly through the suddenly silent room.

"Out, damned sponsor!" Merlin roared.

Macy's Pet Shop is a place of fluent and volatile color with, on one side of the room, the brilliant scarlet, green, blue, purple, and yellow of the Australian lady-gould bird, the Java finches, the cockatoos, parakeets, and canaries, and —on the other—the bright flash of the goldfish, the crimson spark of the baby red-tailed shark, and the bland silver of the kissing gourami, a fish so called because it looks as though it were kissing somebody all the time. One tank in the fish section contains a baby pirhana with his breakfast, a few minnows, swimming innocently near him. At Macy's, the pirhana must be content with cannibalism but, full-grown and in its native habitat, it is said to be the man-eating fish which can strip a man's flesh to its bones in a matter of seconds.

"Some mothers worry about their children buying pirhanas," says Mr. Kase, Macy's fish expert, "but there is absolutely no danger. See?" And here Mr. Kase dabbles his fingers briefly in the pirhana tank. "Baby pirhanas, like baby sharks and baby alligators, do not grow in captivity. There is something about being in a tank that inhibits their growth."

One mother argued this statement rather picturesquely. "Look here," she said to Mr. Kase, "if I had been shut up in a Macy carton at the age of two, I am positive that I would have *outgrown* it!" She went off and consulted the New York Aquarium (now at Coney Island) and the Brooklyn Aquarium (still in Brooklyn). Two days later she came back to Macy's with her little boy.

"You win," she told Mr. Kase, and gave the nod to her son.

"One baby pirhana, one baby red-tailed shark, and one baby alligator!" the child gleefully ordered.

Just about the only drab and colorless object in the Pet Shop is the ant-palace, or "anterium," as Macy's calls it. A revival from a fad of the 1920's, the anterium is a glass enclosure within which a colony of ants toil endlessly, tunneling and building through a mountain of sand. Pallid as it looks, the anterium fascinates children, and older people too. The other day an elderly man came into the Pet Shop and ordered one pair of lovebirds and one anterium.

"The lovebirds are for my granddaughter," he told the salesclerk, "but the anterium is for my wife and me.

"You know," he went on to confide, "there was a time when I couldn't buy a thing but lovebirds, I was that romantic. But now—well, my wife and I have been married almost forty years, and we figure it's about time we left the lovebirds to our kids, and *their* kids, and just sat back and relaxed.

"And I'll tell you one thing," concluded this elderly gentleman, "I can't think of a better way for Momma and me to relax than just sitting back and watching these goldarned ants *work!*"

13

At Last It Came To Be...
The Bigness Which You See

★

ONE DAY IN THE 1930's Jesse Straus, in a hurry to get to his office on Macy's thirteenth floor, stepped into a customer elevator and stood quietly at the rear of the crowded car.

"Going UP!" announced James Cumberbatch, the operator. "Car going to the NINTH floor . . . This car goes only to the NINNNTH floor!"

At the ninth floor everybody got out except Mr. Jesse.

"Everybody out, sir!" sang James Cumberbatch, who had not recognized him. "Going DOWN . . . Car going DOWNNN!"

"I want to go UP," said Mr. Jesse.

"Sorry, sir, this car goes only to the ninth floor. Going DOWN!"

"I'm Jesse Straus," explained Jesse Straus.

"Going UP! Car going UP!" said James Cumberbatch at once.

It is unlikely that such an instance of one-man authority would occur in Macy's today. In industry everywhere the day of the individualist is over. Business in general has become streamlined and highly organized, and the firm of R. H. Macy & Co. in particular is no longer the patriarchal affair that it was under the elder Strauses. Mr. Isidor and his brother, Mr. Nathan, and Isidor's sons, Mr. Jesse, Mr. Percy, and Mr. Herbert, made their personal influence, and often their personal presence, felt in every corner of the store, and Mr. Jesse especially sometimes lit a personal bonfire under any employee he wished to enliven to a better sense of his duties. Nowadays, the business has grown too big and too complex for such autocratic touches, vivid though they were. Authority still comes from on high, but it is delegated through many executive hands working as a harmonious whole. This is a natural development, a sign of the times, neither to be hailed nor deplored, but simply to be accepted as a fact.

The three men who head the Macy Corporation today are Jack I. Straus, Jesse's son and chairman of the board of R. H. Macy & Co., Inc.; Wheelock H. Bingham, president of the corporation and the first non-Straus to be a Macy president; and Donald B. Smiley, who entered the firm as a lawyer and is now the corporation's vice-president and treasurer. (Edwin F. Chinlund, a longtime vice-president, officially retired last year but remains a director of the corporation, chairman of the Finance Committee, and a member of the Executive Committee.) The three top men stroll regularly through the store—that being the only way, they say, to keep in touch with employees and customers and to know just what is going on—and all three are respected and liked by the staff. But it would be hard to visualize any of them, during business hours, commandeering an elevator for his exclusive use as Mr. Jesse did.

A good deal of the "family" atmosphere at Macy's survives in the fact that Jack I. Straus is known to the employees as "Mr. Jack," his son as "Mr. Kenneth," and his cousins in the corporation as "Mr. Edward" and "Mr. John" (sons of Mr. Herbert). This is a pleasant echo of old times, but nobody expects it to extend beyond the Straus family. For one thing, the practice is a simple convenience, preferable to referring to all four Mr. Strauses as "Mr. Straus"; and, even more importantly, it is a tradition firmly rooted in four generations of Strauses. Wheelock H. Bingham and Donald B. Smiley, both popular with the personnel, are nevertheless known to one and all as "Mr. Bingham" and "Mr. Smiley."

The evolution of Macy's from a kind of ancestral manifestation into a sleek, modern structure has been a gradual one, growing along with the needs and habits of a changing world. Possibly its first seeds were planted in 1919, when the business was incorporated into R. H. Macy & Co., Inc., the company which controls all Macy stores, including Macy's New York. Jesse Straus and, later, his brother Percy were the first presidents of the corporation now headed by Mr. Jack, Mr. Bingham, and Mr. Smiley.

Macy's New York, the mother store, had no separate president for the first eighty-one years of its existence, from 1858 when Rowland Macy established it on Fourteenth Street until 1939, when Jack I. Straus was appointed president, a post which he held for the next ten years. In 1949, Macy's New York was made a separate entity, with Richard Weil Junior, who had been with the company for twenty years, including a term as president of Bamberger's, as the store's president. Weil (known as "Bobby") was a son of Minnie Straus, Isidor's daughter, and hence a cousin to

Jack. He was a Yale man, a self-confessed intellectual, a great talker, and a fast-thinking idea man. His impact on Macy's produced varying reactions among his colleagues. "The man's a thinking machine—you can hear the gears clicking," one of his admirers was heard to say, while a less enthusiastic subordinate just murmured wearily, "Ideas, ideas, all the time ideas. Your head gets tired." In 1952, for various intramural reasons, Macy's and Weil parted company, and he has no present connection with the firm.

Wheelock H. Bingham succeeded Weil as president of Macy's New York, thereby becoming the third man and the first non-Straus to hold that office. In 1956, Jack I. Straus became chairman of the board of the parent corporation and Wheelock Bingham was elected its president, with Elliot V. Walter succeeding him as president of Macy's New York. Mr. Bingham, who was only forty-eight at the time, is a young-looking, well-burnished man who first went to work for Macy's in 1926, when he got a summer job in the shoe department during his vacation from Harvard. Selling shoes to stout ladies on hot days was no picnic, he now admits, but he was only nineteen and after all, Jack Straus himself had started out selling stockings. It was Mr. Jack who rescued Bingham from the shoe salon: he asked him to join the Training Squad with a view to being made manager of the newly-opened Varsity Shop, a department featuring men's wear. Bingham, about to enter his second year at Harvard (where he was studying on a scholarship) consulted Dean Greenough, since taking the Macy job would mean leaving college.

"Well," said the Dean, "if you stay at Harvard you will absorb culture, make friends, and gain poise. You've already got the poise, and I think you can acquire the other two in the world outside Harvard. I would try the Macy job for a year."

By 1928 Bingham had become assistant buyer of men's furnishing under Joseph Mayer, whom he succeeded as buyer when Mayer retired the following year. In 1934, when Bingham was merchandising manager of the men's division at Bamberger's and on a buying trip to Europe, Jack Straus, then a vice-president, called him on board ship by one of the earliest shore-to-ship telephones. "You are coming back to New York to be merchandise manager of the children's departments," he announced. Bingham held that job for three years and then became assistant vice-president and, in 1940, vice-president of Macy's New York in charge of the men's group, children's group, domestics, and piece goods. Jack Straus was by that time president of R. H. Macy & Co.

World War II interrupted Bingham's Macy career in 1943, when he joined the Navy as a lieutenant and became its youngest captain. But even the war scarcely interrupted Jack Straus's telephone calls.

One day in 1945 Captain Bingham was seated with other Navy brass at a conference in Secretary James Forrestal's office in Washington when a secretary entered and told him he was wanted on the telephone. "I naturally thought it would be somebody saying we needed a few more airplanes or spare parts in the Pacific, or something of equal Navy importance," remarks Mr. Bingham, recalling this episode. But it was Jack Straus, who had a habit of picking up the phone in his New York office and saying "Get me Bingham," wherever Bingham happened to be. This time Straus's secretary had traced him to Forrestal's office, and Mr. Jack said tersely, "We've bought a store in San Francisco and you're going to head it, so don't give me any back talk."

Bingham, born in Boston, fell in love with California on sight and still has a home there to which he commutes often, and where his wife and two children spend much of their time. When Jack Straus again summoned him (by telephone) in 1952 to be president of Macy's New York, he declined the job twice because he hated to leave California. But—"Macy's is like the Navy," he explains. "When you're ordered to a new duty, you just don't say no."

Bingham's career, an example of the great American dream, also illustrates Macy's sturdy policy of "promotion from within." Another Macy manifestation, fully as dramatic, is the firm's expansion outward. At the latest count, in 1956, R. H. Macy & Co. numbered six divisions, or affiliated concerns, with a total of thirty-three stores, seventeen of which have opened in the past ten years. Many firms have more branches but they amount, in some cases, to scarcely more than a three-clerk office, whereas each Macy branch, with only two exceptions, is a complete, all-round department store, and every branch opening is a major production. The two exceptions are the Columbia and Sea Island stores.

The six divisions are Macy's New York, Bamberger's New Jersey, the Davison-Paxon Company in Georgia and South Carolina, the La Salle & Koch Company in Ohio, Macy's California, and Macy's Missouri-Kansas. The New York store has five branches, in Parkchester, Jamaica, Flatbush, White Plains, and Roosevelt Field; Bamberger's New Jersey includes the affiliated main store in Newark and its four branches in Morristown, Plainfield, Princeton, and Paramus; the Davison-Paxon Company has expanded from its original Macy division in Atlanta, Georgia, to six branches in Macon, Augusta, Columbus, Athens, Sea Island, and in Columbia, South Carolina; the La Salle & Koch Company likewise has grown from its first store in Toledo, Ohio, to four more in Bowling Green, Tiffin, Sandusky, and Findlay; Macy's California consists of the affiliated main store in San Francisco and its five branches in Richmond, San Rafael, Hillsdale, San José, and San Leandro; and Macy's Missouri-Kansas includes the affiliated main store in Kansas City, Missouri, an affiliated store in Wichita, and branches in Joplin, Missouri, and Mission, Kansas. Macy's has announced four new branch stores to be opened in the next year or so; two for the Bamberger Division, and one each for Davison-Paxon and Macy's Missouri-Kansas.

The organization of this empire is an efficient, modern machine. Each division is headed by a president who reports to Mr. Bingham as the operating head of the corporation. Each branch store is headed by a store manager, or administrator, who reports to a designated officer of the division. To a layman, the whole system seems something like one of those Chinese boxes in which each container holds a smaller replica, and all are encompassed and protected by the biggest of all—in this case, the parent corporation, R. H. Macy & Co., Inc.

Only one Macy's branch store ever turned out to be a stunning flop. In 1940, the firm opened a branch in Syracuse, New York. It lost money steadily, and closed its doors less than a year after opening day. Macy executives have an explanation for the disaster. Thinking to offer Syracuse the cream of its merchandise, Macy's had stocked the store with the items found to be the best-sellers in New York. For example, a popular hat for women was then the Dobbs snap-brim felt, so the Syracuse store featured it strongly in various colors. Syracuse women stayed away from it in a body, reasoning no doubt that if they all bought it they would all meet themselves coming down the street. Syracuse was not New York City, these ladies also complained, and they did not wish to be handed large chunks of New York City fads and fancies; they preferred a decent variety from which they could pick and choose for themselves. In the next branch it opened (at Parkchester) Macy's, having learned its lesson, polled the local citizens beforehand as to what they wanted most and liked best. Since that time, all branch stores have been miniature Macy's with the same wide assortment of wares.

For similar psychological reasons, Macy's sometimes changes the name of a newly acquired store to "Macy's," and sometimes—if the store is well-known to local residents by its original name—it does not. Macy's San Francisco affiliate was originally a concern called O'Connor, Moffat, and Macy's Missouri-Kansas started with an acquired Kansas City firm named the John Taylor Dry Goods Store; both of these affiliates, and their later branches, took the Macy name. However, Bamberger's, Davison-Paxon, and La Salle & Koch retained the names by which they were locally known. Macy's decides these questions by taking a survey of the city or town in which the store is located. In San Francisco, for instance, there were certain objections to changing the name of O'Connor, Moffat until the survey showed that more San Franciscans preferred the name of Macy's than wished to cling to O'Connor, Moffat. In Toledo, on the other hand, when the survey proved that La Salle & Koch was better known there than Macy's was, Macy's sensibly yielded.

The problem of adapting a new store to the region in

which it is located could amount almost to a fascinating
game, if the questions were not so deadly serious. Is the
town inland or on the water, and therefore (to name one
small item) will the store sell more picnic baskets or fishing
rods? Is it in a hot climate or a cold one, and therefore what
kind of wearing apparel is appropriate? Is the store near a
new housing development? How are the town's transportation and parking facilities? What are the residents' main
working occupations and recreational hobbies? What is the
average income level? Has the birth rate gone up in this
particular town, and therefore should Macy's branch stock
more infants' and children's wear? . . . The considerations
are endless and, in themselves, a kind of capsule history of
the times.

"One of the most dramatic changes in the department
store business in the past ten or fifteen years," says Wheelock
H. Bingham, "is the decentralization from the big-city store
to the increasing suburban stores, as more and more people
all over the United States move from the cities to the suburbs. Ten or fifteen years ago, the branch store might have
been considered merely a sort of offshoot, as its name im-
plies, of the main store in the big city. Nowadays, the branch
store, while still an offshoot, has grown so in size and numbers that it is one of the most important aspects of the merchandising business."

The changing habits of the American people mean more,
not less, work for the department stores, according to Murray Graham, vice-president in charge of Macy's New York
branches. "More women work at jobs today, and do their
shopping at night," says Mr. Graham, "and therefore department stores must stay open later, and more often, at
night. Besides, families like to shop together these days.

Even if the wife doesn't work, she likes to have the old man come along and inspect any major purchase, like a couch or a living-room rug, before she buys it. As a result, we have 'late closing' two or three or four times a week, depending on the locality."

The average customer's working hours are shorter now, and people who have moved away from the concrete vaults of the city have more leisure to spend outdoors. Consequently, Macy's sells more casual clothes, sportswear, and sports equipment. People also like to eat outdoors and the outdoor grill or barbecue, practically unknown ten years ago, is a feature of almost every suburban home. Ten or fifteen years ago, too, the boat business was all but inert; a few rich men had yachts, and some well-to-do families owned cabin cruisers, but for the average man a boat was an improbable luxury. Today, very few Americans have yachts any more, but the boat-builders have so simultaneously increased and economized their products that almost anybody can own, at least, an outboard put-putter. Furthermore, the average American today, with better housing facilities and more money in his pocket, is raising a bigger family than his father did, and Macy's, the family store, welcomes this trend with emotions just as sentimental as they are commercial. After all, the store is run by men who have anywhere from three to half-a-dozen framed photographs of their children decorating the desks and tables of their executive suites.

Macy's, however crammed with details about its branch stores, never makes the mistake of twisting statistics into generalities. There are nuances. In White Plains, a fairly high-income suburb, the top demand is for blue jeans, pedal-pushers, and other accoutrements of the simple life. On the other hand Flatbush, a substantial, no-nonsense district in a slightly lower income bracket, goes in for "dressier" clothes. The only generality to be safely assumed here is: the richer, the simpler. A small crisis confronted Macy's and other stores last year with the sudden demand for old raccoon coats out of the twenties. The coats had to be really ancient to be chic, according to the dictum of the college campuses where the fad started, and this was a poser since nearly all old raccoon coats had, by that time, been cut up into Davy Crockett hats. Macy's finally and at great pains located a large supply, and it was then that one of the nuances emerged that make branch stores interesting. Flatbush flatly spurned the old moth-eaten things, and not a single raccoon coat was sold there. White Plains ate them up, bought them out, swept the racks clean, and so did Roosevelt Field, which is situated near Westbury, Long Island.

"Oh, maybe the kids in White Plains and Westbury are 'hip,' but the Flatbush kids are *solid*," says a young Macy executive, with a wave of the hand to indicate that both are terms of endearment.

Self-service, a modern convenience which reigns in supermarkets and in some "shopping-centers," is another sign of the times to which Macy's has adapted itself with all the agility of any acrobat. Macy's calls it "simplified selling." It is not "self-service"—after all, a department store without salesclerks would be a dreary and confused place, and would lose its important personal warmth. "Simplified selling," in Macy's lexicon, means simply a greater exposure of merchandise and a more direct way of presenting it to the customers. Macy's basement, its phonograph-record department, and some sections of the children's department use the new system, and in many Macy affiliated and branch stores the method has been preened to a point where the busy housewife can select an article from a counter, hand it to the cashier at the end of the counter, and say "I'll take this."

The average housewife today generally has no servants, or at the most, a cleaning woman once a week plus a sitter now and then; but she has her push-button kitchen, her deepfreezer, her automatic washer and dryer, her automatic dishwashing machine, her automatic garbage disposal, and dozens of other mechanical marvels that her more personally pampered predecessors never knew. Even with this wealth of conveniences, she occasionally comes up against something that only an old-fashioned tool can handle, and this was recently proved by a young modern housewife whose husband happens to dote on imported Portuguese sardines and imported Italian *prosciutto* ham, both canned and sealed in Europe.

"I have a wall can opener, and even an electric can opener," said this young modern housewife. "The only thing I haven't got for opening cans is an atomic ray. And do you know how I have to open those tins of imported sardines and ham? With a hammer, an ice pick, and an old-fashioned hand can opener!"

Macy's has this girl cold. They sell the modern gadgets, all right, but they also sell hammers, ice picks, and manual can openers. With the housewife, modern or old-fashioned, Macy's cannot lose.

In spite of the popular migration to the suburbs and the growing importance of branch stores, Macy's feels that its big-city stores will always retain their eminence as the focal points of the business. This is partly a matter of

acreage, as any Macy executive will tell you. Macy's on
Herald Square, as an example, offers its merchandise not
only in departments but in acres of a single department.
The furniture section on the ninth floor covers two and a
half acres, and housewares in the basement fill one full acre
alone. No branch store can afford that kind of space. Moreover, many suburban families who do their daily shopping
in the local branch store still come into the city, to the main
store, for major purchases such as furniture, refrigerators,
draperies, or household linen. Whether they buy in a main
store or in a branch, these clear-eyed shoppers mostly know
what they want and are willing to pay for it, and Macy's, as
another curtsy to a new era, has produced a new slogan to
fit them. The old magic words, IT'S SMART TO BE THRIFTY,
were appropriate to an age of tight money, uncertain jobs,

and general nervousness, are in fact appropriate to any age, and the store still uses them extensively. But Macy's feels that customers no longer have to be quite so cleverly nudged into buying. The new slogan, NO LOWER PRICES THAN MACY'S, offers the customer a simple statement of fact.

The customer is still, of course, the dearest thing in Macy's life, and the subject of its constant research both in the main stores and in their branches. All of Macy's affiliated stores and branches are hosts, twice a year, to fairly intense visits by Wheelock H. Bingham, Donald B. Smiley, and Abe Hackman, a vice-president who operates the office of Corporate Control. This is another innovation brought about by changing times. In the days of Jesse Straus, Mr. Jesse summoned out-of-town managers to regular meetings in his New York office. When Wheelock Bingham became president of the corporation he decided that, with more branches and with airplane travel so easy, it would be better for the president to pay a call on the main stores and their branches in person, along with a couple of other specialists.

"I'm the 'merchant' of this traveling group," says Mr. Bingham, who also likes to refer to himself at times as "an old rag merchant who has worked for everyone at Macy's except Isidor and Nathan." "Smiley is the financial man, and Abe Hackman is the figure man." The three men spend a week or ten days with each division and its branches, reviewing the merchandise, the expense budgets, the merchandising figures, and other details, and the reports they bring back are invariably a shot in the arm for Macy's.

"How else would we know that some little town which up to now has not spoken suddenly wants a hundred and fifty skin-diving outfits right away?" a nonitinerant vice-president recently asked, wide-eyed.

The traveling trio, like most Macy executives, are young men, considering the eminence of their positions in the company. Bingham is barely fifty, Donald Smiley is forty-two, and Hackman forty-eight. Charles T. Stewart, who in 1956 was elected secretary and general attorney of the corporation, was only thirty-eight years old at the time. At the age of fifty Rowland Macy was already planning his own retirement, not because he had accomplished so much but because, in his day, a man of fifty had begun to grow old. Today's man of fifty has not even yet started on his second wind, and in many cases he has already reached a position somewhere near the top. Because of the better educational facilities of modern times, and the faster recognition of true worth, this youthfulness prevails among Macy's top person- nel. A recent check revealed that 50 per cent of the store's merchandise managers, or administrators (a highly respon- sible job), are in their thirties. "The younger our executives start the better," says Frances Corey, "because it takes any- one a little time to become integrated into Macy's." Mrs. Corey, herself a comely young woman, is a senior vice- president in charge of sales promotion and public relations at Macy's New York. She has held executive posts with other large merchandising firms but, asked to compare them with Macy's, she lifts her hands helplessly. "There is noth- ing like Macy's anywhere," says Mrs. Corey, simply.

Streamlined young executives, although vital to progress, do not give a store the warmth for which Macy's has always been known, and the credit for this distinct flavor must go to the loyal employees who have worked at the store for twenty-five, thirty-five, or even forty years. Last year's ban- quet of the Twenty-Five-Year Club had the largest attend- ance in Macy history, over one thousand, and to the higher echelons this is a soothing thought. It means that people who came to work out of necessity, during the 1930's depression, have relaxed in the security of the big store and have stayed right on.

Even the people who have left Macy's for other pastures carry their Macy experience with them like a banner. To have made good at Macy's is something like a Phi Beta Kappa key or a Hollywood Oscar—it signifies that you have

scored with the best of them and for you there is no looking back. It has been said that any woman who has once been a Macy executive can be picked out of a crowd of hundreds . . . there is a quality in her manner, her step, the way she walks and talks, that identifies her as clearly as though she wore a sign. Certainly this is true of such varying personalities as Bernice Fitz-Gibbon, Estelle Hamburger, Alice Hughes, and Margaret Fishback. The first two of these Macy graduates went on to establish their own businesses, the other two left merchandising for writing careers, and no four women could be fundamentally less alike. Yet all of them retain the aura of the Macy alumna—the intangible quality which seems, to the layman, to be a happy combination of authority, enthusiasm, skepticism, and humor. You would know this kind of girl anywhere, and it is no more necessary for her to tell you "I used to be at Macy's" than it would be for a pool-side acquaintance, after executing a front three-and-a-half somersault from the 10-meter platform, to stroll up and say "I used to be a professional diver."

One of the most typical and yet distinctive of the Macy graduates is Beatrice Rosenberg, who retired last year after thirty-nine years as a buyer and seven years as vice-president in charge of millinery, footwear, and accessories. As Mrs. Harry Kirshbaum, the wife of an architect, Bea Rosenberg presides vibrantly over a wide-terraced penthouse on Central Park West where all of her buoyant salesmanship bounces from her as healthily as it ever did during her long merchandising career. "Communication and Expectation are two great things in merchandising," says Miss Rosenberg, going on to explain; "you communicate your own enthusiam to the other fella, and then you naturally expect him to get excited too." Every Rosenberg gesture unconsciously illustrates this doctrine. When Bea shows you a wooden pepper mill she picked up in Italy, she doesn't just say "It's nice, isn't it?" as most ordinary women would do. She hands you the pepper mill and stands back expectantly, eyes snapping.

"Well," says Bea, finally, "are you going to go out of your *mind?* Are you going to faint dead away? . . . Are you going to DIE?"

Somehow this is so contagious that you feel the only fitting reception of the pepper mill would be a prompt swoon on the spot.

Enthusiasm mixed with a little wonder is the prevailing condition of merchants in this new age, when we wear what we eat, harness what we drink, and produce scientific marvels so fast that one pharmaceutical laboratory in Illinois quickly had to change the name of a new miracle drug before it reached the market. The trade name originally chosen by some harassed executive was "Damital." A few years ago, a startling new fabric called Aralac was introduced to the merchandising world; it looked and felt like cashmere, cost much less, and it was made of milk. Merchants everywhere (Macy's, as it happened, was not among them) found that it was just great, too, unless you wore it on a rainy day. One touch of dampness in the atmosphere, and you began to smell like a cow. A safer novelty fabric, this one recently featured by Macy's, is Curon, which looks like a thin, iridescent sponge-rubber and is used as a heating and insulating lining for lightweight coats. Curon, Macy's declares straight-faced, is made of salt and air. It is manufactured by Curtiss-Wright, a corporation once known only for its airplanes.

Hand in hand with all the excitements of science, expansion, and modern improvements, Macy's tradition marches peacefully on. New cycles may start, but the old ones never end. Last season, an echo of the Burgess Meredith-Tom Ewell days resounded when Kenneth Sylvia, a quiet young clerk in the Gift Shop, turned out to be the author of *The Shadow Years,* a play about Mary Todd Lincoln which had a successful run at an off-Broadway theater and received good notices from Brooks Atkinson of the *Times* and other first-string critics. And only last May Donald Sobol, an assistant in Cotton Fabrics, published his first novel, *The Double Quest,* a tale of chivalry in medieval England.

Like all natural phenomena, including the sea and the earth itself, Macy's, while always changing, will never change. This truth is clear to all observers, with the possible exception of one drunken gentleman whose taxi paused in traffic, on a certain evening, outside Macy's San Francisco store. The passenger peered foggily from the cab window, and the great red letters of the MACY sign stared down at him.

"Man," muttered this gent, impressed, "dig that crazy mixed-up YMCA."

INDEX

Index

*

This book was set in

Baskerville and Bulmer types,

printed, and bound by American Book–Stratford Press.

The paper is Perkins and Squier Company's

RRR Wove Antique

made by P. H. Glatfelter Company.

Typography and design are by

Lawrence S. Kamp

Date Due

SEP 3			
MAR 10			
JUN 28	MAY 1 65 52468		
JUL 22			
JUL 13			
AUG 20	FEB 1 66 90236		
NOV 11			
SEP 16 70 5206			